WITHDRAWN

DATE DUE

GAYLORD			PRINTED IN U.S.A.

COLUMBIA UNIVERSITY STUDIES IN ENGLISH
AND COMPARATIVE LITERATURE
NUMBER 123

THE SILVER-FORK SCHOOL

THE
SILVER-FORK SCHOOL

Novels of Fashion Preceding *Vanity Fair*

BY

MATTHEW WHITING ROSA

KENNIKAT PRESS, INC./PORT WASHINGTON, N. Y.

THE SILVER-FORK SCHOOL

Copyright 1936, 1964 Columbia University Press
This Edition published in 1964 by Kennikat Press

Library of Congress Catalog Card No: 64-15541

Manufactured in the United States of America

PREFACE

IN A more leisured age, such as the one in which the novels discussed in these pages were written, readers hardly concern themselves with any criticism of their favorite reading except for an occasional glance at some periodical review. We today read even more novels than our ancestors did, but we are more critical of them. The novel has now achieved the dignity of a permanent literary form, and the numberless vagaries of structure and subject through which it has passed interest us greatly. Because one long-lived and popular form of the novel has hitherto received little or no critical attention, it seems desirable that someone examine it. This study is not, I hope, unrewarding.

There can be little doubt that the "silver-fork" school has left its mark unmistakably upon the English novel. The vast flood of fiction comprising the school was narrowed, as the subtitle of this study indicates, into the channel of a single novel. By its very success, Thackeray's *Vanity Fair* has so dwarfed its predecessors that they now no longer seem to occupy the position that is rightfully theirs. Coming immediately after the Waverley novels and before the work of Dickens and Thackeray, the fashionable novels inevitably suffer in comparison, but they may still offer an interesting comment on life and letters in the reigns of George IV and William IV.

Because of their popularity, moreover, a study of the novels is of importance to anyone interested in early nineteenth-century bookselling. It is hardly an exaggeration to say that nine-tenths of the fashionable novels bear the colophon of Henry Colburn. He was the first to publish the

PREFACE

diaries of Evelyn and Pepys, and is thus assured of a certain fame, but it is as the publisher of contemporary novelists that he is presented here. In business acumen he equaled any of his competitors, while as a master of the art of advertising he was without rival or successor until the twentieth-century American practitioners burst into flowery blurbs.

The author wishes to express his obligations to the late Professor Ashley H. Thorndike, who suggested the subject of this study, and to Professor Emery Neff, whose sympathetic counsel has been so generously proffered. Others who read it in manuscript, or contributed advice in conversation, are Professor H. N. Fairchild, Dr. Susanne Howe Nobbe, Dr. Henry Wells, and Professor Ernest H. Wright, all of Columbia University, and Mr. Anthony Netboy. Special debts have been incurred to Miss Dorothy Dalton of the American University Union in London, to the late Richard Bentley of Slough, Bucks., and to the Earl of Lytton. For constant encouragement and for aid in reading proof thanks are due to Mr. George E. De Mille and to my wife.

MATTHEW W. ROSA

NEW YORK
May 15, 1936

CONTENTS

CONTENTS

THE SILVER-FORK SCHOOL

I

THE SILVER-FORK SCHOOL

TIME has a curious way of reversing values, and travelers down the old paths of literature are constantly struck by the evidences that their route had once been a popular way. To re-enter the past through the pages of its magazines is to meet with almost completely forgotten books, authors, and schools of writing. A fragment here and there of the ruins may be incorporated in some later building, but usually the successors have built so well that their structures seem homogeneous. Evidence of one forgotten school may be found in the advertising and review columns of the widely popular *Literary Gazette* and the *New Monthly Magazine* between 1825 and 1845. A sameness compounded of sex, fashion, and gentility links titles like *Women as They Are, Cecil, the Diary of a Coxcomb, Arlington, Pelham, A Marriage in High Life,* and *The Victims of Society.* This impression of family resemblance is heightened by the observation that nearly all—including the magazines themselves—were published by one man, Henry Colburn. William Hazlitt, in a withering review in *The Examiner* for November 18, 1827, called them the "dandy school," but other denominations, the "silver-fork school," or "fashionable novels," are perhaps more accurately descriptive. Under any name, they represent a best-seller wave almost without parallel in the intensity and duration of its development.

When Thomas Carlyle, in *Sartor Resartus*, contemplated the dandies for whom Bulwer's *Pelham* had become a confession of faith, or the whole duty of man, he was hardly able to restrain his wrath within the artistic bounds set by Herr Teufelsdröckh's rather genial nature. While the world has not always agreed with the fervent prejudices of the Scotch Puritan, in this case not only Carlyleans, but also literary historians, have agreed in denouncing or ignoring those human documents known as "fashionable novels." Although there is indubitable evidence that Carlyle had read some of them, it is to be feared that the critics have read Carlyle first. And truly, the catastrophes he describes as the result of his own acquaintance with the fashionable novel—ranging from a mere drumming in the ears, an insufferable Jew's-harping and scrannel piping, through a magnetic sleep, to *delirium tremens* and total deliquium, furnish a plausible excuse for neglect. But this dandiacal body, Carlyle tells us, is the positive pole, which, when charged with all the money in the nation and connected with the negative pole, drudgism, will flash; "and then— What then? The earth is but shivered into impalpable smoke by that Doom's-thunder-peal; the Sun misses one of his Planets in Space, and thenceforth there are no eclipses of the Moon."

To turn from the extravagance of that prose back to the subject that inspired it is admittedly a little hard, but so much has been written of the condition of the poor, and so little of the condition of the rich, that a study of the latter may prove to have a certain interest and value. The poor have always been a problem; amelioration of their state demands exact knowledge, and parliamentary committees, local poor boards, and professional sociologists have been busy with inquisitions. Of the rich Englishman, however, it may be said with peculiar propriety that his home is his castle. It was partly to correct a half real and half fancied deficiency in knowledge, and partly to relieve the gloom of the middle classes arising from their daily contemplation of the poor, that the novelists of the "silver-fork school" had proffered their services.

The causes for the dandiacal novel doubtless lie in two stupendous upheavals—the Napoleonic Wars and the Industrial Revolution. The panic brought on by Jacobinism had long delayed ordinary political changes, until the growth of education among the lower classes, the virtual creation of a new and wealthy middle class of industrialists, and the unrest in the huge manufacturing centers, combined with Whig discontent finally to produce the Reform Bill. Enfranchisement was not complete, but the time when great landed proprietors alone ruled England was over. The new aristocracy was based on wealth, not blood. The social stability of the earlier periods was gone, and in its place came a shifting class alignment in which the talents of the *roturier* were best fitted to survive. While economic and political differences widened the gulf between aristocrat and bourgeois, social and fashionable emulation tended to draw them together. Charles Knight observed: "The middle classes were becoming more and more luxurious. There was more elegance in their household arrangements, and more expense. Their manners were less formal, their dress more natural. . . . The young ladies had begun to be educated more with a view to accomplishments than housekeeping utensils."[1]

It is in this social meeting of the two classes that the fashionable novels have their place. Symptomatic on the one hand of the Philosophical Radicals' quarrel with aristocratic privilege, they represent on the other no less clearly the snobbishness of the English caste system. Endeavoring to make social comedy out of such heterogeneous materials, the novelists found their subject matter refractory to handle and their audiences too divergent in taste.

The recurring shocks to which society was subjected began as early as 1811, when the Prince of Wales became Regent, attained their greatest intensity in 1816, when

[1] Charles Knight, *Passages of a Working Life*, London, 1864, I, 220–21.

Beau Brummell left England in disgrace, and subsided to a quiet tremor when George III died in 1820. Certain chronological developments in the fashionable novel tended to obscure the change. The novel itself belongs definitely after 1820, when Hook, Ward, Lister, Bulwer, Disraeli, Bury, Gore, and Blessington flourished, but many of the novels of these writers deal with the period before 1820 and are historical fictions like *Vanity Fair*. *Pelham* and *Vivian Grey* offered new and contemporary figures which represented an abandonment of the Brummell tradition that had been exploited by Lister and Hook. But Mrs. Gore, writing *Cecil* as late as 1841, returned to the buck of pre-Regency days. The years before Waterloo formed her favorite period, treated in novels like *The Cabinet Minister*. She herself attributed the undeniable change in spirit between 1810 and 1830 to the war. The stern presence of the war once over, she says, people contracted a levity brought on by peace, got foreign servants, and England, "not content with hanging up her conquered banners in triumph, or chanting her *Te Deums* with grateful solemnity, suffered her anthems to be overpowered by a Bacchanalian roar, and the senseless giggle of fashionable levity."[2] "Congreve and Vanbrugh are your only comedy," observed Byron in 1814. "Our society is too insipid now for the like copy."[3] Society was perhaps more insipid under William IV than it had been under the Prince Regent, but a host of brummagem Congreves and Vanbrughs sprang up anxious to immortalize it.

Circumstances favored a mass output of fiction. Potential readers had greatly increased because of radical and nonconformist zeal for education. The invention of the steam press and the development of improved methods of paper making, which had helped make possible wide distribution of the Scotch novels, contributed equally to the

[2] Mrs. Gore, *The Money Lender*, London, 1843, I, 5.
[3] Byron, *Journal*, March 10, 1814, II, 397.

success of the fashionable novels. Circulating libraries, whose rise in the 1740's had been contemporaneous with the rise of the novel, assured the publishers of a fairly predictable number of sales. The production of books rose more than fivefold between 1725 and 1825.[4] The fashionable novels, appearing as "shiploads" to Carlyle, must have formed a considerable proportion of the total in 1830. Moreover, it was the day of the three-decker, and they stretch out alarmingly on library shelves. Hosts of writers contributed at least one book, but no more than eight merit attention—Theodore Hook, Thomas Henry Lister, Plumer Ward, Lady Charlotte Bury, Disraeli, Bulwer, Mrs. Gore, and Lady Blessington.

The long life of the school was astonishing, for it lasted for some twenty-five years (roughly from 1825 to 1850), a length of time that would seem incompatible with the intensity of its exploitation. But the fashionable novels displayed the tenacity of life possessed by any widely popular form of literature, and, it may be added, the same resistance to outward change. Once a formula was developed it was never modified, and a second generation of novel readers found fresh at its booksellers the same sort of entertainment which had pleased its fathers a quarter of a century before. One result of this unyielding front to innovation was an ultimate fate resembling that of the one-hoss shay— virtually complete annihilation. But the names of Bulwer, Disraeli, and Hook may recall the literature of the dandies, and recollections of Beau Brummell, Count D'Orsay, George IV, and the Marquis of Hertford may serve to place in time the period of the silver-fork school. Bulwer and Disraeli are still read; their subsequent work has earned them a hearing which perhaps *Pelham* and *Vivian Grey*, despite their wit and charm, might not have received. Mrs.

[4] Charles Knight, *Shadows of the Old Booksellers*, reprinted London, 1927, Appendix.

Gore, possibly the most voluminous writer in all English literature, still has readers, for her novel, *Cecil*, was reprinted in England a few years ago.

The origins of the fashionable novel were confused and uncertain, but after the period of experimentation was over, a formula was evolved which was exceedingly simple and workable. Complexities of plot and characterization were avoided; the overload of thesis carried by so many novels of the 1790's was discarded, and an exclusive preoccupation with verisimilitude became the distinguishing mark of the fashionable novel. Social etiquette at the ball, the dinner, the hunt, the club, and the opera; conversation which seldom extended beyond the shallow conventionalities of polite discourse; and a zealous attention to the details of food and clothing supplied the material for hundreds of novels by dozens of novelists.

Had none of the fashionable novels surpassed this standard, however, hardly any historical value could atone for their lack of intrinsic merit. The formula was too simple to produce novels which might live beyond the brief span of a season. If it had not been for the few writers, who, while fulfilling all the minimum requirements necessary to secure readers, went further and created real characters, Carlyle's indictment might well stand. But the intellectual dandies of Disraeli and Bulwer manage to combine some measure of mental alertness and serious endeavor with the frivolous graces, and even the Regency beaux and dandy chaperons of Mrs. Gore occasionally deviate into sense. Both because of their place in old traditions of literature and life and because of their own interest, the fashionable novels deserve more attention than has hitherto been given them.

Clearly enough, the fashionable novel grew out of the eighteenth-century novel of manners, but later borrowings and accretions from the picaresque romance and the German apprenticeship novel complicate the story. The intellectual dandy is, in essence, a picaresque rogue who has substituted a decorous ride on Rotten Row for his ancestor's canter on moonlit heaths. The exchange of the rough and hearty Tom Jones for the elegant Mr. Henry Pelham shows how accurately literature reflects life. Wisdom instead of physical adventure became a quest for youth, for often the young German apprentice to life appeared as a most natural offspring of the picaresque rogue. Much of Bulwer's and Disraeli's sentiment came from Goethe's *Wilhelm Meister*, but its theme was ignored by most of the fashionable novelists, and, indeed, is hardly germane to the fashionable novel itself. Far more important is the general debt to the transcripts of contemporary manners written by Fanny Burney and Maria Edgeworth.

In the latter years of the eighteenth-century prose fiction was reaching out and absorbing for its own those domains of life that had hitherto been reserved for the essay, the poem, and the play. People who wished to reform the world, those who wished to frighten it, those who wished to satirize it, joined hands with those who wished merely to entertain it. The new feeling for humanity engendered by Richardson and Rousseau received a powerful impetus from the industrialization of England, and in the lurid glare of the French Revolution, established institutions no longer seemed imperishable. There arose a new interest in the past, and sharper attention was paid to the manners, customs, and aims of the present. It was then that the historical novel arose, waiting for a Scott to transform it; it was then that its ally, the novel of terror, appeared. Above all others, moreover, it was the period of the thesis novel, whose writers, Bage, Holcroft, Godwin strove to erect their new and stainless edifices on the ruins of the old world. Reform was the cry everywhere, heard even by those novelists who professed no higher aim than to spread before their readers the manners and trifles of the day.

But the brave new world had many of the old creatures in it. The sentimental novel had seldom failed to endow its delicate heroes and heroines with rank and fortune, and this aristocratic bias was too powerful to disappear even from the revolutionary novels. In Robert Bage and Thomas Holcroft it merely changed its direction. The simple folk who reveled in creaking Gothic machinery loved the shades of dead lords and ladies, and until Scott found romance in the medieval serf, the historical novelists dealt exclusively with feudal splendors. As for those novelists who chose their subjects from the contemporary world—Fanny Burney and Maria Edgeworth—they too found it most expedient to write about fashionable people.

For many reasons, however, Maria Edgeworth was not a fashionable novelist. Her apprenticeship in novel writing seems to have been a reversal of "The Rake's Progress." And, unlike a rake, who may sometimes repent, and feel the better for it, Maria never felt quite comfortable when she allowed her artistic conscience to take precedence over her parental awe. Those *Parent's Assistants* and *Early Lessons* in which she and her father annotated the gospel of Rousseau for a young English audience measure the extent to which she subordinated her mind to his. The voice was Maria's, but the moral was Richard's.

This will partly explain, perhaps, why her two volumes of *Tales from Fashionable Life*, 1809–12, are not fashionable novels, and why her first full-length novel, *Belinda*, 1801, whose scene scarcely shifts from a mansion in fashionable Berkeley Square, is not what the young Bulwer would have understood by the term. They are, in reality, illustrations of moral lessons preached to the fashionable world, the text of which had been announced in *Essays on Professional Education*. The theory upon which she worked was sound enough. Indeed, Mrs. Wharton remarks that "a frivolous society can acquire dramatic significance only through what its frivolity destroys. Its tragic implication lies in its power of debasing people and ideals."[5] But Miss Edgeworth's early novels are unsuccessful because, while they deal with London society and anticipate the fashionable novels in form and content, she was not familiar with higher English society when she wrote them. Wishing to satirize the follies of the great, she was often forced to set puppet characters working out their unconvincing destinies in an artificial setting. The shuddering, fanatical horror with which she looked at London's fashionable world was foreign to the nature of Bulwer, Disraeli, and Mrs. Gore, and only an insincere pose with Lady Charlotte Bury and Lady Blessington.

Indeed, it may be doubted whether Miss Edgeworth came as close to the spirit of Lister's *Granby* and Mrs. Gore's *Cecil* as did Fanny Burney. *Evelina* and *Cecilia* do not bear the weight of heavy theses, nor are many of the characters mere puppets. Living in the midst of London's literary and musical circles, Miss Burney had the intimate knowledge of society denied Miss Edgeworth. Her presentation of the *haute monde* as it was before the French Revolution is light-hearted caricature, its freshness unmarred either by the reformative zeal of Miss Edgeworth or by the masculine coarseness of Fielding and Smollett.

Some of the light-heartedness of Fanny Burney's comedy was recaptured by the fashionable novelists. Mrs. Gore thought that she and her contemporaries were reviving the traditions of Congreve, Cibber, and Farquhar. "It is from the ashes of our long-extinguished high-life comedy that this swarm of triflers has arisen." One remembers, too, that Sheridan had given high-life comedy a brilliantly

---

[5] Edith Wharton, *A Backward Glance*, New York, 1934, p. 207.

new, if short, vitality when England was enjoying its brief hour of peace and prosperity before the American Rebellion and the French Revolution. We are proud of the literary products of these other periods, even though for a century or more we have been a little reserved about the moral values of Etherege, Wycherly, and Congreve, contenting ourselves with encomiums on their wit. But they, at least, are read, and occasionally acted, while the fashionable novels hardly attain to the dignity of a footnote in a compendious history.

What is the difference between the comedy of the age of George IV and that of the earlier periods? The novel has usurped the place of the drama, but that is only a symptom, not a cause. The social comedy of the eighteenth century is partly preserved in novels still read today. One reason for the impermanence of the fashionable novel probably lies in the fact that the school culminated in a single great book— *Vanity Fair*. Curiously enough, Thackeray, who for many years, too many, indeed, attacked snobbery and burlesqued Disraeli, Bulwer, and Mrs. Gore, wrote the supreme example of the fashionable novel. Many obvious minor lines of connection between *Vanity Fair* and its predecessors (a resemblance between Thackeray's Lord Steyne and Disraeli's Lord Monmouth, for example, or between Rawdon Crawley and any of the innumerable bucks of Lister, Mrs. Gore, or Bulwer) immediately come to mind. But there is a greater likeness between the fashionable novels and *Vanity Fair* than is to be found in any comparison of individual characters and scenes. *Vanity Fair* enlarges and restudies the entire world of the fashionable novelists. Thackeray, although he saw that world more clearly and recorded it more faithfully than his predecessors, is nevertheless the successor of Bulwer, Disraeli, and Mrs. Gore, whose novels he so despised. His success has thrown his predecessors into a shade from which they have never emerged.

And because this is true, a study of the fashionable novels will throw considerable light on Thackeray.

Fashion as material for study is singularly evanescent. Of the day only, like one's newspaper, fashion becomes ridiculous—old-fashioned—overnight, and when a century has passed, impossible of anything but the faintest re-creation. "Herculaneum may be discovered under the ashes; but a few years heaped on the manners of a society bury it deeper than all the dust of volcanoes. Memoirs which are the history of such manners are themselves no more than anecdotes."[6] Between Pope's *Rape of the Lock* and Edith Sitwell's *Elegy on Dead Fashion* there is hardly a middle approach: satire when the fashion is living, light elegy after it is dead. It may be, too, that the silver-fork school of novels was written with "too-finely-sharpened pens, dipped in a too-scented India ink . . . on pale blue silver-edged paper";[7] it may be that entranced by the delicate charm of their creations the novelists forgot the struggle for "repeal, retrenchment, and reform," which we today still find living, and by thus forgetting, ensured our forgetfulness of them. But if the people who throng the pages of the fashionable novels are gone beyond recall, the novelists themselves have still a little reality, and their work and its interaction with their lives may inform and amuse us.

The men and women in the fashionable novels who might once have danced at the same balls as Becky Sharp, or nodded from a club-window as Jos Sedley waddled painfully by on his way to a curry, are mere phantoms compared to the sharp realism of Thackeray's creatures. They are not human beings first and pose and pretense second, but pose and pretense completely. They must have been so even to

[6] Barbey D'Aurevilly, *Du Dandysme et de Georges Brummell*, translated by D. B. Wyndham Lewis as *The Anatomy of Dandyism, with Some Observations on Beau Brummell*, London, 1928, p. 11.

[7] *Ibid.*, p. 13.

their contemporaries; to us who see them but dimly in the shade cast by their successors in the late nineteenth century, they are shadows of a dream. But the shadows, after all, were reflected on the white pages of substantial volumes. Though the lineaments remain faint, one may, perhaps, sharpen an outline, or reveal more clearly the reason for a pose.

II

THE DANDIACAL BODY

THE fashionable novel tells us, in effect, that the world is a place of make-believe and sham, and that nowhere is this so true as among the members of fashionable society. The deliciousness of its comedy increases in the very ratio in which it is faithful to all the outward trappings of that society. In striving for the utmost correspondence between fictional characters and the picture of the aristocracy drawn from Debrett's *Peerage*, the *Court Journal*, and the tailor's style book, it must be admitted that the novelists occasionally omitted the saving spark of life and humor, and turned out for our inspection curiously glossed but stuffed shirts. But, though the fashionable writers frequently overshot their mark, and like Shelley's Peter Bell the Third,

> . . . touched the hem of Nature's shift,
> Felt faint—and never dared uplift
> The closest, all-concealing tunic . . .

their aim was a clear and perhaps worthy one. To draw convincing pictures of the upper classes was the first and most important duty. Whether the critic approves or not, his quarrel cannot be so much with what the novelists attempted to do as it is with their occasional failure to achieve the avowed purpose. Mrs. Gore once remarked, "A novel of fashionable life does not pre-suppose a tissue of puerile vulgarity."[1] But *The Westminster Review* lamented in 1829 that the passion for fashionable novels sprang "much less from a rational desire to acquire a knowledge of human nature, as modified by the accidents of high birth

---

[1] Mrs. Gore, *Women as They Are*, London, 1830, II, 235.

and fortune, than from an anxiety to glean a few airs and graces, to be played off in succession . . . until the toe of the peasant, once more intruding upon the heel of the courtier, all wits are again upon the rack to invent new distinctions."[2] Whether the higher aim was satire, philosophical reflections on truth and beauty, or insipid rhapsody, depended on the individual writer.

The limited subject matter which the fashionable novelists permitted themselves had a corresponding effect on the richness of their characterization. For the most part, they shut themselves off from the middle and lower classes which form the inexhaustible reservoir of English comic figures, and confined their observations to the least varied group in society. Their plots were not essential enough to demand much care or originality, and like the Restoration dramatists, the novelists availed themselves of a succession of stock characters. Abundant as these were, they were hardly new, for the great majority—braggarts, flirtatious *jeunes filles*, jealous lovers, foolish lords, and the like— were simply pulled from the showman's box of tricks, dusted off, and set to perform again. Only a few, notably the buck, the dandy, the woman of fashion, the marrying mother, and the social climber really underwent a thorough renovation, and repainted and furbelowed, were made ready to amuse a fresh audience.

From Brummell to D'Orsay, from the buck to the dandy, is a jump of only fifteen or twenty years, but the great changes during that time are manifest even in the circumscribed domain of men's clothes. Brummell's chief achievement in dress had been the introduction of white starched cravats. His valet, in a well-known story, when questioned as to the meaning of a pile of apparently clean but discarded cravats, remarked glibly, "Oh, those are our failures." Difficult to adjust, and uncomfortable to wear,

[2] *The Westminster Review*, X, 173, January, 1829.

the cravat had the virtue of cleanliness, while it furnished a fitting accent to the invariable blue coat with brass buttons, the buckskin breeches, and the polished top boots. The whole was very English, clean, simple, and masculine. But after the war, trousers began to come in from Paris. For a time excluded from formal affairs, they were finally accepted in spite of being possibly the ugliest leg-coverings that could be contrived. Ten years of foreign innovation led to the fantastic and effeminate dress of Bulwer and Disraeli. Over the intellectual dandy hovered the scent of perfume, while on his curled locks gleamed "thine incomparable oil, 'Macassar!'" There were rings on the fingers, and a suspicion of rouge on the cheeks. Waistcoats, which had formerly been subdued by the chaste cravat, became gorgeous vestments frequently spangled by turquoises or seed pearls. The coat was made of velvet or had velvet cuffs. The inimitable Disraeli, strolling along Regent Street complacently accepting the stares of the passers-by upon his blue surtout, his black stockings with red stripes, or astounding the officers at Gibraltar with his morning and his evening canes, would have shocked the fastidious Brummell.

Many of the extravagances that mark a parallel between the 1820's and the 1660's come from their common feeling of social uncertainty. The restoration in 1660 was so recent that aristocracy did not feel sure of itself. In the early nineteenth century the fear of Jacobinism which had distinguished the nineties was dying, but aristocratic privileges were steadily going down before the rising power of the landless rich. One or two trivial instances may illustrate what this meant. Her Majesty's Theater, known as the Italian Opera in the Haymarket, was controlled in 1814 by a committee of patronesses, the Duchesses of Marlborough, Devonshire, and Bedford, Lady Carlisle, and others, without whose express invitation it was impossible to buy a ticket for the stalls and boxes. By 1820 this restriction had ceased, and the opera, open to all, had lost its prestige; unfortunately, in addition to this perhaps venial loss, the quality of its music had suffered. The most famous and most exclusive of Regency clubs was White's. In it, as in Brookes's, Boodle's, and the rest, gambling for high stakes was customary, but after the establishment of Crockford's in 1827, the palm for high play passed to that institution. Many a wealthy member, blackballed elsewhere, made Crockford's his only club.

It was because of changes like this, accelerated by the influx of new families from the mercantile and manufacturing classes, that a few aristocrats were led into absurdities like Exclusivism.[3] Their desperate efforts to preserve some of the last vestiges of privilege were made slightly ridiculous by their choice of battlefields—Rotten Row, the ballroom at Almack's, or the clubs of St. James's. The real struggle was being waged far off in Manchester, in Birmingham, or amid the gleam of burning ricks in Kent or Essex.

Thomas Carlyle, grimly composing *Sartor Resartus* in remote Ecclefechan, bitterly reproached Pelham and the sect of the dandies for their lack of earnestness. With England on the brink of revolution, the mere mention of other clothes than those for the spirit angered him into forgetting the duty of a critic to read carefully the work to be criticized. A second reading of *Pelham* might have saved him from the rather grudging admission of error which he made years later after having become acquainted with Bulwer. The last fault of which anyone could accuse Pelham was a lack of earnestness. Not only Pelham, but also Vivian Grey are surprisingly earnest when studied by anyone not

---

[3] Exclusivism, flourishing in the 1820's and 1830's, was a curious defensive movement on the part of certain aristocrats. Their dismay at the breaking down of class lines led them to organize artificially what had hitherto existed quite naturally, and society, mistaking an economic war for a social, fought a bloody battle on the wrong front.

prepossessed with the notion that a dandy must necessarily be a mental lightweight devoted only to the cultivation of the sillier formalities of social intercourse.

Pelham, to put aside for a moment the more flowery "adventures of a gentleman," as a young man is elected to Parliament. As preparation for taking his seat, he studies political economy, starting with James Mill and ending with the more popular of Jeremy Bentham's works. Ricardo's remarks upon finance are made to serve as an introduction to private ethics approached by way of public ethics. Unfortunately, before Pelham is admitted to the House, his election is contested, and he finds himself defeated. Familiar with the younger and idler members of Parliament, he makes himself useful to Lord Dawton, leader of the Opposition, by rounding up members, writing pamphlets, and performing confidential duties for which he has been promised the first open seat within the minister's gift. When the Whigs win, however, the minister forgets him in favor of some more powerful and less independent party worker. But Pelham, convinced of the righteousness of his side, refuses to join a new party being organized by his friend, Lord Vincent, because he cannot approve of the new party's principles. He likewise foregoes the power of revenge with which his friendship for Lord Guloseton, the gourmand, provides him. Surely Pelham's devotion to the principles of party and to measures in which he believes ought to have given him some claim to the suffrage of Carlyle. Instead, Carlyle seizes Bulwer's ironical essay on clothes in *Pelham* and treats it with elaborate seriousness as dandiacal doctrine. He effectively contrasts the Irish poor slaves with the dandies, but he was hardly fair to *Pelham* or Bulwer.

Vivian Grey's earnestness resembles Pelham's, although Vivian's political aspirations hitch themselves to a spectacular rocket rather than to a genuine and regular star.

Instead of joining the Opposition and biding his time, Vivian strives to create and lead an entirely new party. The whole affair is the veriest moonshine, of course, the party's only realistic feature being its prompt collapse. But Vivian is not an idler; no young man who trains his political sense on the neo-Platonists, organizes a party, and kills a man before he is twenty-one, can be said to be really a loafer.

Although Mrs. Gore's *Cecil* did not appear until 1841, years after Carlyle's attack, it is interesting to see how carefully she has assimilated the spirit of the Regency buck to her coxcomb. Far more than the intellectual dandy, the idle though magnificent buck deserved the reproaches of sober citizens. In his heyday, however, no prophet arose to denounce him, and on a comparatively diligent successor fell the burden of reproof. Pelham and Vivian represent their time perfectly because they are contemporaries of their young authors; Mrs. Gore has made alive once more in Cecil's customary indifference to serious matters, the careless life of men like Brummell.

Curiously enough, a distinction in real life between the buck of 1810 and the intellectual dandy of 1830 has not been made clear by the novelists. The bucks were inarticulate, and like the peacock, confined their self-expression to gorgeous plumage. To the dandies was added the gift of song. Even a partial list of the Carleton House clique contains a fair proportion of names which are in some way familiar—Brummell, the Duke of Argyle, the Marquis of Hertford, Lords Alvanley and Worcester, Sir Lumley Skeffington, Sir Henry Pierrepoint, Sir Henry Mildmay, Charles Standish, Captain Gronow, and Don Mackinnon. Of this group, Hertford is the best known because he appears as Lord Monmouth in *Coningsby* and as Lord Steyne in *Vanity Fair*. Mackinnon owes what little fame is his to his association with Byron. Sir Lumley Skeffington wrote plays long since forgotten, but only Captain Gronow, by his entertaining memoirs, may be said to have perpetuated his name by writing. The men who once filled the bow window at White's have achieved a certain immortality, not because they were writers, but because they were the material of which literature was made. Novelists and biographers saw in the dandies a source for endless stories, but the dandies, Byron observed, "disliked literary people and persecuted and mystified Mme de Stael, Lewis, Horace Twiss, and the like, damnably."[4]

Any list of dandies would be composed almost entirely of literary men—William Harrison Ainsworth, Bulwer, Campbell, Dickens, P. G. Patmore,[5] and Thackeray, to name a few. "Ainsworth was frequently mistaken for D'Orsay . . . 'the glass of fashion and the mould of form—really a complete Adonis,' as poor Haydon put it."[6] Even Count D'Orsay, the King of the Bucks, wrote a little. That the literary dandies so seldom put themselves into books shows that they did not consider a writer, purely as a writer, of very high social standing. Byron expressed the view neatly in *Beppo:*

> One hates an author that's all author, fellows
> In foolscap uniform turned up with ink,
> One don't know what to say to them, or think,
> Unless to puff them with a pair of bellows;
> Of coxcombry's worst coxcombs e'en the pick
> Are preferable to these shreds of paper,
> These unquench'd snuffings of the midnight taper.

Bulwer, indeed, compared the boorish attitude of the English unfavorably with the graciousness of the French,

---

[4] Quoted in W. A. L. Bettany, *The Confessions of Lord Byron*, New York, 1905, p. 391.

[5] Young Patmore boasted two kinds of trousers, one for walking and one for sitting. He once sat down in the walking pair with disastrous consequences.—W. C. Hazlitt, *Four Generations of a Literary Family*, London and New York, 1897, I, 165.

[6] S. M. Ellis, *William Harrison Ainsworth and His Friends*, London, 1911, I, 263.

and Carlyle considered the German man of letters better situated than the English.

The intellectual dandy, however, had to be endowed with two attributes of the literary man, a knowledge of books and an inclination to study. Fortunately for the novelists, to give an air of learning to ostensible social butterflies was comparatively simple, for the cult of the amateur had been long established in England. One remembers Congreve's request of Voltaire and Voltaire's blunt reply, "Do you think that I would have come this far to meet a mere gentleman?" Henry Luttrell, author of the pleasant poem *Advice to Julia* and the novel *Crockford House*, was lamented even by the worldly Rogers for giving nearly his whole time to persons of mere fashion. Byron, who dashed off poems between tea and dinner, or while dressing, and for a long time refused to accept money from Murray, boyishly played the same game. Pelham, therefore, like Luttrell and Byron, would be deeply mortified to admit publicly the hours he spends reading; his learning must appear as a natural growth, but we are told that never a day passes during which he does not devote six hours to his books. Lord Vincent, whose conversation is made up of stores rifled from all the classics, has a similar horror of appearing pedantically learned. Vivian Grey, after the years are over in which he studied twelve hours a day, must blossom like another natural wit whose store needs no replenishing from reading.

To place too much emphasis on the earnest qualities of the dandies, however, is to commit the same error as Carlyle. After all, the dandies were young men about town, not cloistered monks, and the sins of young men are perhaps even more revealing than their virtues. It must be admitted that the vices of the 1800's, although basically the same as those of the 1820's, gambling, drinking, and whoring, were not nearly so scarlet as they had been under good

King Charles. The effort of the intellectual dandy was to pass through all the dangerous and fascinating pleasures of life unscathed, and just a little aloof. Dash and brilliance are reserved for the *salon*, the ball, or the dinner. Roistering in the streets, "tipping the Charlies," has become at this time somewhat collegiate, thanks to Brummell, "who induced the ingenuous youth of Britain to prove their valor otherwise than by threshing superannuated watchmen."[7] But Pelham engages in one escapade of the sort with a group of young bloods who get drunk,[8] engage in a fight with Cyprians (the Restoration bawds have become Cyprians), go down in defeat before a superior force of watchmen, and much reduced in numbers, start out in search of some recommended young women. Pelham leaves at this juncture and wakes up in the morning with a headache. The realism is Byronic:

> Let us have wine and women, mirth and laughter,
> Sermons and soda-water the day after.

Although the dandies may have drunk and roistered less than their fathers, they gambled more. The difference between the fairly restricted gambling among men of the same social class at White's, Boodle's, or Brooks's, and the type of gambling at Crockford's has been cited to show the greater spread of the habit by 1830. Perhaps never before or since has the gambling mania so gripped England. Captain Gronow, writing about 1860, says that many a family still felt the poverty brought on by their unwise progenitors. The fashionable novels, far from seeking to palliate the craze, may be said to have tried to stop it. While few actu-

---

[7] Mrs. Gore, *Cecil*, London, 1845, pp. 102-3.

[8] Cecil apparently became perturbed over that part of Pelham's adventures which involved buying gin in a low dive, and mourns such actions. The dandies of the Brummell school, he says, "drank their claret without forcing buckets of gin down the throats of the swell-mob . . . their victims were sought and found in their own order of society."—*Ibid.*, p. 104.

ally denounce gambling, it is noticeable that Pelham and
Vivian seldom gamble and then only out of idle curiosity.
Lister's *Arlington* contains a gambling scene of great power
and repulsiveness. In Disraeli's *The Young Duke*, there is
described a twenty-four hour session that almost makes a
beggar of the young Croesus and purges him of all gambling
desires henceforth. The habitual gamblers in *Pelham* are
mostly blacklegs, thieves, or murderers. The moral effect
thus produced is direct enough, but gambling was conducted on such an incredible scale then that in the absence
of exact figures one cannot be quite sure of the actual re-
straint practiced by the dandies. Pemberton Milnes, the
father of Richard Monckton Milnes, Lord Houghton, once
seriously denied that he was a gambler, claiming as proof
the fact that he had only twice lost over a thousand
pounds at a sitting.[9]

The gambler in the fashionable novels is likely to be a
sportsman as well. Racing, hunting, and fishing were the
chief recreations of the English gentleman then as now, but
the dandies despised sports just because of their universality.
Turned loose among a group of horsemen, fishermen, and
hunters, Vivian and Pelham are more at a loss than they
would care to admit. Vivian, for the sake of political ends,
endures the jargon of the field, but Pelham, dragged off to a
race, soon loses interest and wanders off in search of his
eccentric companion. The young Duke follows the common
course, and acquires a tremendously costly stable, only to
see his horses defeated in races at great cost to his pocketbook and his egotism.

Because of the grave danger of being considered effeminate in avoiding common male pursuits, the dandies found it
necessary to excel in other arts. What can a man do who
eschews the chase, gambling, and racing, and who associ-

[9] T. Wemyss Reid, *The Life, Letters, and Friendships of Richard Monckton
Milnes*, London, 1890, p. 30.

ates with women from preference, but prove his manliness
in other and less generally practiced arts? Pelham boxes,
fences, and is skillful with the shortstick. Vivian Grey
fences, and is so adept with the pistol that he kills a man in
a duel. But dandies at play, like dandies at study, never
display themselves in public. Only Cecil, who admittedly
lacks Pelham's and Vivian's claims to intellectuality, dares
ride, fence, and hunt openly.

Young bloods or bucks like Rawdon Crawley devoted
much of their energies to such athletic pursuits as boxing
and four-in-hand driving. When we meet Rawdon in
Vanity Fair he has already fought "three bloody duels."
The difference, of course, between Pelham and Rawdon is
that Rawdon's physical prowess, or, if you will, brutality,
is frankly his only strength. To Pelham or Vivian manual
dexterity is definitely of secondary importance, while with
other dandies athleticism like Rawdon's represents only a
temporary stage of development.

In the 1820's the rise of Tom-and-Jerryism under the
sponsorship of the renowned Pierce Egan was a phenome-
non the dandies took care to resist. That a generation of
young barbarians found the cult of the athletically rowdy
even more attractive than their fathers had was sufficient
reason why the intellectually gifted youth of the late
1820's should reject it. So, outwardly at least, the companions of Rawdon Crawley and Corinthian Tom moved
far asunder from those of Pelham. Only in surreptitious
drill did Pelham and Vivian reveal how strongly they were
marked by the quaint vulgarities of Pierce Egan.

Ultimately, perhaps, the tone of a society depends on
the relationship between the sexes. Because some of the
squeamishness which Thackeray deplored in the sixty-
fourth chapter of *Vanity Fair* had already appeared in the
twenties and thirties, an absolute comparison of social
intercourse in this period with that in earlier periods like

the Restoration is difficult to make. On the whole, the Regency seems to have been slightly more moral but a good deal sillier. Bulwer, in *England and the English*, attributed, a bit unfairly one would think, this silliness to women. The average man and nonintellectual dandy, he says, despised "Blues"; and women, forced to associate with the lighter males, tended to become like them. The original deficiency would seem to have existed in the obtuse male, but some of Bulwer's experiences with women had been unfortunate. Disraeli was far more gallant and grateful.

Silliness is not, however, a failing of the older women who act as mentors in the novels. Many a fashionable novel is, like *Vanity Fair*, a novel without a hero; few lack a mature woman of the world. The novelists, apparently believing that worldliness should be imbibed at its source, were forever advising young men to seek feminine companionship for the cultivation of manners. The mother of Don Juan was

> . . . a walking calculation,
> Miss Edgeworth's novels stepping from their covers,
> Or Mrs. Trimmer's books on education,
> Or "Coeleb's Wife" set out in quest of lovers,
> Morality's prim personification . . .

But women like Lady Frances Pelham, Lady Ormington, the mother of Cecil, Lady Harriett in *Cecil*, and Mrs. Dallington Vere in *The Young Duke* believe in education for this world, not for the next. All are married or widowed; two are mothers, and only one is under thirty. Poor Juan, freed from his mother's solicitude, flew direct to the charming Julia, but the emergent dandies were more cautious amorists. Before making serious overtures of marriage, they sought counsel from the experienced.

Disraeli's Mrs. Dallington Vere and Mrs. Gore's Lady Harriett are ideal examples of the fashionable lady. The former was "a most successful woman, lucky in everything, lucky even in her husband; for he died. He did not only die; he left his whole fortune to his wife.''[10] Lady Harriett is also a wealthy widow—how often in the fashionable novels does that condition appear as the summit of earthly bliss—selected by the dandies as their muse. It is to her that Cecil confides his social direction after leaving Oxford. Her attitude towards him is the coquettish mixture of maternal affection and occasional flirtation typical of these dandy chaperons. She is too old seriously to consider Cecil as her lover, but she is not so old that the desire to add him to her satellites is gone. Her forte, like that of Lady Frances Pelham, is good advice, but a certain amount of propriety prevents it from being quite so candid. She coaches Cecil in the social amenities, the proper houses to visit, the kind of clothes to wear, and introduces him to her own circle. She firmly suppresses his awkward collegiate flattery, and endeavors to make him a perfect gentleman after the Brummell pattern.

In drawing these people the novelists were often using actual persons. The dandy chaperon was no mere literary convention, but possibly the most real of the characters described in the novels. The novelist could hardly help knowing one, but in the rare event that he did not, he was plentifully supplied with sources by the gossip of the day. The seven patronesses of Almack's were always available in their individual or corporate form. Lady Melbourne, to whose engagingly cynical judgment Byron submitted his endless difficulties with Caroline Lamb, Augusta Leigh, Lady Oxford, Lady Frances Webster, and his wife, undoubtedly offered the novelists their most striking model, but no one succeeded in putting her on paper successfully, nor in producing a scene equal to the one in which she and Lady Bessborough begged Byron to relinquish Caroline. Both Lady Blessington and Lady Holland fancied them-

[10] Disraeli, *The Young Duke*, New York, 1870, Book 2, chap. iv, 24.

selves in the rôle of Egeria, although to writers who did not know them a far greater appeal lay in their damaged reputations.

Lady Blessington, of course, was not the only society woman with literary connections. Lady Charlotte Bury wrote dozens of novels, but survives today chiefly because of her diary describing her services as Lady-in-Waiting to Queen Caroline. Mrs. Caroline Norton was the granddaughter of Richard Brinsley Sheridan, and a novelist and poet in her own right. Lady Morgan was a society woman of a sort, and has even been suggested as the original of Becky Sharp. From Lady Morgan the list of prominent women declines into more purely literary figures like Emmeline Wortley, "her person more beautiful than her poetry," [11] and L. E. Landon, whose melancholy tomb at Capetown furnishes a silent commentary on her tearful verse.

Besides the dandy and the woman of fashion there are only two other figures who are of enough interest in the fashionable novel to demand special mention. The first of these is the mother who lives a vicarious existence in the lives of her marriageable sons and daughters.

Tennyson's "Proputty, proputty, proputty—that's what I 'ears 'em say" is fashionable marriage in capsule form. As late as *Vanity Fair* there is little or no change from the emphasis on making a good match seen in the works of Fanny Burney, Maria Edgeworth, and Jane Austen. Mrs. Stanhope in *Belinda*, it will be remembered, has such a reputation for intrepid marriage brokerage that eligible young men flee her as they would the devil. The novels, of course, have their share of love matches, but one in which a parent is actively involved is almost sure to be one in which the young man is approved because of membership at Melton or Crockford's. The number of mothers who are

[11] Disraeli, *Home Letters*, July 3, 1833, p. 124.

familiar with the genealogy, fortune, and prospects of every personable male in London is astounding. The skill required for the successful maneuvering of a squad of sons or daughters is much greater than that required by a mere general. The off season is an interval between campaigns which must be studied and prepared for as carefully as a campaign in Flanders.

The title of Lady Charlotte Bury's novel, *The Maneuvering Mother*, shows how directly the type was sometimes treated. Lady Wetherall succeeds in making good matches for all of her five daughters except the youngest, who insists on marrying for love. The moral is found when the four matches turn out unsuccessfully while the love match flourishes. The story told of Jane, Duchess of Gordon, lacks such a neat moral, but raises the intriguing mother to unbelievable heights of resourcefulness. She also had five daughters and boundless ambitions for their future. She married three of them to Dukes, one to a Marquis, while one, Louisa, was loved by Lord Brome, the son of Lord Cornwallis. Everything was being settled when Cornwallis suddenly broke off the match. The Duchess, understanding his action to be due to supposed madness in her husband's family, told him, "I know your reason for disapproving of your son's marriage with my daughter; now, I will tell you one thing plainly—*there is not a drop of the Gordon blood in Louisa's body.*"[12] Whether Lord Cornwallis was convinced or just frightened by this terrible woman is not known. At any rate, the marriage took place.

The determined gleam in a mother's eye is used in a perverse way by T. H. Lister in *Arlington*. Sir Gerald Denbigh, wishing, for personal reasons, to break up a match between Arlington and Lady Rochdale, intimates to her parents that they are being criticized as too eager to for-

[12] *Recollections of the Table Talk of Samuel Rogers*, New York, 1856, p. 143.

ward the affair. Their dislike of being thought capable of such actions postpones the marriage. ten years.

The other minor character of interest is the social climber. The wealthy man who wishes to enter the social class above him is not a new type, for Massinger, Fletcher, and Shirley present some, but in the early nineteenth-century period he took on greater importance. More recently, the figure had been best treated by Miss Burney and Miss Edgeworth. The Regency was oversupplied with actual people who thus achieved fame or notoriety. Perhaps the most famous was Mrs. Coutts who was said to have devoted her immense fortune to purchasing the Duke of St. Albans. In her lifetime she was fair sport for every satirist. Captain Gronow tells of a less celebrated Mrs. Beaumont, who, coming into a large fortune, although she herself was of low origin, resolved to invite none but persons of rank to her *salon*. Poor Gronow once asked her if he could invite a friend of his who was a captain in his own regiment. Mrs. Beaumont's reply was, "I want no more captains at my balls; you should consider yourself lucky in getting an invitation." He left, Gronow continues, "and, reflecting on the injustice I had done Mrs. Beaumont in presuming to appear at her assemblies, I never again perpetrated the offence."[13]

People and circumstances similar to these throng the pages of the fashionable novels. Reginald Cressingham in *The Man Of Fortune* by Mrs. Gore, comes unexpectedly into an income of £55,000 a year, most of which he dissipates in endeavoring to buy his way into society. His only success is admittance to Crockford's. Harris in *Cecil* is a young man of neither wealth nor position who determines to force his way into society by means of a studied insolence which his toadying instinct knows is best calculated to succeed in the atmosphere of English snobbery. Theoreti-

[13] Rees Gronow, *Last Recollections*, London, 1866, pp. 161–63.

cally the climbers fail, but despite the notorious conservatism of the aristocracy, many parvenus succeeded. Though, like Becky Sharp, they were often unsuccessful in the end, their sheer numbers compelled that protective measure on the part of the aristocrats called Exclusivism.

Interesting and valuable as fashionable novels may be for their portraits of individual types, they are primarily social documents concerning a distinct class. The novels deal with a compact and homogeneous social group in which there is considerable class solidarity and class consciousness. More strongly than any other contemporary body in England or elsewhere, the English leisure class felt the urge to do the same things, to think the same thoughts, to act in accordance with established methods of procedure. The assaulting forces, which were coming up from below to capture the luxuries of hereditary privilege, did not so much want to destroy the privilege as to share its possession. The defensive tactics employed against the intruders occasionally took the form of active punitive measures, but the more usual defense was an intensified cultivation of the group's customary pursuits. Such pursuits centered inevitably about their monopolies—the accustomed possession of wealth, leisure, and the land. There can be no doubt that the essential spirit of the English upper class arose from ownership of the land, coupled with a love for it engendered by actual residence upon it. Elsewhere in Europe ownership was customarily divorced from residence. The aristocracy of France, for example, centered its interests in Paris. Certain characteristic modifications of English institutions were due to this devotion to the land. Establishment for the greater part of the year on scattered estates with only periodic reunions in London meant that society was not predominantly urban or metropolitan, but rather that the social unit was the country house, one of the "stately homes of England." And since control of the land meant power to govern the country, positions in the government, in the army and navy, in the State Church, went to members of this class.

The management of the land itself was the primary duty and joy of the leisure class. The man of property considered that he and his estate represented England, indeed, that the two together were England. Hardly secondary to his concern in his own small part of the country, therefore, was his interest in the politics by which the whole was governed. The fashionable novelist, wishing to give an accurate picture of the upper classes, found a twofold problem. He solved it, for his own purposes at least, by assuming a duality of belief and action which cannot have been far from the truth. Since stories lay in London, society and politics received a disproportionate emphasis which the novelist sought to correct by frequent sermons on rural virtue.

The manor life, however, was not a mere pastoralism having no more connection with actual life than the idea of the noble savage has with an Iroquois. In books addressed to a people whose lives were spent more in the country than in the city, it was impossible for even the most superficial novelist to be as stupid about rural realities as would have been a Parisian. During the eighteenth century there had been too much attention paid to improved farming methods and to the enclosure of farm lands for an aristocrat to consider agricultural pursuits ignoble. Royalty itself was not above discussing its technicalities. Farmer George had actually contributed practical articles to *The Annals of Agriculture*—while peers like Townshend and others had dignified the calling. Thus, while no fashionable novels are as practical handbooks to farming as, let us say, the *Georgics* of Vergil, their attitude is outwardly respectful. Some, by members of the silver-fork school, in fact, study the gentry only on their estates. *The Banker's Wife, or,*

Court and City, 1843, by Mrs. Gore is of this description. In her *Women as They Are*, the young wife of the stern states-man is so hurt by the unjust scandal cast on her town con-duct that she insists that her husband take her to his Irish estates. The translation from the Cabinet to the farm was one often made by English lords, and not one which would have caused much commiseration except among the frothier elements in the capital. The custom of primogeni-ture practically ensured the dedication of the elder son to the life of an English gentleman. Pelham, after his un-successful political efforts, marries and retires to the peace of his estates, determined, it is true, to achieve a political return, but not counting the period of retirement as lost. It enabled him to cultivate the classics, and furnished a convenient bridge from the ecstasies of his honeymoon to re-entrance into the world of affairs. Vivian Grey has little to do with country life, for Disraeli was a city product, and he had not yet found his task of comforting the harassed Tories. Mrs. Gore makes the most continued use of this country material as background. In *Stokehill Place, or, The Man of Business*, 1837, her best study of the country squire type, we have almost nothing but country life portrayed. Even Cecil slips into a sort of liking for the country, never as an actual cultivator of the soil, but as one pleasantly enough attached to the rural beauties of Windsor. Robert Plumer Ward's *Tremaine*, 1825, is, apart from its theology, a long panegyric on country life, one whole-somely corrected and disciplined by the proper study of mankind. The model is the scholarly Horace on his Sabine farm, but there is enough shrewdness in the portrait to prevent the studious waters from becoming brackish. Tremaine is frankly bored, and if it were not for the in-fluence of his old friends, the rector and his daughter, the chances are that the retreat would soon have exhausted its charms.

A composite picture might be made of the typical landed gentleman as he appears in the fashionable novels. Even when individuals differ most in personal qualities, they are usually more alike than unlike in their fundamental characteristics. Our average country gentleman is interested in up-to-date methods of farming; he is an earnest advocate of enclosure, but concerned for the welfare of his tenants. His reading is fairly wide. He is a subscriber to either *The Edinburgh* or *The Quarterly*, according to his politics, and to one or more monthlies like *Blackwood's* or *The London Magazine*. His library is stocked not only with the standard literary works, but also with treatises on scientific agriculture. Occasionally he is interested in political science and reads Ricardo, James Mill, Jeremy Bentham, and Adam Smith. He is thoroughly attached to his estates and usually regards a season in London with aversion, often being dragged there only by the importunities of his wife and daughters. As a Justice of the Peace he sits through the Quarter Assizes with the utmost dignity, zealously ignoring legal intricacies. The tie between him and his brother magistrates is usually close, especially upon those questions which touch them as a class. Perhaps the topic upon which they unite most readily is poaching, but even this unforgivable crime is sometimes treated with a strange broadmindedness by an enlightened minority. Unfortunately for the sake of readers interested in the aristocratic reaction to poor laws, rick burning, or the trend to the cities, the fashionable novels are silent on such controversial items. The most that can be said is that an occasional group will unite in "virtuous horror of the three R's—Repeal, Reform, and Retrenchment."[14]

As one recalls the numberless country gentlemen who appear in the novels, one is willing to grant the fashionable novelists credit for many sympathetic portraits. Those

[14] *London Society*, London, 1863, IV, 145.

qualities in the country squire which appear as virtues in
their proper setting are seldom made a butt for city wits.
Occasional ridicule of the squire may be partially dis-
counted for two reasons; its source, which is usually the
giddy London crowd; and its object, since it is directed
more against dress and style than against the manor house
in general. Clothing made by the local tailor may be of
superb wearing qualities, but it is sure to have subtle errors
in cut which are ever so much more amusing to the critic
than glaring anachronisms. Next to clothing comes the
squire's lack of familiarity with the small talk of the
coteries. The phrase, "Not to know . . . argues yourself
unknown," had an annoying vogue at the time. It was
miraculously effective in reducing the tyro to a feeling of
humble inferiority. A concern with the more serious kinds
of reading instead of a superficial acquaintance with the
latest novel or poem is another example, to the smart set
in the city, of the stodginess of the gentleman interested in
his estates.

What has been said of the country squire is not entirely
true of the great landed gentry in the novels. A man of
this latter class is so bound up with his public and semi-
public functions that he almost ceases to be a private
gentleman. The year becomes a royal progress from his
mansion in Park Lane to his estate in Norfolk, to his castle
in Yorkshire, with a biennial stay in Wales or Ireland.
From the day of his birth to the day of his death the events
that mark the years become public celebrations. Such an
individual almost inevitably becomes sunk in his honors
until all realization of his personal significance is lost in
the symbol he has become. Look for example, at Lord
Rossville in Susan Ferrier's *The Inheritance*. He is not a man
so much as an incarnation of family pride. Although he is
not unmistakably the Duke of Argyle for whom Susan's
father was bailiff, he was undoubtedly drawn from wide

knowledge of the type. Lord Ormington, to whose title
Cecil eventually succeeds, is not an ass like Rossville, but
he is so methodical and pompous that he communicates
with his wife and Cecil through an attorney. His nightly
departure to the House of Lords is a rite conducted with
the ceremony of a papal court. Lord Windermere in Mrs.
Gore's *Women as They Are*, is another example of the
stilted pomposity of the great gentleman. Try to imagine
Lords Rossville, Ormington, and Windermere, swayed by
such trifles as a daughter's marriage, or indulging in an
antipathy to London in the Season. Impersonations of the
pomp and circumstance of England, they never relax.

The fashionable novel—one might almost say the
English novel—is largely concerned with that difficult
gentleman, the younger son. The present Duke and Duchess
of Omnium need give hardly a thought to the next Duke
except to give him a regular schooling and a trip abroad.
But for all the younger brothers the problem is complicated by the necessity of finding posts for which they are
not too obviously disqualified. The problem at one time,
according to the *Colloquies*[15] of Robert Southey, was far
simpler. In medieval and Tudor days the younger sons
either fought in the wars, scattered over the world in search
of adventure, or immured themselves in abbeys. With the
closing of these ways of escape, and with the gradual rise
of a government carried on by influence, it had become the
practice to enter younger sons in the numberless posts
under government. Thus the army and navy, the Church,
Parliament, and the diplomatic service were the private
preserves of upper-class families enabled to transfer the
support of their unendowed children to the nation. While

[15] Robert Southey, *Sir Thomas More, or Colloquies on the Progress and
Prospects of Society*, London, 1829, VII, 236. Addison's Will Wimble
shows how the footloose younger son worried the eighteenth-century
moralist.

the practice solved the pressing problems of parents and younger sons, it rather complicated the carrying on of government by providing for official use an extensive collection of young men of strictly amateur standing and efficiency.

From the very nature of the literature with which we are dealing, it is obvious that the young men who enter politics will be of chief interest. Churchmen are at once ruled out, except insofar as they or their wives may be of subsidiary interest; people like Mrs. Bute Crawley are occasionally met. The navy after Waterloo found itself eclipsed by the army because the country had gone mad over that victory on land. While much distinction was still attached to the bearer of a commission in one of the regiments, the Guards as a whole represent a masculine society, an awkward garrison set down in the midst of St. James's. Fashionable opinion vacillated on this subject, depending partly on the country's state of war or peace, and partly on personal whim. Lady Ormington in *Cecil*[16] has a horror of Guardsmen, whose mammoth frames are so likely to demolish her delicate *bric-a-brac*. There followed a period when adverse criticism died down—Brummell held a commission—but by the time that the eccentric man of genius had appeared, the army was again out of favor. Vivian Grey, considering what career would offer him the most scope, says, "The Services in war time are fit only for desperadoes (and that truly am I); but in peace, are fit only for fools."[17]

Despite the immense returns from the profession of law, it seems to have been more a career for the sons of attorneys than for gentlemen. The low birth of many of the Lord Chancellors would have rendered their success almost im-

[16] *Cecil* was published in 1841, but Lady Ormington's opinions are presumably expressed about 1800.

[17] B. Disraeli, *Vivian Grey*, New York, 1870, Bk. I, ch. ix, p. 9.

possible in any other field of endeavor. More than the services, the Church, or politics, a legal career required hard, persevering labor. Vivian Grey again: "The Bar—pooh! law and bad jokes till we are forty; and then, with the most brilliant success, the prospect of gout and a coronet. Besides, to succeed as an advocate, I must be a great lawyer, and to be a great lawyer, I must give up my chance of being a great man."[18]

In Mrs. Gore's *The Cabinet Minister*, 1839, there are presented circumstances that will make clear the distinction between law and politics as vocations. Grenfell is a poor youth with good patronage. Conscious of abilities, he enters the Temple[19] and plans to win his way to the Bench by hard and sober work for many years. But before long he is seduced by the charms of society, and by one woman in particular who specializes in being the protector of brilliant youths like him. She has certain political connections, not so many as she in her love of the semblance of power imagined she had, but enough, at any rate, to wean him completely from his dull books. Rationalizing his desires for the scintillating wit of Carleton House he is not long in convincing himself that he is much more likely to succeed quickly in Parliament than in law.

Although the connection of the fashionable novel with the political novel is hardly our concern here, it should be noted that long before the appearance of *Coningsby*, writers like Ward, Hook, Lister, Bulwer, and Mrs. Gore were using political figures in their books and accustoming readers to a political *milieu*. Actual political ideas are scarce, but many novels have as principal characters either active politicians, retired and disillusioned practitioners, or young

---

[18] *Ibid.*

[19] The dismay shown by Major Pendennis when he visits his nephew in the Temple illustrates the ultra-fashionable attitude toward that charming spot.

and hopeful aspirants to fame. Members of the first group
appear more often as background figures than as actual
protagonists of the novels. A prime example is the old lord
who uses Pelham as a messenger and pamphlet writer.
Unconscionable scoundrels whose devotion to the machinery of party has made them soulless automatons, they
do not present a pretty picture, but it is difficult to say
that such pictures are overdrawn. The best study of a
placeman is that of Augustus Hamilton in Mrs. Gore's
novel, *The Hamiltons, or, Official Life in 1830*. He devotes all
his energy to staying in office, only to be thrown out when
the Tories lose. Then in *Cecil* there is Lord Votefilch whose
only concern is that all the remote Votefilches get jobs.
Because of this ceaseless nepotism the Votefilches thrive
like the slightly more famous family of the Tite Barnacles.

The politician who has become disillusioned by the
sordid strife of party politics is extremely common. Because conditions in England were bad and certain aims
like Catholic emancipation and Parliamentary reform were
at times apparently hopeless of attainment, the Byronic
pose of satiety fitted the circumstances exactly. Consequently we find high-minded men, thwarted in their early
idealistic notions, turning aside from reform into self-
communing solitude. Ward's Tremaine is one who had
found political chicanery too gross for his sensitive spirit.
Cleveland, in *Vivian Grey*, has had more experience, but
his alternately sullen and brilliant moods make him a
good example of the Byronic misanthrope. Some, like
Bulwer's Godolphin, entertain such harsh opinions of
political life that they refuse to enter it at all. Because
most of them are purely conventional figures, it is a little
hard sometimes to be sympathetic with these Don Quixotes
as they tilt at windmills.

The men who retire from politics after long service because of disappointed ambitions or deception by their

party are often more convincing, although Disraeli's Marquis of Carabas, an old party hack, is only an outline. Without Cleveland's picturesqueness and without enough merit to rebel openly, he is sinking into senility when Vivian comes along and revives him. Mrs. Gore's cabinet minister furnishes another example of disappointed party service, this time to a member of the Tite Barnacles. In short, the story woven around the disappointed statesman was one of the most common.

Descriptions of the campaigning necessary to enter Parliament were much used in the novels. They gave opportunities for wit, humor, and satire. The scenes are not limited to the actual vote gathering on the hustings, but extend to the systematic house-to-house canvassing. Pelham, for instance, encounters a pretentious family sitting down to a very casual meal to which he invites himself, protesting that he never could resist such delicious cold boiled mutton. There are similar scenes in Ferrier's *The Inheritance*, Hook's *Sayings and Doings*, Lister's *Granby*, *Vivian Grey*, Massie's *Sydenham*, and dozens of later novels. At other times the campaigning is used to show the ruinous cost to candidates. Reginald Cressingham in Gore's title story in *The Man of Fortune and Other Tales* impairs a fortune of £50,000 a year in fruitless attempts to buy victory at the polls. There is a similar theme in "The Daltons," one of Hook's first series of *Sayings and Doings*.

In using politics as a demonstration of the careers of their heroes the novelists did not often set their stage in Parliament itself. Instead, they dealt with those extra-Parliamentary functions in which women play so large a part, and used the actual incidents of party warfare simply as an aside, as matter with which they expected their audiences to be familiar. Thus they lent unity and interest to their parties in country houses, their dinners at city houses, and to their balls and *conversazioni*.

Unfortunately, most fashionable novels show little concern with political issues. The chief question is, "In or out?" And except for the genuine conviction shown by men like Bulwer and much pretentious reflection displayed by many of the others, there is no mention of anything save the lowest motives. In a sense, the novels represent politics from the insiders' point of view. With professional realism they reduce issues to the simplest common denominator, "Will this position bring us votes or not?" or, "What is there in this for us?" Sad as it may be, this attitude is at least refreshingly honest and free from the cant with which such a decision, once made, would be presented to the voters.

Whether the interest shown in politics is enlightened or selfish, however, it is manifest that in 1830 there is a much greater realization of the responsibilities of the ruling classes than there had been in 1670. Closely allied as the novels are to the Restoration drama and descriptive as both are of the same social stratum, the novels show a greatly increased amount of sober work being done by the aristocrats.

The seriousness of the dandy continues to be mingled with the lighter elements of his character in the Grand Tour. As a very old and well-established custom with the English upper classes, it was renewed with great zest after the reopening of the Continent. After leaving the University, the average young man, usually accompanied by a friend or tutor, left for Paris on the first leg of a journey through France, Germany, Spain, Italy, and the Near East. The aim was the indefinite one of "broadening the mind," which included perfecting his languages, extending his knowledge of foreign cuisine, and gaining an intimacy with the best Parisian and Roman society. Visits to Geneva and Ferney were pilgrimages to the shrines of Rousseau and Voltaire. Crossing the Alps and standing in the Colos-

seum in the moonlight was paying homage to Byron. .
Whether the tour was profitable intellectually or not often
depended on the quality of the tutors, some of whom were
very conscientious fellows. An amusing story is told of
Charles Richard Sumner, a clergyman tutor to Lord
Mountcharles, the eldest son of Lady Conyngham. Lord
Mountcharles fell in love with a comparatively plebeian
Swiss girl at Berne, and actually threatened to marry her.
The tutor sent a special messenger to Lady Conyngham,
who replied forthwith, "Marry her yourself." The gallant
tutor did so, and the Lady and King George never let him
regret his heroic services, for at thirty-six he became
Bishop of Winchester.[20]

Society has never, perhaps, been more international than
it was in the eighteenth century. With the French wars
came a decided change that even Waterloo could not overcome. The exotic macaronies of Fanny Burney's day grew
old and had no successors, but the fashionable novelists
had traveled enough to give their characters something
of an international flavor. Disraeli used in *Vivian Grey*
material which had been accumulated in France and
Germany a year or two earlier. Mrs. Gore lived in Paris
and Brussels for several years, and the pictures of Parisian
society to be found in novels like her *Greville, or, A Season in
Paris*, and her *Cecil* are authentic enough. Lord Normanby
turned the usual travels of a young aristocrat to advantage in *Matilda* and other books. Practically all the
novels of Lady Blessington show traces of her seven-year
sojourn abroad. Another internationalist was Lady Charlotte Bury. Bulwer's comments on French society in *Pelham*,
England and the English, *Godolphin*, *The Disowned*, and
elsewhere, were based on his own grand tours. Thackeray,
therefore, in conducting Jos and Becky, George and Amelia,
to Waterloo was only continuing an old tradition. Indeed,

[20] William Toynbee, *Glimpses of the Twenties*, London, 1909, p. 158.

both in *The Newcomes*, and in the long description of the tedious German watering place where Jos Sedley met Becky again, he was, like many another novelist, unconscionably stretching his material.

At any rate, the dandies effectively renewed the Grand Tour, and wandered over Europe each after his own fashion, soberly studying foreign manners, or carelessly tasting of wine and love. They had to go in the spirit either of Childe Harold or of Don Juan, for they were fast in the grip of the *Zeitgeist*.

Politics, agriculture, and the Grand Tour are all very well, but the fashionable novelist knew that he was never giving his readers their supreme thrill unless he devoted many pages to the mysteries of the London Season. Between May and July the fashionable family dropped its manorial duties and forsook the bourgeoning countryside to gather within the confines of a dozen London squares. There in that tiny portion of the great city, during these few months, was played the arduous game which so intrigued the readers of fashionable novels. For it was an arduous game, as intricate as a chess match in its spirit of intrigue and advancement.

W. H. Mallock tells of Lady A., who lent her house in Hertford Street for use during August to her niece, Mrs. Marcus Hare, but was very particular in stressing the point that she was never to allow the front shades to be raised. Tactful curiosity disclosed that the kind relative was afraid that if people saw her house was being inhabited they might infer that she herself was in town during such an unfashionable month.[21]

The season was short, fortunately for the people who yearly submitted to its strict discipline. Mallock concluded that intelligent people endured it because it was only part

---

[21] W. H. Mallock, *Memoirs of Life and Literature*, London, 1920, VI, 72–73.

of life. Nothing is more stressed in the fashionable novel
than the exhaustion and world weariness commonly induced. Hook, for example, speaks of "the poor dancing
girls of Almack's, who, before the season is three parts
over, are jaded, and worn, and haggard."[22] Late hours,
overheated rooms, and rich suppers night after night preceded by a wearisome round of social visits and by calls on
dressmakers and hairdressers during the day had a cumu-
lative effect that by the end of the season left the victim
exhausted.

The most typical form of entertainment was the private
or public ball. The former, if it were to be given with the
proper effect, required the use of a large and expensive
house. Lady E—— of T——, a well-known social philosopher, advised Mallock in his early days, "You should
never be seen at a ball in a two-roomed house, a house, for
example, like the houses in Eaton Place."[23] Thus, though
Mrs. Gore assures us, "mob-assemblies went out with
George the Fourth,"[24] there was nothing Bohemian about
society. Stately, formal ceremonial was the rule. The
public balls were really only semi-public in nature—in
fact, a series of subscription affairs at Almack's was far
more exclusive in its membership than any private ball.

Properly to write of Almack's would require the satirical genius of the author of *The Rape of the Lock*, but since
Pope lived too early for a glimpse of that mystery, we shall
have to be content with lesser figures. Fortunately most
of the diarists, poets, novelists, satirists, and essayists who
entered or aspired to enter its portals wrote of it. "At the
present time," wrote Captain Gronow in 1863,[25] "one can
hardly conceive the importance which was attached to

[22] Theodore Hook, "The Man of Many Friends," in *Sayings and Doings*, London, 1825, Series II, p. 118.
[23] W. H. Mallock, *op. cit.*, VI. 72–73.   [24] Mrs. Gore, *Cecil*, p. 333.
[25] R. H. Gronow, *Reminiscences*, London, 1863, p. 43.

getting admission to Almack's, the seventh heaven of the fashionable world." Even in 1841, when the pathos of distance had not thrown a charm over its memory, *Bentley's Miscellany* contained "Almack's, a Sketch," by an "American," of which the following is a fair sample,

It is a place where the very soul of enlightened society centers; where the most splendid and noble of the noblest aristocracy of the noblest and most enlightened nation of the earth assemble; where the spiritual and ineffable quintessence of the sublimate of fashion, refined from the clarified essence of wealth and rank, is collected in one hot and luminous focus . . . the very temple, and, as it were, the most holy place of fashion.[26]

These are fine words and ironic, but they hardly exaggerate the common feeling. W. H. Mallock,[27] when a young man at Torquay, met an old dandy, Mr. Bevan, who sixty years before had flourished in Stratton Street as Amphitryon under the patronage of the Prince of Wales. On his wall, next to some sketches by D'Orsay, was a frame containing some tickets of admission to Almack's.

The rooms themselves, known as Almack's Assembly Rooms, were built in 1765, on King Street, St. James's. Almack, the builder, had established the club known by his name the year previous. This club later became Goosetree's and then Brookes's. The Assembly rooms were used for various lectures, readings, and concerts, and later by a women's club. The grand ballroom, forty by one hundred feet, was decorated in neo-classic style with gilt columns and pilasters, medallions and mirrors, and lighted by gas lamps in cut-glass lusters. Its capacity was once extended to 1,700 people. By the time of the Regency its proprietorship had passed to a Mr. Willis, and its once bright gilding had become somewhat dingy. Its social luster was undimmed, however, under its new patronesses—Lady Cow-

---

[26] *Bentley's Miscellany*, 1841, X, 640–44.
[27] W. H. Mallock, *op. cit.*, pp. 47–48.

per (later Lady Palmerston), the most popular, according
to Gronow;[28] the very rude and ill-bred Lady Jersey (the
original of Zenobia in Disraeli's *Endymion*); Lady Sefton,
kind and amiable; Princess de Lieven, haughty and exclusive; Lady Esterhazy; Lady Londonderry (later Lady
Castlereagh); and Mrs. Drummond Burrell.

This elaborate organization had a twofold motive. The
primary desire was exclusiveness, of course, but mingled
with this was the desire to lessen the cost of balls, which
for private affairs had risen to ruinous heights. The persons
admitted were of such undoubted blood and wealth that
they had no need of lavish expenditure to establish their
rank, and so Almack's was not expensive as such things go.
For the dozen or so balls every Wednesday night of the
season, the subscription was only ten guineas. The refresh-
ments were of the simplest sort, bread and butter and tea.
Simplicity was the keynote, but it was the simplicity of
shining steel, for the patronesses ruled with absolute
autocracy. Family connections, wealth, and reputation had
all to pass the censors, with the final judgment depending
on personal acquaintance with one of the board. Countless
stories are told of the difficulty of admission. For example,
only six of the three hundred socially important officers
of the Guards ever got in.[29] But perhaps a somewhat
lengthy quotation from Luttrell's poem, *Advice to Julia, a
Letter in Rhyme*, 1820, would be better than further description.

> For oft I've marked how *one* rejection
> Has spoiled a blooming nymph's complexion.
> A *second* has been known to leave her
> In strong convulsions or a fever.
> I waive the stories I have heard
> Of what has happened from a *third*.
> Nor marvel that a prize which, won,
> Is capital, and yields to none

[28] Gronow, *op. cit.*, pp. 43 ff.   [29] Gronow, *op. cit.*, pp. 43 ff.

In this world's lottery—when lost,
Not health alone, but life should cost.
All on that magic LIST depends;
Fame, fortune, fashion, lovers, friends:
'Tis that which gratifies or vexes
All ranks, all ages, and both sexes.
If once to Almack's you belong,
Like monarchs, you can do no wrong;
But banished thence on Wednesday night,
By Jove, you can do nothing right.

. . . .

Hence the petitions and addresses
So humble to the Patronesses;
The messages and notes, by dozens,
From their Welsh aunts and twentieth cousins,
Who hope to get their daughters in
By proving they are *founder's kin*.
Hence the smart miniatures enclosed
Of unknown candidates proposed;
Hence is the fair divan at Willis's
Beset with Corydons and Phillises,
Trying, with perseverence steady,
First one, and then another Lady,
Who oft, 'tis rumored, don't agree,
But clash like law and equity;
Some for the Rules in all their vigor,
Others to mitigate their rigor.

. . . .

The vainest Beauty will renounce
Her last imported blonde or flounce;
The gamester leave a raw beginner;
The diner-out forego his dinner;
The stern reformer change his notions,
And waive his notices of motions;
The bold become an abject croucher,
And the Grave—giggle for a *Voucher*;
Too happy those who fail to nick it,
In stumbling on a *single ticket*.[30]

[30] Pages 10–12.

The costume of men attending was strictly prescribed—knee breeches, white cravat, and *chapeau bas*. Gronow is authority for the story of Willis's refusal to admit the Duke of Wellington when he appeared one night in black trousers.[31] The conservatism of Almack's was not quite so apparent in the dances, however, for the Scotch reels and old English country dances which had been the favorites up to 1815 were promptly superseded when Lady Jersey introduced the quadrille from Paris. The cotillon was considered disgraceful by some, Mrs. Gore calling it "the ordeal of a chaperon's patience and a lover's magnanimity."[32] Byron's dislike of the waltz, too, is well known.

The patronesses were very strict about not admitting anyone after the hour set, midnight, with the result that the carriage line was often badly confused when latecomers from the opera hurried to the door. Formerly, when the opera had also required tickets of admission issued by patronesses, guests who attended both functions had been sifted twice. The humble American who wrote in *Bentley's Miscellany* was hardly far from the simple truth with his "essences and quintessences."

While Almack's represents an Amazonian type of organization, the clubs, being the spheres of male domination, are far more numerous in a masculine city like London. Parliament was often called "the best club in London," a phrase dating from the eighteenth century, but not really true until just after the middle of the nineteenth. Earlier than that the words represent an enthusiastic toast, nothing more. The clubs in existence before the Regency had mostly grown out of chocolate and coffee houses. White's, the oldest, was a chocolate house in 1698. Its burning in 1733 was immortalized as picture six of Hogarth's *The Rake's Progress*. Finally after rebuilding in 1755, it

---

[31] Gronow, *op. cit.*, pp. 43 ff.
[32] Mrs. Gore, *The Diary of a Débutante*, New York, 1836, p. 66.

settled at its present home, 38 St. James's Street. White's
was the possessor of the famous bow window whence
Brummell viewed the passing scene. Across the street from
this Tory stronghold was Brookes's, the Whig headquar-
ters, established toward the end of the eighteenth century.
The Cocoa Tree Club was another Whig organization,
slightly older, and more conservative. These three, with
Arthur's, were the chief clubs for the nobility and gentry
until the Regency, when clubs multiplied. There are various reasons for this increase, one being the large number
of good cooks deprived of employment during the French
Revolution. Watier's, for example, owed its existence to a
gentleman who, dining at Carleton House, lamented the
bad fare at his club. The Prince interested himself in the
poor chap's mutton diet, and calling his cook, Watier,
proposed that he start a dining club. It was there that
Brummell made most of his gambling fortune, but the pace
of the macao played was so fast, however, that the club
lasted barely a dozen years.

The most famous of the new clubs was Crockford's,
although it had somewhat the nature of a gambling house.
Crockford practiced his father's trade, fishmongering, in
Billingsgate, until he achieved some skill in gambling and
horse racing. There are various accounts of his rise to
affluence. At any rate, in 1827 Crockford erected a magnificent clubhouse at 50 St. James's Street, next to White's.
It was classical in style, with tremendous staircases of rare
marbles, the decorations alone costing £94,000. He engaged Ude, probably the most celebrated cook who ever
practiced his art in England, as chef at twelve hundred a
year, and made no charge for meals. So famous was the
club for its dinners and wines that many gentlemen dropped
a hundred or two annually at the gaming tables in order
to have the entrée. Annual dues were twenty-five pounds.
There was a committee of gentlemen in ostensible charge

with whom Crockford had an agreement to supply the hazard bank with a nightly capital of five thousand pounds while Parliament was in session. Other games, whist, faro, *rouge et noir*, macao, dice, were played, but hazard was the chief interest because a single victory could bring thousands. Crockford's gains when he retired in 1840 were estimated at £1,200,000. He had absorbed in thirteen years the surplus cash of a wealthy generation.

While the membership of the club was large, its tone was excellent. The ten to twelve hundred English members on the rolls were augmented by practically every foreigner of distinction temporarily in London. Brilliant must have been the scene in the magnificent chambers from midnight on when the playing tables were surrounded by as notable a group as has ever been assembled in London. The Goddess of Chance has rarely had such a temple erected in her honor, and at the altar—the hazard table—sat the high priest, Crockford.[33]

The gambling mania was not confined to the legitimate clubs. It permeated high and low society. *The Gaming Calendar*, 1820, by Seymour Harcourt, estimated that before the French Revolution the number of "hells" was six. With the influx of French *emigrés* and the return of Englishmen from Paris with new ideas about gambling, the number rose to fifty. Two cony-catching pamphlets of the time give some indication of the stir caused by this deluge. One, *The Greeks, a Poem*, 1817, is supposed to have been written by a gambler living in exile in France, and judging from its date, is probably an attempt to masquerade as the work of Brummell, who had just retired to Calais. "Greek" is a cant term for professional gambler; "pigeon" is the equivalent of modern American "sucker."

[33] There is a sympathetic portrait of Crockford himself in Disraeli's *Henrietta Temple*. An account of the club may be found in Mr. Michael Sadleir's *The Strange Life of Lady Blessington*.

For here, gallant Greeks! my sad fortune deplore,
No *pigeon* takes wing to the Gallican shore;
And the nation, composed of sly slippery elves,
Admits of no *plucking*, except by themselves.[34]

The Pigeons describes the victims who were plucked by
the Greeks. The first pamphlet contains a list of gambling
houses and addresses, and denounces gamblers and warns
pigeons under such transparent disguises as Sir G[odfre]y
W[ebste]r, and Lord A[lvanle]y.

A certain number of gambling houses, both patrician
and plebeian, following the lead of the Palais Royal in
Paris, administered not only to the demand for gambling
but to the appetite for venery.

Ye haunts of St. James's! ye Cyprian Fair!
How sweet your amusements! how *winning* your air![35]

Resorts like this are delicately alluded to in *Pelham,
The Young Duke, Sydenham,* and other novels chiefly by men.

When young men gamble, they generally lose and resort
to the people who live by supplying advance funds on
anticipated inheritances. "Jew" King, for example, was an
expansive chap, not above making puns on his own name,
with a taste for art, and an oriental villa up the Thames.
His competitor was Solomon, miserly, secretive, the
archetypal money lender. But the generation of dandies
hardly contributed anything new to the lore of the usurers,
because the tradition is too old in English literature.
Under a statute dating from the time of Charles II, gambling debts were not legally collectable if for more than ten
pounds. This was a way out for pigeons who felt cheated,
but debts of honor took precedence over a gentleman's
other obligations. Many a dandy who in his youth had
taken the Grand Tour found it necessary in old age to
take another.

[34] Quoted by John Ashton, *The History of Gambling in England*, London,
1898, p. 106.   [35] *Ibid.*

This was a period intensely interested in gastronomy, and its literature, though small, was choice. Two books in particular were the source of most gustatory discussions of the sort in fashionable novels. Louis Eustache Ude, whom we have mentioned before as chef at Crockford's, had formerly been in the service of the Earl of Sefton and the Duke of York. His authority was pontifical, therefore, and his *The French Cook*, 1813, ran through twelve editions in twenty years. More famous, however, than Ude's book, and of a different type, was the immortal *La Physiologie du gout*, 1825, of J. A. Brillat-Savarin. With Brillat-Savarin for philosophical, and Ude for practical guidance, the fashionable novelist was well equipped.

The common person had resort to Mrs. Rundell's cookbook, one of John Murray's most profitable copyrights. Ude's successor at Crockford's, Charles Elme Francatelli, who ultimately became cook to the royal family, wrote a *Gastronomy*, which Richard Bentley published. Alexis Soyer, chef to Lord Chesterfield, published a *Gastronomic Regenerator* in 1846. Lady Charlotte Bury herself edited a cookbook, but it was a mere matter of scissors and paste, lacking soul.

George Saintsbury is inclined to credit Thomas Walker's *Original* and Thackeray's essay, "Memorials of Gormandizing,"[36] rather than the work of any Frenchman with revolutionizing the native English theory of dining. Walker, a Cambridge man, and former London police magistrate, was desirous of expressing himself on "three subjects of interest and importance—the Art of Dining and Giving Dinners, the Art of Travelling, and Art of attaining High Health—all from experience."[37] To do so he

---

[36] George Saintsbury, *A Consideration of Thackeray*, London, 1931, p. 11.
[37] Quoted by A. Hayward, *The Art of Dining*, New York, 1899, p. 104. A sixth edition of Walker's *The Original*, edited and arranged by William A. Guy, was published in London, 1885.

started (on May 20, 1835) a weekly paper called *The Original*, which he continued until his death the following January. The paper is a most curious hodgepodge of downright superstition and sound sense regarding health, and "aristology"—to adopt Walker's name for dining. He was one of the first to advocate simplicity in a meal, regarding which there had been little change for the better since Waterloo.

Gronow, whose zest for the minutiae of living was most commendable, has preserved a sample menu of an English dinner of about 1814. He implies that it was a more or less invariable collection of comestibles. There were two soups, mulligatawny and turtle; three fishes, salmon, turbot, and smelt; mutton or roast beef; fowls; tongue and ham. French dishes, just coming in and neglected by nearly every one, occupied the side tables. Plain boiled potatoes were served with every course except the soup, but including the sweet. Vegetables were supplied with a sauce, a commendable effort toward blending flavors spoiled by being brought on cold. The mechanical part of eating was fearfully complicated by the necessity of placing a sample of everything on the fork at one time. Wines accompanied every course, sherry and hock being the favorites. After dinner, of course, when the women left, the men spent an extra hour or two over their port. It was in reaction against such Gargantuan feasts that the fashionable novelists reveled in dotting their pages with mention of soups, sauces, and sweets named after French immortals.

But a change in the "silly direction of Frenchifying" cookery was not all that was wanted. Too often "capital Scotch broth" became merely *potage de mouton à l'Ecossais* as in the eighth chapter of *Vanity Fair*. Walker's essays helped to crystallize sentiment for a native English development of the art.

Out of two articles in the *Quarterly* for 1835 and 1836 by

Abraham Hayward, the first a review of Walker's papers, grew Hayward's *The Art of Dining*, 1852. This very learned essay is too formal and cold to be a real contribution to the warm and generous art. Thackeray's essay, a letter from M. A. Titmarsh to Oliver Yorke in *Fraser's* for 1841, was in most pleasant contrast to Hayward's authoritativeness, and a genial normal development of Walker's occasional eccentricity. In their sturdy English tone Thackeray's pronouncements might have suited the English eaters of Gronow's meal, while their French quality was a refreshing simplicity in contrast to the overdecorative meals which fashionable novelists loved to describe to their readers.

Fashions in dining, gambling, and dancing, of course, change lightly with the years, and if it were not for the great importance allotted to them by the fashionable novelists such discussions would hardly merit attention in a literary history. Indeed, to study the fashionable novel even under such broad headings as characters and classes is, of course, to omit part of the picture. The long life of the *genre* and the great number of its practitioners make similarities and differences caused by time and individual approach of the utmost importance. The people who wrote the novels were not mere cogs in a machine turning hot-pressed paper and ink into sumptuously bound three-volume tales for the circulating libraries, although some of the large-scale producers, Mrs. Gore, for instance, may have thought so in moments of discouragement. The light novelist has his fingers on the pulse of his age. His equipment is crude, perhaps, no elaborate battery of sensitive instruments, only a delicately attuned response to every superficial movement of the patient. In the following chapters we shall have to see how that response varies with the time and the individual observing it.

III

THE FASHIONABLE NOVEL FROM SUSAN FERRIER
TO T. H. LISTER

THE 1790's were years of idealism, of schemes for political justice, for prison, marital, and educational reforms. By 1820 the disillusioning effects of war and commercial expansion had cooled these generous ardors, and a nation of shopkeepers once more saw profits as the main purpose of existence. Wealth, quickly but unevenly distributed, sought culture to bolster up its new pride of place. The didactic tale of fashionable life, hitherto used to preach contentment to the lower middle class by showing the shallowness of riches without virtue, gradually changed to meet the requirements of a new audience. The writers, who, by making the didactic novel a medium for spreading the rudiments of manners among the newly rich and the newly literate, changed it into the fashionable novel, are Susan Ferrier, Theodore Hook, R. Plumer Ward, and Thomas Henry Lister.

The fashionable novel was firmly established with Lister's *Granby* in 1826. In it the moral lessons, which had become less and less essential in the novels of Susan Ferrier and Theodore Hook, virtually disappeared. As the moral obsession declined, the desire for accuracy in the portrayal of rank and setting grew. Susan Ferrier, Theodore Hook, and Plumer Ward, no matter how much they may have owed to Maria Edgeworth's theory about the purpose of fashionable fiction, wrote expertly about a society which they knew. They brought the fashionable novel to the point where Mrs. Gore, Lady Blessington, and Lady Charlotte Bury could begin. At the height of the vogue, people read fashionable novels as much to learn etiquette as to be amused.

SUSAN FERRIER

There can be no pretense that Susan Ferrier was of the silver-fork school. She was Scotch, and characters who converse in the broadest of Scotch dialects use pewter. Her custom, however, of depicting fashionable London characters against a background of Scotch scenes and Scotch people gives her a peculiar interest that is intensified by her occasional pronouncements on the theory of fashionable conversation. While her peasants remain far more alive than her English gentlefolk—what modern reader would trade Uncle Adam for a dozen Lord Rossdales?—she at least tried to deliver fashionables from their customary stilted and Frenchified speech.

Her output was scanty, only three novels in all—*Marriage*, 1818, *Inheritance*, 1824, and *Destiny*, 1830. It took her several years to compose *Marriage*, in which she was helped by Miss Clavering, a niece of Lady Charlotte Bury. The method seems to have been a collaboration in which Ferrier did most of the writing, while mutual criticism decided on details. Miss Clavering submitted several chapters, but in the book as published, only part of Chapter XIV, "The History of Mrs. Douglas," is hers.

Both of them had definite ideas about the novel. On May 10, 1813, Miss Clavering wrote to Miss Ferrier,[1]

I don't like these high life conversations; they are a sort of thing by consent handed down from generation to generation in novels, but have little or no groundwork in truth.

On a perusal of Chapter XIV as it was first submitted to her, Susan wrote to her friend,

What you have written I like very well except the speech of the Duchess of M——, which is the style of conversation of

[1] J. A. Doyle, editor, *Memoir and Correspondence of Susan Ferrier*, London, 1898, p. 115.

duchesses in novels. Far from giving occasion to describe character, I know nothing more insipid or uniform than fashionable
manners and conversation, and to attribute designs to them from
their conduct is ninety-nine times out of a hundred quite a
mistake.[2]

From this critical agreement it may appear that each
could detect factitious conversation when the other wrote
it. Fashionable conversation always displeased critics, but
novelists serenely continued with their pomposities. The
unique nature of Edinburgh society, described affectionately
in *Marriage*, was undoubtedly responsible for Miss Ferrier's
and Miss Clavering's dislike of ostentatious duchesses.

The circle is so confined that its members are almost universally
known to each other; and those various gradations of gentility,
from the cit's snug party to the duchess's most crowded assembly,
all totally distinct and separate, which are to be met with in
London, have no prototype in Edinburgh. There the ranks and
fortune being more on an equality, no one is able greatly to exceed his neighbor in luxury and extravagance. Great magnificence
and the consequent gratification produced by the envy of others
being out of the question, the object for which a reunion of individuals was originally invented becomes less of a secondary
consideration. Private parties for the actual purpose of society and
conversation are frequent, and answer the destined end; and in
the societies of professed amusement are to be met the learned,
the studious, and the rational; not presented as shows to the
company by the host and hostess, but professedly seeking their
own gratification.[3]

Because of this feeling for the integrity of Edinburgh
society, Miss Ferrier threw the weight of her disapproval
chiefly on London people, or on Scotch people in London.
Her chief incentive to attack was a lusty sense of the
ridiculous. She delighted in puncturing the inflated egos of
Lords Rossville and Altamont with the sharp sword of wit.
Individuals she could understand, whether they were
Scotch or English, but London itself she conjured up as an

[2] *Ibid.*   [3] Susan Ferrier, *Marriage*, London, 1929, p. 116.

iniquitous Babylon to be attacked, not with laughing satire, but with thundering denunciation. She was even more convinced than Maria Edgeworth that attendance on a London season meant the loss of fortune and of morals. Gertrude, at the end of her London career in which "she was hailed as the leader of every fashionable folly,"[4] suffers every whit as much as members of the family in Edgeworth's *Patronage*.

The London season was now drawing near a close, and Lady Rossville had run her full career of folly and extravagance. As bills came pouring in upon her from all quarters she was startled at the magnitude of the sums she had expended, and for which she had nothing to show but a parcel of gewgaws, which had ceased with their novelty to afford her any pleasure.[5]

That was the financial effect. The moral contamination was worse.

She was the idol of the day, and she breathed only in an atmosphere of adulation, baleful alike in its effects on the head and the heart.[6]

In *Marriage*, poor Lady Juliana, not thrown into the social whirl comparatively late in life, like Gertrude, but born in it, had even less chance of becoming something worthy.

Under the auspices of a fashionable mother and an obsequious governess the froward petulance of childhood, fostered and strengthened by indulgence and submission, had gradually ripened into that selfishness and caprice which now, in youth, formed the prominent feature of her character.[7]

One cannot look, therefore, to Susan Ferrier for an urbane attitude toward London society. In the diction of the fashionable novel, however, she made more than one praiseworthy attempt at improvement.

I disapprove very decidedly of Frenchifying Lady Ju's conversa-

4 Susan Ferrier, *Inheritance*, London, 1929, p. 688.
5 *Ibid.*, p. 737.   6 *Ibid.*, p. 688.   7 *Marriage*, p. 5.

tion . . . it is not, nor has been, I'll answer for it, the least the mode this century.[8]

By this very sensible stand she reduced to a minimum the occurrence of French words. She used them only for almost untranslatable terms like the names of foods, or commonplaces like *tête-à-tête*, *canaille*, *àpropos*, and her characters cannot be accused of senseless repetition of them when English words would have been more suitable. A severe pruning, however, has left Lady Juliana a few; they indicate in her, perhaps, life copying art. In any case, all the French words in *Marriage* and *Inheritance* combined would hardly serve for a single chapter in *Evelina* or *Belinda*. Despite this practical demonstration of the ability of the English language to express fashionable fatuity, Ferrier had almost no followers. Either French did come into general fashionable use in London, which is quite possible, or else the tradition was too strong for one writer to overcome. The novelists who followed her remained adherents to the Burney-Edgeworth practice.

THEODORE HOOK

Theodore Hook was the first novelist since Fanny Burney to escape the handicap of an imperfect knowledge of London's fashionable life. He was hampered neither by the disability of sex nor the craving for correctness in his enjoyment of the "various gradations of gentility, from the cit's snug party to the duchess's most crowded assembly." When a character in Edgeworth or Ferrier goes to London one shudders and yearns to cry out a word of warning. Hook's people are at home there; they have become immunized to the noxious vapors, and while they may suffer, they do not require a village sanatorium for cure. London is both a disease and a cure.

The period during which Hook flourished is known in

[8] J. A. Doyle, *op. cit.*, p. 115.

part as the Regency, but Hook, like Beau Nash and Beau Brummell, might well have given his name to an era. He was its dominant social figure, not in the same sense as Charles II, George IV, Nash, or Brummell, perhaps, but in a way unique with him. Of the half dozen actual people who appear in novel after novel—Prinny, Wellington, Croker, Eldon, the Marquis of Hertford—Hook is easily the chief. He is the Stanislaus Hoax of *Vivian Grey*, the Lucius Gay of *Coningsby*, the Mr. Wagg of *Pendennis* and *Vanity Fair*. But even the best of novelists can do no more than faintly adumbrate his amazing powers. His own books, says Lockhart, "are nothing without the commentary of that bright eye, the deep gurgling glee of his voice—the electrical felicity of his pantomime."[9] For the first time since the passing of the Restoration and Sentimental comedy, society had a writer born of its own flesh, nourished on its own traditions, one who loved the city with as much fervor as Charles Lamb.

Hook was born in London in 1788, the same year as Byron. His father composed music, and for him in 1805 Theodore wrote the words for a comic opera. The boy was seventeen then, and had already besieged the managers with manuscripts. His education, after Harrow, where he was a schoolmate of Byron's, and a short trial at Oxford, came from the Green Room of the theaters, where the city is as concentrated as it is in Clerkenwell. The first operetta he followed with numberless farces and sketches, what we should call vaudeville today. From these the young man developed a weakness for broad farcical situations that hurt his more serious work thenceforward. All the emphasis was thrown on developing character in a hurry by the stressing of a single feature, on word plays, and slapstick.

Hook was gifted beyond any other person in English

[9] *The Maclise Portrait Gallery*, edited by Wm. Bates, London, 1898, p. 232.

literature with the ability for rapid extemporaneous composition. Introduced into a roomful of people, he could produce apparently without reflection endless verses so apt in their application, so clever in their conception, that his fame rapidly spread beyond theatrical circles, and young Hook found himself the most assiduously cultivated guest in the capital. No party was complete without him, so he lived in the midst of a whirl and bustle that would have kept a less prolific author from any composition whatever. As a result of his social prowess he incurred the notice of the Prince Regent, who secured for him a place as treasurer in Mauritius. A shortage of funds entrusted to him led to his recall and ultimate imprisonment, although it is doubtful whether he was to blame for anything beyond utter carelessness.

He became in 1820 the editor of *John Bull*, established by the King and Tories as a medium for attacking the Queen, whom George wished to divorce. From this Hook derived a quite adequate income, although he lived from day to day in danger of a horsewhipping because of his connection with the scandal sheet. He always denied any knowledge of it, while the office was represented by a "coarse, half-brutal, but tall and powerfully built Irishman, of the grade of a day-laborer . . . to answer all applicants to see the editor, his one sentence generally being enough—'I'm the Idditor, sir, at your sarvice.' "[10]

His first acknowledged book-length production, *Sayings and Doings*, was published by Colburn in 1824. There are four short tales, each one based on some familiar proverb, the "saying," while the story represents the application, or the "doing." Hazlitt thought the book exposed Hook's stupidity,[11] but it proved extremely popular, and the publisher called for another. The second series appeared in

[10] S. C. Hall, *Retrospect of a Long Life*, New York, 1883, pp. 70–72.
[11] *Examiner*, November 18, 1827, "The Dandy School."

1825, and the third in 1828. One story in the first series, "Merton," had been published as long before as 1808, under the title of *The Man of Sorrow*, by "Alfred Allendale." It was stillborn, and Hook revised it for its rebirth.

In *Sayings and Doings* appear all the elements that were to make up the stock-in-trade of the fashionable novelist. Here are the balls, the dinners, the hunts, the teas, the gossip, the electioneering, the opera, the theater, the clubs, the marriage settlements, the love marriages, the fashionable marriages, the gambling, and the dissipation—everything, in fact, that makes up the daily round for those fortunate souls who possess accounts at their bankers and live in London. In this charming world Hook was thoroughly at ease. His immediate predecessors were ladies whose refusal to compromise with Vanity Fair is admirable, no doubt, but a trifle dull.

The first story in the first series, "Danvers," will help us understand his use of society material. The plot is old, for Hook never took the pains to devise new ones. Danvers Burton has a wife and five children, who all live happily together in a fairly opulent middle-class way. An old nabob uncle leaves them a fortune, whereupon they proceed to go to pieces as promptly as ever Maria Edgeworth could have predicted. Frustrated in an attempt to enter society, Danvers turns to Parliament. Successive defeats impoverish even the store the nabob had piled up, and possessed finally of only the wife's dowry, the Burtons retire to the country.

An original feature of *Sayings and Doings* was the electioneering, so cleverly and satirically described that it gained a popularity which brought it forth again and again in subsequent novels by Bulwer, Disraeli, and Mrs. Gore. Then, too, some of the scenes, particularly the *conversazione* at the Marchioness of Hatfield's home when the shy and middle-class Mrs. Burton is forced to enter a little party of some fifty persons, lent new interest to old material.

Series Two contained "The Man of Many Friends," which is a conventional tale of a young man who wasted his substance in London. The gambling scenes, the treatment of the gulling of the youth by his steward and friends, the waste of money on horses, women, and tailors is all done with a skill and convincingness that make one wish that Hook had taken the pains to write a thoroughly realistic novel about London life, one in which he could have thrown overboard his antiquated and stereotyped plots. His was the realistic method working in the factitious framework of farcical plots.

The form of prose *fabliau* into which Hook chose to throw his stories emphasizes the relation of his work to Maria Edgeworth's. Given an outline of the story and the proverb to be illustrated, a reader might conceivably mistake his work for hers. The story of "Danvers," for example, is an illustration of the saying, "Too much of a good thing is good for nothing." "The Man of Many Friends" expounds the adage, "Practice is really better than precept." Maria Edgeworth could have written stories with these plots and theses readily enough. But Hook was able to support his theses with material drawn from personal knowledge, while he was not one to allow any scheme to bother him overmuch. He succeeded in making the pseudo-didactic tale of real life very popular. Thackeray and Dickens adopted it in their turn, and improved upon him.

ROBERT PLUMER WARD

The hold of the didactic novel seemed never to be broken when in 1825 a new novel by an anonymous writer became a best-seller. The book was longer and more substantial than anything Hook had ever done, and had for theme one he had never used—a wealthy young patrician's search for an occupation which should satisfy his scruples. The book was obviously by someone who had occupied a high station in politics, as Colburn, the publisher, liked to point out, and yet a good portion of the novel dealt with a purely religious theme. *Tremaine, or, The Man of Refinement*, was its name, and Robert Plumer Ward its author.

Before writing *Tremaine*, Ward had already achieved an impressive bibliography, composed not of items of fiction, but of works on foreign relations, law, and politics. His life had consisted of anything but the pleasures of society when he decided to turn fictionist. Educated at Christ Church, Oxford, and the Inner Temple, he was called to the bar in 1790, and in 1802, as a *protégé* of Pitt, entered Parliament. Upon retiring from active participation in law and politics, he cast about for a method of rendering his experiences beneficial to his fellows. The reading of modern novels convinced him that what was needed was a return to the sound principles embodied in such works as *Rasselas*, the *Spectator Papers*, and the novels of Maria Edgeworth. He found that the modern novel neglected moral principles, lacked edification, and did not attempt to reconcile man with God and nature—aims which to him were the only excuses for the writing of novels. They were written, it seemed to him, either by jesters like Theodore Hook, who couldn't conceivably have anything worthwhile to say, by atheists like William Godwin, or by frivolous artists like Jane Austen.

If it should be asked why I have recorded the series of retired scenes, and sometimes abstruse conversations which compose the following narrative, my answer is a very simple one: in the present state of the world, they may possibly do good, and cannot do harm . . . if it detach but one man or one woman, from the headlong career which most are pursuing, and induce them to look for a while into themselves, as God and nature intended them to do, its end will be answered.

It is curious that a novel which justifies such a preface should ever be considered a fashionable novel. Most of it is rotund moralizing, but it paraded a number of elegant people and the reviewers considered it a social document. Colburn, whose sense of judgment in such matters was unerring, exploited it to a fashionable audience.

Ward had chosen to submit the book to Colburn anonymously, but he wished some actively practicing literary man to correct the style before it was published. Colburn named his reader, P. G. Patmore, as best fitted to judge whether the style was popular and contemporary. Because of Ward's whim, neither Patmore nor Ward knew whose were the papers they so solemnly exchanged through Ward's solicitor, Austen, and Colburn. After a second novel had been revised in this way, the author and his adviser became friends, and Patmore never quite recovered from the honor.[12] Colburn had tried to turn his own ignorance of the author's name to account by fathering the novel on likely individuals. Curiously enough, one gentleman, the Hon. Richard Ryder, declined the attribution publicly.[13]

Tremaine, the man of a single bent or humor, was a well-worn literary type when Ward decided to revive him in 1825. His chief characteristic is a delicate refinement which is so extreme that one is immediately reminded of Mackenzie's *Man of Feeling*. The shock of acceptance kills the man of feeling; the horrible indelicacy of most young ladies has kept Tremaine from ever proposing. Unable to engage in any pursuit for long because of his refusal to compromise, he has tried several accepted methods of finding a place in the world—travel, study for the ministry, and participation in politics, but at the time the book opens he has fled to the studious quiet of his estate, resolved to emulate Horace. The good Dr. Evelyn and his daughter, Georgiana, prove the means which are to draw him from the ivory tower which he had already begun to

[12] He recorded it at great length in his *My Friends and Acquaintance*, London, 1854. [13] *London Magazine*, May, 1825, pp. 128–31.

find overrated. Georgiana returns his love, but his inability to profess belief in the Christian way of life forces her to refuse his proposal. He withdraws from their society and threshes out his problem until he is brought to a state of mind where Dr. Evelyn is able to overcome his last remaining scruple by an invincible argument based on immortality, Providence, and the problem of evil and free will which extends over half the second book. The final capitulation of the forces of atheism finds Georgiana and Tremaine with their religious differences harmonized and therefore ready to marry.

A fashionable novel? Surely not, if the term has any definite meaning, and yet this very book is credited with having been a society sensation because of its flattering handling of fashionable life. The people who acclaimed it for its correctness welcomed it because of their willingness to let the world identify them with stainless people like Tremaine, Dr. Evelyn, and Georgiana. Insult people, browbeat them, ridicule their actions, and they will be only too willing to call the writer liar; mirror them as people of refinement and the path of the reformer is automatically smoothed. The anonymous author of this book obviously belonged to the charmed cricle. He was neither crude and mawkish in his praise, nor bitter in his iconoclasm. Others had described the silly fringe at great length while murmuring that, of course, the better part of society was not like that. Ward had happily reversed these tactics.

Tremaine, with two hundred of its pages turned over bodily to a disquisition on Christianity, had showed, however, a woeful lack of imaginative power. In it Ward almost unnecessarily asserted that what he was writing was a philosophical treatise.

"Essay? surely, Sir, it begins to be a novel!—" "By no means! and I will maintain it before any bishop, professor, or critic in Christendom, that it still is that treatise of moral philosophy I intended when I set out. I am to relate facts, and if love be a subject of moral philosophy, how can I help it?"[14]

The whole bent of Ward's mind was didactic, and he knew well enough that he could hardly claim to be a novelist in the ordinary sense of the word.[15] The *Quarterly's* review of *Tremaine* stressed this failure by pointing out that Ward too often secured his effects by the introduction of temporary characters who deliver their preachment, and fade away.

Ward's second novel, *De Vere, or, The Man of Independence*, 1827, did more to establish the truth of Canning's malicious remark that Ward's law books were as interesting as novels and his novels as dull as law books. *De Vere* studies another man of a single bent, yet the contrast with *Tremaine* is sharply drawn. Tremaine is the man satiated with experience who seeks his renascence in the country. De Vere is of the opposite type—the innocent idealist whose salvation lies in experience of the world. His youth has been circumscribed, but after Christ Church he spends three years traveling on the Continent, preparatory to entering Parliament. His seat in the unreformed House is kept for him by a friend, pending his readiness to assume it, but this substitute proves to be so useful a tool to Lord Mowbray, De Vere's kinsman and a Minister, that they plot to keep De Vere out, fearing that he will not go along with the party. He becomes indignant finally, and takes his seat as a partial follower of the Opposition leader, Wentworth.

There are many portraits of actual political characters

[14] *Tremaine*, pp. 157–58.

[15] Ward wrote to Patmore thanking him for a review Patmore had written: "What pleases me most in this review is the handsome and forcible manner in which you vindicate my claim (laughed at by the flippant and very shallow) to be something more than a writer of novels of fashionable life. I cannot say that I am much flattered to be so considered, and in short, pretend to be an essayist, only in another form." (January 13, 1839.) Patmore, *op. cit.*, p. 110.

in the novel. Wentworth was designed by Ward as a composite of Pitt, Canning, and Bolingbroke: the anecdotes are Pitt's; the love of letters and conversation, Canning's; the remainder, Bolingbroke's. Mowbray was in part the Duke of Newcastle. Ward drew portraits of himself as the Man of Imagination and the Man of Content. Contemporary criticism took for granted the political as well as the social implications of the book. *The Quarterly Review*, for example, thought "nothing more true and graphic than some of the political" scenes.[16]

Ward's contribution to the fashionable novel ended with *De Vere*. He wrote other books,[17] it is true, after an interval of twelve years, but they adhered to the same general type, and made no advance. His importance lies almost solely in his appearing in print so close to the time when the fashionable novel reached its greatest popularity. He succeeded in transferring to his books the excessive seriousness which had characterized the favorite novelists of his youth, and in investing the upper classes with a gentleness and good taste hitherto lacking in novels about them. Moreover, he aroused Disraeli's interest in novel-writing, and then by carrying the political interest to a high pitch, as in *De Vere*, farther than Disraeli had gone in *Vivian Grey*, he thus foreshadowed such political and fashionable novels as Bulwer's *Pelham*, Massie's *Sydenham*, and Mrs. Gore's *The Hamiltons*.

THOMAS HENRY LISTER

Up to a certain point, Edgeworth, Ferrier, Hook, and Ward do not vary greatly in their use of material—whether

---

[16] *Quarterly Review*, June, 1827, XXXVI, 285.

[17] *Pictures of the World at Home and Abroad*, 1839, London, consists of three stories all displaying his aristocratic prejudices. *De Clifford; or, The Constant Man*, 1841, endeavors, among other things, to explain the features that distinguish *nous autres*, or members of the *haut ton*; concludes tritely enough, that it is "that indescribable something."

they got it by the exercise of imaginative power as Edgeworth did, or by actual experience, as Hook did. To the
women novelists society was a hotbed for the sprouting of
moral lessons. Hook, having seen some of the rascalities of
society, was willing to neglect the question of moral
sanctions, but even he continued to write more in the well-
established forms than might be expected of a person of
his upbringing. As for Ward, who really should have published twenty years earlier, there can be no debate—he is
simply an anachronism. However, in 1826 appeared
Granby by Thomas Henry Lister, aged twenty-six, and
Vivian Grey, by Benjamin Disraeli, aged twenty-one—two
first novels absolutely untouched by the naïve assumption
that fashionable society is necessarily worse than any
other.

Lister is the less important of the two, largely because
of Disraeli's subsequent work and fame, although there
can be little doubt that *Granby* is a better novel than *Vivian
Grey*. Lister was an older man with the normal education
of a gentleman—Westminster, and a period at Trinity,
Cambridge. When Disraeli wrote his first novel he was still
a boy, his limited knowledge of society atoned for by an
illimitable imagination. Little wonder that for sober value
Lister surpassed him.

The plot of *Granby* hardly displays sober value, however,
for Lister based it on the old device of exchanged heirs.
Stern parents oppose young love, and only when the poor
hero proves to be the rightful heir do they relent. The
movement is slow, progressing through spasmodic, melodramatic actions like that in which Granby denounces his
cousin as a cheat. One feels that this and similar occurrences, such as are to be found in Lister's *Arlington*, where
the finding of the body of the murdered lord in the first
chapter makes one expect a detective in the second, are put
in mainly to sell the book.

Lister's real merit must be sought in his handling of dialogue. Such a judicious mixture of wit, humor, and tomfoolery results from the banter of the dandy Mr. Trebeck[18] with the inexperienced, nineteen-year old Caroline, as could hardly be improved. The skillfulness with which Trebeck plays on the provincialisms of his country neighbors is an example of Lister's ability to demonstrate rather than merely describe the wit of his characters. The sentimental lady, Harriett Duncan, an excellent likeness of Lady Caroline Lamb, furnishes a perfect foil for Trebeck. The picture of the politician, Sir Henry Jermyn, who votes with the ministry at night and talks radicalism in the morning, shows great satirical power.

The distance we have traveled from Maria Edgeworth may be seen in Harriett Duncan's remark, "Do tell me your favorite novels. I hope you like nothing of Miss Edgeworth's or Miss Austen's. They are full of commonplace people that one recognizes at once." Whether Lister did or did not share Lady Harriett's feeling is immaterial; apparently the feeling existed. The qualification we had to make in Hook's novels—that they continued to use the form of their didactic predecessors—does not apply to Lister's. The fashionable novel, as opposed to the novel which for didactic or romantic reasons uses fashionable people, was firmly established by Lister's *Granby*.

There are better fashionable novels than *Granby*, no doubt, but few that fulfill all the requirements of the *genre* more adequately. There is some politics; there are sumptuous balls, spirited house parties, excited gambling scenes, heightened by gossipy conversation everywhere—at the breakfast table, at the morning embroidery session, at tea, at the dinner table, and in the drawing-room. There is

[18] Captain Jesse in his life of Brummell says that the Beau considered Trebeck to be a portrait of himself. It is not probable that Lister could have shot so far wide of the mark. Brummell was simply flattering himself.

ridicule of the middle classes, an intellectual dandy with enough wit to give him edge, and a beautiful heroine less insipid than usual; there are social climbers, clever but homely daughters who despise men, and, most indispensable of all, there is Almack's. All of these elements have seldom been so well shuffled and spread out for the delectation of readers.

Lister's second novel, *Herbert Lacy*, 1828, inferior to *Granby* in wit and portraiture, deals with the conflict between ancient family pride and new wealth. The hero succeeds in overcoming the prejudices of his relations and the villainous interference of the girl's trustee.

Bulwer privately termed *Herbert Lacy*, "neat, or even elegant mediocrity; but . . . no rival to *Pelham*."[19] When, as editor of *The New Monthly*, he came to review Lister's next novel, *Arlington*, he revealed only mild enthusiasm.[20] The reason for Bulwer's dislike of Lister may have been, as Mr. Sadleir suggests, that Lister was a Tory. His fashionable novels were about the only representatives of their kind in Murray's list, but when in 1838–39 that publisher disposed of his novel copyrights, Colburn acquired *Granby*.

Arlington, 1832, is notable chiefly for its careful presentation of two types of dandies, what may be called the intellectual and the picturesque. Of the two, the intellectual, Sir Gerald Denbigh, who is probably drawn in part from D'Orsay, is the more interesting. Distinguished neither for personal charm nor good looks, he affected to despise clothes, while assiduously cultivating an agreeable wit. Instead of remaining a lonely clothes' model on the sidewalks or in the club windows of St. James's, he became the most celebrated diner-out in London. Refusing steadily to attend mass parties, he kept raising his social value until a hostess felt assured of success at her house party or dinner

[19] Quoted, Michael Sadleir, *Edward and Rosina*, Boston, 1931, p. 122.
[20] *The New Monthly*, June, 1832, XXXIV, 250.

if she could secure him. The picturesque dandy, Henry Beauchamp, obviously drawn from Brummell, is endowed with physical beauty and a genius for style, but his mental and moral level is not so high as Denbigh's.

He was the glass of fashion in which all the aspiring young coxcombry of London dressed themselves, and wore the Beauchamp hat, or the Beauchamp collar, and tried to walk, ride, or drive in humble imitation of the inimitable original.[21]

This book employs another of Lister's favorite situations. Miss Watson, a bouncing young lady from the country, is talking to Denbigh in ignorance of his social status. She says she is afraid to go to London because she would not know how to talk to smart people. Denbigh asks her how they talk.

"Mix a great deal of French with one's English," pursued Miss Watson, "and have the names of singers and dancers, and the fashionable shops quite pat. Then one ought to know a great deal of scandal; and all about the parties that are going on; and all the marryings that are to be; then I should be *so* afraid of getting into disgrace, by going where one ought not to go" [i.e., Russell Square, or the City].
"I am told," pursued Miss Watson, "that what is of most consequence, is to get to Almack's. If you get a ticket for that, you'll be invited everywhere else directly; and if not, nobody will take any notice of you. Almack's is of immense consequence, and fashionable people think of hardly anything else; and the Patronesses can do almost anything; and it is *such* a favor to let people in—even the Prime Minister must beg very hard."[22]

These paragraphs come from Lister with a good grace. The fashionable life as he portrayed it bears little resemblance to this burlesque view.

By 1832 Lister's satire was no longer prophetic. The faults of Bulwer, Disraeli, Lady Blessington, and Lady Charlotte Bury are neatly tallied in these adroit paragraphs. The French which Susan Ferrier decried had be-

[21] *Arlington*, pp. 129 ff.   [22] *Ibid.*, pp. 300–304.

come the inevitable proof of blue blood. Dancers and singers were almost a Disraelian specialty; and as for the names of shops, they had become an indispensable part of Mr. Gore's topography. By indicating the contempt in which Russell Square and the City were held, Thackeray, in *Vanity Fair*, was able to recall the flavor of the period.

IV
BULWER LYTTON

TRACED through his writings, Bulwer is such an elusive creature that in selecting one phase of his work and saying, "Here is the real Bulwer!" the critic is sure to be confounded. A convincing Bulwer appears in novels so disparate as *Pelham*, *The Pilgrims of the Rhine*, *The Last of the Barons*, *The Caxtons*, and *The Coming Race;* in poetry like *King Arthur* and *The Siamese Twins;* in plays like *Richelieu* or *Money;* in social studies like *England and the English;* and in the *History of Greece*. A study of the fashionable novel can therefore hope to touch upon only a single side of the multifarious Bulwer. He completed just one fashionable novel, but there are indications both in his earlier and later work of a continued interest in the problem of upper-class life.

His novel, *Pelham*, a dandy's hornbook with an influence that extended beyond literature into life itself, is without doubt the most important of the fashionable novels. Carlyle's attack on it in *Sartor Resartus*, although based on an unaccountable misapprehension, was a tacit recognition of Bulwer's position of supremacy in the realm of dandy literature. That position would have been longer maintained if his publisher, Henry Colburn, had not willed otherwise, and refused to consider *Greville*. With *Greville* an unfulfilled promise, however, the works which are the most important for us are—*Pelham*, *England and the English*, and *Godolphin*, the novel which marked his escape from the fashionable novel into the "metaphysical."

Bulwer planned a first novel as early as 1823, began writing a year later, but did not publish *Falkland* until

Colburn accepted it in 1827. It attracted little attention
in the papers, but because a few critics found it a convenient illustration of current immorality in fiction,
Bulwer ultimately yielded and disowned the bantling.
Meanwhile he thought it pleasant to regard it as Goethe
regarded *Werther*. In the preface to the 1835 edition of
Pelham he wrote: "I had rid my bosom of the perilous
stuff. I had confessed my sins and was absolved. I could
return to real life and its wholesome objects."

Before this purge was complete, however, Bulwer had
unburdened himself of one short story, *Mortimer, or, Memoirs of a Gentleman*, which represented the cynical reaction
to Falkland's sentimentality. The title character is almost
the first and is by far the wickedest of Bulwer's young men.
So pronounced, indeed, is Mortimer's badness that his determination to seduce his fiancée, whom poverty had made
ineligible for marriage, hardly seems extraordinary. At
the scene which is to represent the consummation of his
plans, he is detected by her brother. Mortimer kills him
in a duel and flees to the Continent. There he spreads his
groat's worth of repentance over a lengthy sojourn, finally
returning to London to find Ellen an orphan in an insane
asylum. Still only moderately repentant, Mortimer visits
her, secures her release, and cares for her until she dies.

The story is not quite so sordid as this bare outline
indicates since the quick deterioration of Mortimer's character is so obviously a literary convention. The studious
author had had less experience of life than of books, and
they were reflected powerfully in his imagination. Dr.
John Moore's *Zeluco*, Henry Mackenzie's *Man of the World*,
and Richardson's *Clarissa Harlowe* had excited in him the
pessimism frequently present in ardent natures.

Mortimer and *Falkland* have this much in common—
they are either wholeheartedly sentimental or wholeheartedly cynical in their attitude toward life. Neither of

them gives any sort of rounded view; each is partial, incomplete. But Bulwer's reading broadened to include Fielding, Smollett, and LeSage, and in his next novel, *Pelham*, a deliberate attempt at redressing the balance is visible, though through it run all the strains which he had employed before. The achievement of this balanced view was partly due to a study of Goethe, whose *Wilhelm Meister* had been translated by Carlyle in 1824. An analysis of *Pelham*, therefore, entails the disentanglement of these strains.

Mortimer, the short sketch from which *Pelham* was developed, was written about the middle of 1824, but was not published then. Several years later, just after Bulwer's marriage in August, 1827, he decided to develop the work, but no longer found its spirit congenial. He utilized part of it, however, in the new work appearing in 1828. Finally in 1835 he published *Mortimer* in the same volume as a new edition of *Pelham*, along with a preface which purported to describe the reasons for the change.

Its ["*Mortimer's*"] commencement is almost word for word the same as that of *Pelham*; but the design was exactly opposite to that of the latter and later work. *Mortimer* was intended to show the manner in which the world deteriorates its votary, and *Pelham*, on the contrary, conveys the newer, and I believe sounder, moral of showing how a man of sense can subject the usages of the world to himself instead of being conquered by them, and gradually grow wise by the very foibles of his youth.[1]

As a description of the differences between the two this paragraph can hardly be bettered, but when Bulwer goes on to ascribe this change to his recollection of Mme de Stael's remark that the gay and sentimental on the stage was always a success, he becomes fanciful.

Granting the claims of both *Mortimer* and *Pelham* to represent the author's opinions, it is manifest that a great inner change had taken place in Bulwer between 1824 and

[1] *Pelham*, London, 1835 edition, Preface.

1827. He had obviously gone beyond the petty view of society held by Maria Edgeworth and Fanny Burney. Hook and Lister had tempered their predecessors' simple morality, and by the time of *Pelham* Bulwer was abreast of them. There can be little doubt that it was Goethe, rather than Mme de Stael, Hook, or Lister, who rescued Bulwer from the doldrums of *Falkland* and *Mortimer*. As early as 1826 he had listed *Wilhelm Meister* as the subject of a proposed essay. In an article, "Conversations with an Ambitious Student in His Last Illness," published in *The New Monthly* for 1830, he more accurately estimated his indebtedness to Goethe's apprenticeship novel, when he described it as a book "which had a marked influence upon my own mind."

Carlyle's translation of *Wilhelm Meister's Apprenticeship* was slow in reaching an audience, but Bulwer so immediately absorbed the novel that it colored all his subsequent work. His reading of Goethe was so fresh in 1827, however, and so commingled with the bracing heartiness of the eighteenth-century realists, that its effect in *Pelham* is felt chiefly in an underlying seriousness. In the later *Godolphin*, the direct debt to Goethe becomes very apparent, but *Pelham* might have been very much what it is, as far as form is concerned, if *Wilhelm Meister* had never been read.

The apprenticeship novel includes the picaresque romance in its complex literary heritage, and basically, perhaps, *Pelham, or, The Adventures of a Gentleman*, is a version of the picaresque romance. It is the continuator of *Gil Blas*, *Tom Jones*, and *Roderick Random*, but with the crude *picaro* replaced by the intellectual dandy. In a novel like *Pelham*, therefore, the danger of confusing the influence of the picaresque romance with that of the apprenticeship novel is very great. Certainly when Bulwer had finally assimilated the borrowings from Goethe into his own "metaphysical" novel, the result, in *Ernest Mal-*

travers and *Alice*, was no longer a fashionable novel, although it was still about fashionable people.

The apprenticeship novel and the picaresque romance in their simplest forms may both be reduced to the formula, *The boy grew older*. The Germans have a word, *Bildungsroman*, for the apprenticeship type which helps us to understand the essential difference between the two forms. In the picaresque romance, the boy, while growing older, learns slowly and painfully from his blunders. In the *Bildungsroman* the hero much more consciously builds up a reasoned attitude toward experience. Through the power of imagination he is enabled to see the wider implications of what happens to him, and to profit accordingly.

If the line of distinction between the two types could always be drawn thus sharply there might be little doubt that *Pelham* is a *Bildungsroman*, the result of deliberate imitation of Goethe. Bulwer, in the preface to *Mortimer*, seemed to think so, but to quote a preface by Bulwer as evidence about one of his novels is a trifle dangerous, especially a preface written years after the event. Bulwer's powers of self-criticism were limited by his reverence for the subject.

To accomplish its formative program the apprenticeship novel adopted from the picaresque romance the custom of conducting the hero through all sorts of social groups. Thus two aims were fulfilled; the hero is educated, and the reader is given a view of society in its infinite variety. *Pelham* is a fashionable novel, but the *Weltbilt* which it offers is as varied as that of *Wilhelm Meister* or *Tom Jones*. International society in London and Paris, low life in its English raciness are spread before us garnished with the appropriate sauce of commentary. There are English sportsmen, eccentric scholars, shrewish wives, selfish gourmets, politically-minded lords and tailors, blacklegs, thieves, murderers, gamblers, jockies, Cyprians, marrying mothers, silly daughters—a veritable directory of English types. Acquaintances, occasionally becoming more than casual, offer their life stories (compare Fielding's "Man of the Hill" and Goethe's "Story of a Beautiful Soul") and the novel pauses while whole chapters intrude themselves to the destruction of unity and the confusion of critics. In *Wilhelm Meister* there are frequent group discussions of *Hamlet* and the stage, the philosophy of education and of religion. In fashionable novels like *Pelham*, or Mrs. Gore's *Cecil*, the dinner table, the drawing-room, or the ballroom drops its normal function and becomes a puppet theater in which the novelist ventriloquizes on marriage, politics, or the fashionable novel.

Is this from the English or the German forerunners? Probably from the English, with the Goethean influence felt chiefly as an urge to deliberate artistry.

One undeniable result of the reading of *Wilhelm Meister*, however, was to encourage a view which sees life as a pilgrimage; the chastening effect of sorrow and disaster in the life of the hero is likely to be stressed beyond anything met with in the picaresque romance. Thus an important phase of the apprenticeship novel, the worship of sorrow concept, *Heiligtum des Schmerzes*, had its reflection in the English imitators. "And perhaps for this reason, among others, the apprenticeship of most of the nineteenth century novel heroes consists of a passing through some sort of baptism of fire, coming out purified and ennobled by sorrow . . . in the manner of Bulwer's or Disraeli's young poets and politicians."[2]

Although the problem of Goethean influence upon *Pelham* is puzzling, something quite the contrary is true of the Byronic. There are portions of *Pelham* every bit as Byronic as *Falkland* and Bulwer's early poems. Sir Reginald

[2] Susanne Howe, *Wilhelm Meister and His English Kinsmen*, New York, 1930, p. 89.

Glanville, Bulwer asserted in 1835, was drawn purposely after the Byronic model as a foil to Pelham. Certainly he is just such another writhing hypochondriac as Falkland. The tendency to self-analysis and confession displayed in both *Vivian Grey* and *Pelham* as well as in later books like *Cecil* is something unknown to the picaresque romance. In English it too came from Byron, though originally from Rousseau.

All that darker thread of story woven around Glanville is not, however, Byronic. The scenes in the solitary hut, in the graveyard, and in the desolate spot where Tyrrel is murdered, are pure Gothic from the novels of Ann Radcliffe. The melancholy scenery, matching the fierce characters in mood, is an example of Bulwer's tendency to see nature through the eyes of an early Romanticism. As for that part of the story laid in the low dives of London, that too has only extraneous interest as fashionable-novel material; T. H. Lister alone uses it. The Minerva Press strain of horror met something congenial in Bulwer's nature, and for vividness and suspense the scenes in which Pelham enters the criminal resort to get evidence to clear his friend are hardly to be surpassed. Certain episodes laid in cabbies' gin palaces had already been exploited in the novels of Pierce Egan. To Corinthian Tom and Bob Logic are due also some of Pelham's concern with boxing, a fad which had been epidemic some years before, when a still younger Pelham had been the contemporary of Byron. *Pelham* shows, indeed, more than most novels, traces of its sources; its originality lies chiefly in its skillful blend of various fictional strains presented with freshness and wit.

The book and its hero succeeded in setting a fashion both in literature and in life.[3] Just as the beaux had aped

[3] The book was both parodied and imitated. As an example of the first see *Pelham, Second Series*, in *The Age*, October 11, 18, 1829. The best of the direct imitations is *Sydenham; or, Memoirs of a Man of the World*, by

Brummell and the Prince of Wales, the dandies followed
Pelham. Pelham wore black evening clothes, and men to
this day wear like formal garb. Pelham insisted on suits
without padding, and Stultz and Trufitt had perforce to be
content to fit men as God made them. He turned his con-
tagious example against street rowdyism, Byronic postur-
ing, and misanthropic moping, and the ideal English
gentleman changed over night. Under the lead of Brummell
he had learned to change his linen; under Pelham he almost
changed his moral nature.

What Pelham was in 1828, the dandies of St. James's
were to be next season. By the time of the book's second
edition, Bulwer had learned this pleasant fact, and hastened
to note it.

I think, above most works, it contributed to put an end to the
satanic mania,—to turn the thoughts and ambition of young
gentlemen without neckcloths, and young clerks who were
sallow, from playing the Corsair, and boasting that they were
villains. If mistaking the irony of Pelham, they went to the extreme of emulating the foibles which that hero attributed to
himself—those were a thousand times more harmless, and even
more manly and noble, than the professions of misanthropy, and
the mawkish sentimentalities of vice.[4]

Pelham did not succeed without a struggle. During its
first two months it nearly perished from lack of sales, al-

W. Massie, 1830, two volumes. Volume one is purely social, dealing with
such notables as Brummell (Mr. Beaumont), the Prince (Lord Snowdon),
D'Orsay (Mr. Paulet). In Volume two, Sir Matthew Sydenham com-
pletely drops his dandyism, and becomes an M. P. The scene shifts to
Devonshire House (Claverton House in the novel), the Beefsteak Club
(Brooke's), and Westminster, while Brougham (Broughton), Canning
(Anstruther), Sheridan (Singleton), conduct the destinies of the Whigs
up to the death of Canning in 1827.

4 The name "Pelham," despite Bulwer's pride in the book's redemp-
tive qualities, became a nickname for a fast young man about town.
The Devil in London, a satiric, scurrilous sheet, reported, March 3, 1832,
"as fashionable intelligence the fact that 'Henry Pelham, Robert Peel,
John Scott, and an "Earnest"' had been arrested in a raid on a brothel in
Charles Street." Sadleir, *Edward and Rosina*, p. 174 *n*.

though Colburn was doing his skillful best for it.[5] A few favorable reviews, however, in *The Literary Gazette* by William Jerdan, in *The Examiner* by Albany Fonblanque, and in *The Atlas* gave the necessary impetus, and in the third month sales picked up. Unfavorable reviews, fortunately, came too late. *The Edinburgh Review*, which never seemed to find time to notice Bulwer's novels, much to his chagrin, did not get around to it until April, 1832. The reviewer considered its satire so bland and impalpable that nine out of ten mistook it for eulogy, for "under the guise of satire in *Pelham* there was an anxiety to engage our sympathies and enlist our prejudices on behalf of the man of fashion."[6] Carlyle wickedly called Pelham, "a Mystagogue, and leading Teacher and Preacher of the Sect" of dandies, but his pronouncement was delayed so long that it probably led only to a revision of the new edition of 1835.

Bulwer, however, was sensitive to criticism. After the appearance of *Sartor Resartus* in 1833–34, he made extensive alterations in the novel. From Chapter XLIII alone of the first editions he cut out about one and one-half pages of offending matter. Elsewhere he altered incidents in an obvious effort to tone down some of the irritating egotism of Henry Pelham. In Chapter XLIV he inserted this paragraph:

And here, as I am weary of tailors, [he had cut their number from three to one] let me reflect upon the divine art of which they are the professors. Alas, for the instability of all human sciences! A few short months ago, in the first edition of this memorable work, I laid down rules for costume, the value of which fashion begins already to destroy. The thoughts which I shall now embody, shall be out of the reach of that great innovator, and applicable not to one age, but to all. To the sagacious reader, who

[5] This appeared in *The Age*, July 20, 1828, p. 227. "The Marquis of . . . and his gaming coterie, are hit off to the life in the new novel of *Pelham; or, Adventures of a Gentleman*, which is said to be written by an ancient friend of his lordship."

[6] *Edinburgh Review*, LV, 208–19.

has already discovered what portions of this book are writ in irony—what in earnest—I fearlessly commit these maxims; beseeching him to believe, with Sterne, that "everything is big with jest, and has wit in it, and instruction too—if we can but find it out!"[7]

The phrase, "sagacious reader," betrays a hint of Bulwer's impatience with the misunderstanding displayed by Carlyle.

Following this explanation the revised edition cast its material on clothes into the philosophical form of twenty-two maxims. The first edition had been far more specific in its discussion of clothing. In the coat, for example, "wrinkles behind should be carefully avoided . . . this can never be the case where any padding is admitted." "The gigot sleeve is an abominable fashion." Then follows a dissertation on rings. The waistcoat "is one which influences the whole appearance more than anyone not profoundly versed in the habilatory art would suppose . . . nothing tawdry—nothing common must be permitted." "A white waistcoat with a black coat and trousers, and a small chain of dead gold, only partially seen, is never within the bann of the learned in such matters; but beware, oh beware your linen." "For the rest, I cannot sufficiently impress upon your mind the most thoughtful consideration to the minutiae of dress, such as the glove, the button, the boot, the shape of the hat, &c."

In at least two other places Bulwer removed lines which tended to destroy a reader's sympathy with Pelham. *The Age*,[8] pretending to quote other journals, had observed that *Pelham* must have been written by a "perfumed coxcomb," "a daring adventurer," "a satirist," or "a philosopher." Possibly to remove the first reproach, Bulwer excised a scene from Chapter XLIV in which Pelham subdues an unruly horse.

[7] *Pelham*, London, 1877, pp. 180–81.
[8] *The Age*, August 3, 1828, p. 242.

"Believe me," said I, escaping from them all, throwing myself on a sofa in the next room, "riding is too severe an exercise for men, it is only fit for the robuster nerves of women. Will any gentleman present lend me his essence bottle?"

Then again, in the first edition, Pelham sets a dog fight going at Lord Chester's. Bulwer retained the the fight but eliminated this last sentence:

I flung myself into an armchair, and gave way to an excess of merriment, which only enraged the spectators more. Many were the glances of anger, ma^ ^he murmurs of reproach directed against me.[9]

These revisions v Bulwer felt compelled to make are not very exten ^ ^^^ all. Even in the first edition the ironical note is so pervasive that one wonders how the *Edinburgh* ever persisted in its owlish solemnity. The ironical tone is struck on the very first page:

I am an only child. My father was the younger son of one of our eldest earls, my mother was the dowerless daughter of a Scotch peer. Mr. Pelham was a moderate Whig, and gave sumptous dinners;—Lady Frances was a woman of taste, and particularly fond of diamonds and old china.

Vulgar people know nothing of the necessaries required in good society, and the credit they give is as short as their pedigree. Six years after my birth, there was an execution in the house. My mother was just setting off on a visit to the Duchess of D——p; she declared it was impossible to go without her diamonds. The chief of the bailiffs declared it was impossible to trust them out of his sight. The matter was compromised—the bailiff went with my mother to C——, and was introduced as *my tutor*. "A man of singular merit," whispered my mother, "but so shy!" Fortunately, the bailiff was abashed, and by losing his impudence he kept the secret. At the end of the week the diamonds went to the jeweller's, and Lady Frances wore paste.

I think it was about a month afterwards that a sixteenth cousin left my mother twenty thousand pounds. "It will pay off our most importunate creditors, and equip me for Melton," said Mr. Pelham.

[9] *Pelham*, London, 1828, II, chap. viii.

"It will just redeem my diamonds, and refurnish the house,"
said Lady Frances.

The latter alternative was chosen. . .

Or this:

"My dear child," said my mother to me, affectionately, "you
must be very bored here. To say truth, I am so myself. Your uncle
is a very good man, but he does not make his house pleasant;
and I have, lately, been very much afraid that he should convert
you into a mere bookworm; after all, my dear Henry, you are
quite clever enough to trust to your own ability. Your great
geniuses never read."

"True, my dear mother," said I, with a most unequivocal
yawn, and depositing on the table Mr. Bentham on "Popular
Fallacies"; "true, and I am quite of your opinion. Did you see in
the *Post* of this morning, how full Cheltenham was?"[10]

The Tories who mistrusted the political elements in
Pelham showed a much more acute sense of reality than
Thomas Carlyle. Disraeli, in his *Vivian Grey* a year or two
before, had created a Carabas Party which bore little resemblance to anything in the actual political situation. In
1825, seven years before the Reform Bill, party strife ran
high, but lent itself less to fictional use than in 1828 when
the issues were rapidly clarifying amid an intense public
interest. Disraeli, at twenty-one, had not thought out his
political beliefs; his Young England party was as yet
unborn. Consequently the political action in *Vivian Grey*
occurs in a vacuum. There is a party, but no principles;
politicians, but they bear little resemblance to the Whig or
Tory leaders. The political events in *Pelham*, however,
while they seldom have a factual basis, made the Tories
uneasy. Pelham has political principles which he is not
ready to sacrifice to expediency. To an invitation to join a
new party to be formed for personal reasons, Pelham
replies:

. . . I would sooner feed my poodle on paunch and liver, instead
of cream and fricassee, than to be an instrument in the hands of

[10] *Ibid*., chap. xxxviii.

Lincoln and Lessborough; who talk much, who perform nothing
—who join ignorance of every principle of legislation to indifference for every benefit to the people . . . who level upwards and
trample downwards.[11]

Bulwer's connection with the Benthamites had been
fairly close during the middle twenties. When he entered
Parliament in 1831, it was as a Reform member for St. Ives.
Tory and Whig readers who saw Pelham becoming the
sartorial leader of an increasing group of young and careful
dressers must have wondered what would happen if Pelham's brand of political sincerity should become general.

Distrust by the hard-shelled Tories of Bulwer's obvious
radicalism was coupled with Carlyle's obtuseness to produce a joint attack by two of the strangest allies that ever
shared a bivouac. In *Fraser's Magazine*,[12] April, 1830, the
year in which Carlyle finished *Sartor Resartus*, appeared an
anonymous review, "The Dominie's Legacy, or, Fashionable Novels." This was followed in June[13] by an article
called "Mr. Edward Lytton Bulwer's Novels; and Remarks
on Novel Writing," signed Ned Culpepper, the Tomahawk.
Herr Teufelsdröckh in *Sartor Resartus* probably refers to
these articles when he mentions a dissertation on the
dandies, but the chances are that Carlyle did not write
these reviews.[14] This much is certain, however, that on
November 30, 1831, Carlyle wrote to Macvey Napier, "I
once proposed to Mr. Jeffrey to make a sort of sally on
Fashionable Novels . . . . The Pelham-and-Devereux manufacture . . . ought to be extinguished in British literature."[15]

The Tomahawk's article took a high ground from the
start, declaring that

[11] *Pelham*, London, 1877, chap. liii, p. 220.
[12] *Fraser's Magazine*, I, 318–35.   [13] *Ibid.*, pp. 509–33.
[14] For arguments *pro* and *con* see *Times Literary Supplement*, Jan. 20,
1927; letter of J. A. S. Barrett: *Modern Language Notes*, Baltimore, May,
1931, Miriam M. Thrall, "Two Articles attributed to Carlyle," pp.
316–32.
[15] R. H. Shepherd, *Life of Carlyle*, London, 1871, I, 80.

the word Fashionable Novel was a contradiction in terms, inasmuch as novel-writing predicated philosophical views for the elaboration of utility to society at large; and that as fashionable society, in particular could not, from the peculiarity of its composition, bear the test of philosophy, no real and true novel could be written on the characters to be furnished by such a society.

One might have supposed that any lack of utility to society at large would have been severely dealt with by the *Westminster* in its article in January, 1829.[16] Apparently, however, it preferred to leave a defense of utilitarianism to *Fraser's*.

Less philosophical, but more downright was the verdict that there were too many mediocre novelists, the worst of which were in the pseudo-fashionable class. "Here [Bulwer] is a fellow of a better stamp, but of the same die, nevertheless."

Shifting its attack from the philosophical, the article arraigned Bulwer's novels as subversive of morality. It claimed that his books did not make the reader better or wiser, nor did they "brace up manly energy, and promote heroic virtue." Probably no other novelist of Bulwer's sincerity has been so plagued by the cry of the moralists. Alaric A. Watts, the pious editor of annuals, was shocked by *Falkland*, and even Mrs. Lytton, Bulwer's mother, suffered from some of Falkland's religious conjecturings. *Paul Clifford* and *Eugene Aram*, of course, were held up as praising highwaymen and murderers. It is difficult now to decide how much of this moral reprobation was genuine. At any rate, the bulk was nothing but shrewd manipulation by unscrupulous critics who found the cry of immorality an extremely easy and effective method by which to indulge their various dislikes of Bulwer.

Solomon's writing about pitch was invoked to show the bad effects of Pelham's excursions into low life. *The*

---

[16] *Westminster Review*, X, 173-91, "Fashionable Society."

Westminster had said: "There is, however, a keen although playful earnestness in much of the observation, that proves the anxiety of the author to mix up a portion of Epicurean dignity, in his abstract notions of the finished gentleman."[17]

But in *Fraser's* even Lady Roseville's defense of Pelham's noble heart was not allowed to go unchallenged. "The English of all this . . . 'Despise not a fop, for there may be something noble in him' . . . a most precious recommendation of fops and foppery!"[18] Beyond the admission that Bulwer is not the worst of his school there is hardly a word of praise in the whole article.

This attack is typical of the running guerrilla warfare that existed so long between Bulwer and *Fraser's*, but to infer from *Fraser's* criticism of Bulwer that the fashionable novel as a type suffered similar attacks would be an error. Unfortunately for Bulwer his writings combined with certain personal characteristics to irritate many critics. People were always accusing him of affectation, and were unable to distinguish the man's ideas from his personality. Lockhart, when asked by Sir Walter about the author of *Pelham*, replied that he had not even read it because he so heartily disliked its author, a Norfolk squire and puppy.

The bias of early nineteenth-century periodical criticism is, of course, notorious. Bulwer offended in two ways; he was a Radical Reformer, and his books were published by Henry Colburn. Where political antipathies did not arise to plague a Colburn author, business differences between Bungay and various Bacons were sure to do so. Because Colburn advertised in his own ruthless way, all other publishers united in hatred of the innovator. Bulwer, as one of Colburn's leading authors, had always to share some of Colburn's troubles.

[17] *The Westminster Review*, X, 179, January, 1829.
[18] *Fraser's Magazine*, I, 516, June, 1830.

But the young writer had a best seller to his credit, and Colburn, well aware of the necessity of supplying the public with what it wanted, urged Bulwer to write him another best seller. Bulwer's extravagant mode of living demanding a large income, he agreed, and wrote *The Disowned* in a few months. Naturally enough, rapid writing produced an inferior product, and Bulwer hardly needed the expressed disapproval of *The Examiner* and *The Westminster* to realize the truth. *The Disowned* is a fashionable novel of a sort, but the plot is too complex, and the tone is that of Horatio Alger. The poor, friendless hero makes his way to the top by sheer merit; at the end is revealed what one suspects from the beginning, that Clarence Linden has a much fancier name—Clinton L'Estrange.

A letter from the Duke of Haverfield to Clarence, however, inserted in the course of the narrative is as clever and witty as anything in Bulwer.

. . . *La pauvre petite Meronville!*—What an Ariadne! Just as I was thinking to play Bacchus to your Theseus, up steps an old gentleman from Yorkshire, who hears it is fashionable to marry *bonas robas*, proposes honorable matrimony, and deprives me and the world of La Meronville! The wedding took place on Monday last, and the happy pair set out to their seat in the North. Verily, we shall have quite a new race in the next generation—I expect all the babies will skip into the world with a *pas de zephyr*, singing in sweet trebles—

"Little dancing loves we are!
—Who the deuce is our papa?"[19]

The Disowned, though not a great success, sold well enough for Colburn to renew his demands for another of the kind. Greatly to Bulwer's credit, however, he determined to write satire anyway, but the righteous impulse was not sufficiently strong to carry the new novel, *Greville*, to an end. Instead, Bulwer abandoned *Greville* after completing seven or eight chapters and outlining the rest, and

[19] *The Disowned*, London, 1877, p. 289.

started *Devereux*, which was published by July, 1829. The £1,500 which the book earned probably assuaged his fallen pride, while his failure in a new *genre*, the historical novel, spurred him on to eventual success in his series of "Last" studies.

Greville represents a continuation of the *Pelham* tradition. That it was not finished is a loss to the fashionable novel and to fiction generally, because it is apparent from what has been published that the book would have been one of his happiest. Bulwer in a philosophizing mood is occasionally dull and pretentious, but for purely mundane subjects he retained an acute eye and a sharpened pen.

The very first paragraph has the old *Pelham* flavor.

Everyone knows that England is the most charming country in the world, especially for those who like to be amused. In that moral air the people are so wise that mirth would be altogether out of character. It is only in their parliaments that they stoop to levity. They there concentrate the witticisms of a whole nation in one individual and they call that individual Sir Joseph York. In a social state they exclude the impertinence of *bon mots*, and exult in a stupendous monotony of *ennui*.[20]

The fragmentary nature of the novel reveals a serious weakness in Bulwer's method of displaying character. That Greville is the result of direct statement and description rather than of observed action is understandable enough, since even the completed portions of the book have the appearance of outline, but one feels in all of Bulwer's novels too great a reliance on unsupported assertion. Such a cheap and easy substitute for real conversation did not escape the notice of other prolific novelists, and the works of Lady Charlotte Bury and Lady Blessington abound in so-called witty and brilliant characters about whom no trace of wit and brilliance can be found.

Short as it is, *Greville* might well have improved Bul-

---

[20] *The Life, Letters, and Literary Remains of Edward Bulwer, Lord Lytton*, by his son, London, 1883, II, 335.

wer's reputation as a shrewd commentator on society, for
enough of the novel exists to display a scope as wide as
Pelham. Chapters were to be devoted to "Low Life," a
satire on breakfast, the opera, a conversation on fashionable novels, and to a *fête* at Greville's country seat, while
scattered throughout were barbed comments of the sort
so common in *Pelham*.

Lord and Lady Bellenden were great Tories; and they set up for
being remarkably domestic, in opposition to those rascally
Whigs who were always jesting at anything like morality and
good feeling.[21]
The hostess was a woman of the world, and in the world she
had three daughters and eight hundred friends: In the old classical
times a man generally asked his friend to marry his daughter; in
the present time it is the woman who asks it. There is some
difference in the result; in the former age the friend generally
accepted the offer, in the present he generally refuses it.[22]
They paused at the Athenaeum. The Captain was not a learned
man, neither was Sir James. What of that? The Captain's grand-
father had sailed round the world, and Sir James was going to
start for his country. Such claims to notice, literary bodies
rarely neglect.[23]
It is a charming place that Athenaeum. The people are so well
informed; 'tis a pity that they don't know each other. And so
very entertaining, 'tis a pity they never converse.[24]

Greville is such an entertaining work that it is a pity
Bulwer never finished it, but his pocketbook and Colburn
decreed otherwise. The substitute, *Devereux*, is an historical
novel of Queen Anne's time. *Paul Clifford* and *Eugene Aram*,
which followed closely, are thesis novels dealing with
the careers of a gentleman freebooter and a scholarly
murderer.

Bulwer's new novel *Godolphin*, 1833, although it deals
once more with fashionable people, is one of his frequent
anonymous experiments.

Recollections of the tremendously poetical tempera-

[21] *Ibid.*, p. 345.   [22] *Ibid.*, p. 342.   [23] *Ibid.*, p. 342.   [24] *Ibid.*, p. 351.

ment lavished on Falkland and of his misanthropy inspired by satiety might have caused prospective readers to shy away from a novel which apparently promised to renew the horrors of a pseudo-Byronism. The mood was pretty well outworn by 1833. Bulwer, however, had disavowed his belief in the Wertherian reaction to life in *Pelham* a little too soon. In *Godolphin* he wore his rue with a difference, but much of it was the same rue.

When Bulwer wrote *Mortimer* and *Falkland* he was very young. The patterns which the world impressed on young men had been drawn by Maria Edgeworth in jet black and snowy white, and by Byron in, shall we say, purple. The cult of rural virtue which had been growing in popularity. throughout the eighteenth century, had reached a final expression in Cowper's line that God made the country and man made the town. Bulwer's submission to that attitude was complete in *Falkland* and *Mortimer* but very limited in *Pelham*. With *Godolphin* the incorrigible romanticism in Bulwer's nature broke out again. This time, however, the tragedy is in the protagonist's nature, not in society. Godolphin runs off to the mountains to heal his wounded spirit, taking with him for companion a simple untutored girl, and, in general, behaving like Goethe's Werther or Ward's Tremaine. But the world is not out of step; Godolphin is out of step with the world. Trouble arose because of an irreconcilability between the author's own nature and the demands of his thesis. His own sympathies inclined toward Godolphin, but his duties as a novelist demanded that Godolphin be presented in an unsympathetic light.

Like *Pelham*, *Godolphin* takes its "absolute groundwork in what is called 'the Fashionable World.' "[25] But the difference between *Pelham* and *Godolphin* is so great that the

[25] *Godolphin*, New York, 1877, Preface, pp. vii–x.

effect of this groundwork is demonstrated in an entirely different manner, as the preface of the latter makes explicit.

In a word, dispel all his [Pelham's] fopperies, real or assumed, he is still the active man of crowds and cities, determined to succeed, and gifted with the ordinary qualities of success. Godolphin, on the contrary, is a man of poetical temperament, out of his place alike among the trifling idlers, and the bustling actors of the world—wanting the stimulus of necessity—or the higher motive which springs from benevolence, to give energy to his powers, or definite purpose to his fluctuating desires; not strong enough to break the bonds that confine his genius—not supple enough to accommodate its movements to their purpose. He is the moral antipodes to Pelham. In evading the struggles of the world, he grows indifferent to its duties—he strives with no obstacles—he can triumph in no career. Represented as possessing mental qualities of a higher and richer nature than those to which Pelham can pretend, he is also represented as very inferior to him in constitution of character, and he is certainly a more ordinary type of the intellectual character.

For although it must follow from the inherent difference in the design of the two works thus referred to, that in *Godolphin* there can be little of the satire or vivacity which have given popularity to its predecessor, yet, on the other hand, in *Godolphin* there ought to be a more faithful illustration of the even polish that belongs to luxurious life,—of a satiety that pleasure inflicts upon such of its votaries as are worthy of a higher service. The subject selected cannot admit the same facility for observation of things that lie on the surface—but it may well lend itself to subtler investigation of character—allow more attempt at pathos, and more appeal to reflection.

Godolphin is a curious novel, compounded of even more diverse elements than *Pelham*. The basic strain is that of Gothic romance imposed upon a contemporary scene. In this work, as in *Falkland*, he availed himself to the full of his Radcliffean talents for wild and picturesque characters and scenes. Godolphin, who at sixteen had exhausted the world, is as definitely Radcliffean as the surroundings of his ruined priory. "The large oriel window—the Gothic arch—the broken, yet still majestic column, all embrowned and mossed with age, were still spared, and now mirrored themselves in the waveless and silent tide."[26]

Talk of Whigs and the position of women is obviously incongruous amid such antique splendor. What he did fumblingly in *Godolphin*, he was to do more skillfully in *Alice* and *Ernest Maltravers*. Both *Eugene Aram* and *Paul Clifford* show that his interest in problems of individual and social conduct was intense and probably derived from the problem novels of William Godwin, Bage, and Holcroft. Bulwer the romanticist and Bulwer the witty commentator meet anew in *Godolphin*, which adds to these two strains the Goethean to complete its full savor. Far more than in *Pelham*, he used characters and incidents whose prototypes may be found in *Wilhelm Meister*. Percy's connection with the strolling players is only the most obvious instance. Goethe's Philine is Bulwer's Fanny Millinger; Goethe's Mignon has her counterpart in Lucilla.

All this conscious use of models was a heavy load for a novel to carry, and it is little wonder that Bulwer was not wholly successful. In seeking to cast a veil of the ideal over the actual he was necessarily led to add still more weight through the use of allegory. Saville is plainly a Mr. Worldly Wiseman, Constance is Ambition, Lucilla is Innocence.[27] As Percy goes through life, one after another of these attracts him. Saville is the first to go; Lucilla holds him longer, but she succumbs to the cultured and intellectual Constance, who alone promises to reclaim him, but the future is cut off by Godolphin's accidental death. The frustration does not arise out of circumstance; rather is it a knife which serves to cut the thread of the story already

[26] *Ibid.*, p. 22.

[27] "There was a sort of allegory of real life—like that which Goethe would affect—in the manner in which at certain epochs of his existence our Idealist was brought into contact with the fair actress of ideal creations."—*Ibid.*, I, 106.

grown too long to terminate naturally. Bulwer later recognized the artistic failure of the conclusion.

Between the first and second editions of *Godolphin* he made changes which emphasize the differences between it and the conventional fashionable novel. In the first version it is recognizably a fashionable novel despite the inclusion of much more theory drawn from Radcliffe, Godwin, and Goethe than was customary. In the second edition Bulwer had come closer to what he called a "metaphysical" and what Disraeli (whose term has met with wider recognition) called a "psychological" novel. To the contemporary reader of fashionable novels, *Godolphin* must have seemed merely another example, overburdened, perhaps, with a mass of Gothicism, allegorical interpretation, capitalized abstractions, and astronomical lore. But, deep below the wrappings, lay the proper materials of the fashionable novelist, the origin of Almack's, here attributed chiefly to Constance; the change in English society between 1815 and 1832; the usual amount of politics, this time seen from the standpoint of Lady Erpingham's *salon*; the customary lament over the wearing effects of fashionable life; and most characteristic of all, the presence of at least three unmistakable public characters. For in Lord Saltream, Bulwer had mercilessly set down the eccentricities of John William Ward, first Earl of Dudley, Foreign Minister in Canning's Cabinet in 1827. Coming so close upon Dudley's death in an institution for the insane in 1833, the use of his peculiarities was in questionable taste. Another reviewer drew attention to the figures of Lady Jersey and Sheridan, but they are minor characters not too easily recognized. Set on the hunt by easy success with Lord Saltream, the reader might readily conceive that Constance and Godolphin are meant to be Lady Blessington and Count D'Orsay. Constance has suffered so much in her youth from her dependent position in the Erpingham household, that when she marries Lord

Erpingham and finds herself in a secure position, she devotes her energies to the suppression of genealogical
qualifications for admission to society. She sets up a new
requisite—that of fashion—which is to be independent of
family position, wealth, or office. The accolade of fashion
is to be bestowed on candidates of outstanding leadership
in the arts, politics, or wit. There is a suggestion here of
the Countess of Blessington. Gore House provided the best
society in London simply because its hostess attracted men
of intellect. But although there are some resemblances, the
comparison cannot be carried far; the similarities between
Godolphin and D'Orsay come to much the same thing,
consisting merely of faint echoings of ideas undoubtedly
discussed by Bulwer, Lady Blessington, and D'Orsay.

In the second edition, not reached until 1840, Bulwer
decided to strike out individual portraits. Accordingly all
references to Lord Saltream were deleted, while the book
was further shortened in the more conventional portions
reminiscent of all fashionable novels. The result was a
work still further removed from *Pelham*, and more in ac-
cord with the description put into the mouth of Fanny
Millinger:

I want someone to write a novel, which shall be a metaphysical
Gil Blas; which shall deal more with the mind than Le Sage's
book, and less with the actions, which shall make its hero the
creation of the world, but a different creation, though equally
true; which shall give a faithful picture, in the character of one
man, of the aspects and the effects of our social system; making
that man of a better sort of clay than the amusing lackey was,
and the product of a more artificial grade of society.[28]

Although the first edition of *Godolphin* is close to a
fashionable novel, the second shows that a definite break
with the form had been made by Bulwer. *England and the
English*, published in September, 1833, contained his final
defense of the *genre*, and gave some of the reasons for

[28] *Ibid.*, chap. xx, p. 43.

abandoning it. We shall see in the next chapter that Disraeli's leave-taking of the fashionable novel was not a grateful one. He turned from it abruptly when he found something else to do. Bulwer also found something else to do, yet, although he thought the work of the fashionable novelists almost completed, he recognized their value for their time.

His praise of society novels is negative, perhaps, but all praise is likely to grant them importance chiefly as symptoms of the unsettled state of society. Twenty years later, in the 1850's, long after society had recovered from its turbulence, Mrs. Gore continued to produce symptoms, yet the patient had supposedly recovered. Bulwer treated them seriously as a solvent of manners, and as an ally of the Radical reformers in their fight against privilege and an outmoded social structure. He was far from blind to their frequent vacuity, however, as the following passage from *The Disowned* shows.

"How do you do, Mr. Linden?" said a tall and (though somewhat passée) very handsome woman, blazing with diamonds; "are you just come?"

And here, by the way, I cannot resist pausing to observe, that a friend of mine, meditating a novel, submitted a part of the MS. to a friendly publisher. "Sir," said the bookseller, "your book is very clever, but it wants dialogue."

"Dialogue?" cried my friend—"you mistake—it is all dialogue."

"Ay, sir, but not what *we* call dialogue; we want a little conversation in fashionable life—a little elegant chit-chat or so; and, as you must have seen so much of the *beau monde*, you could do it to the life; we must have something light, and witty, and entertaining."

"Light, witty, and entertaining!" said our poor friend; "and how the deuce then is it to be like conversation in fashionable life'? When the very best conversation one can get is so unsufferably dull, how do you think people will be amused by reading a copy of the very worst?"

"They *are* amused, sir," said the publisher, "and works of this kind *sell!*"

"I am convinced," said my friend; for he was a man of a placid temper; he took the hint, and his book did sell![29]

Be it noted that this good-natured raillery does not alter a whit the values which Bulwer attributed to the fashionable novels in *England and the English*.

And going from the press to the lighter novels of the day we find them giving a picture of the aristocracy which has nauseated the public.[30]

The Utilitarians railed against them, and they were affecting with unspeakable rapidity the very purposes the Utilitarians desired.[31]

What the world would not have dared to gaze on, had it been gravely exhibited by a philosopher, (so revolting a picture of the aristocracy would it have seemed) they praised with avidity in the light sketches of a novelist.[32]

These values are heightened in some degree by bad writing, for the reader is directly nauseated with the books, and indirectly with their subject. In a well-written novel like *Pelham*, the result is a compromise. Pelham himself amuses and stimulates; many of the circle in which he moves revolt us. The whole book is sprayed with Bulwer's irony which acts like a solvent to fashionable pretensions.

Thus, the fashionable novel, like any other weedy growth, bore in itself the causes of its decay. The popularity of the form led to overproduction, and the readers who had borrowed so eagerly from the circulating library either sickened from the surfeit of bad stories, or lost interest in the subject when the novel was good. Bulwer, displaying here as ever his uncanny sense of the literary market, stopped production, pronounced his grateful benediction, and moved to newer and less crowded fields.

[29] *The Disowned*, London, 1877, chap. xxix, pp. 158–59.
[30] *England and the English*, London, 1833, p. 216.
[31] *Ibid.*, pp. 251–52. [32] *Ibid.*, pp. 251–52.

V

DISRAELI

A RATHER close and illuminating parallel may be made out between the early literary careers of Bulwer and Disraeli. They were born a year apart, Bulwer in 1803 and Disraeli in 1804. After each had made a few attempts at writing, Bulwer with verse and a single unnoticed novel, Disraeli with a political pamphlet or two, they both obtained a considerable measure of fame and notoriety with a best seller. Disraeli's *Vivian Grey* came first, in 1826–27; Bulwer's *Pelham* followed a year later. Thus set on the way to fortune by their successful entrance into the profitable field of fashionable novel writing, through the same publisher, Henry Colburn, both cast about for ways of escape. Bulwer wanted to write more trenchant satire than *Pelham*, but Colburn protested and he perforce wrote *The Disowned* purely for money. Disraeli actually published his satire, *Popanilla*, in which he rashly told what he thought of fashionable novels. But the same pressure from the publisher which led Bulwer to *The Disowned* led Disraeli to *The Young Duke*, although *Popanilla* remained to remind him of his indiscretion. *Contarini Fleming, a Psychological Romance*, and *Godolphin*, a "metaphysical" romance, appeared in 1832 and 1833, respectively. Both these books were influenced by Goethe's *Wilhelm Meister*. The new field which *Godolphin* opened became Bulwer's opportunity to escape from his publisher, for although his versatility led him into poetry, history, and novels of all sorts (historical, prophetic, realistic, and romantic), his sincerest work is to be found in *Godolphin*, *Alice*, and *Ernest Maltravers*. Not until he wrote his political novel, *Coningsby* (published in 1844), did Disraeli find his best way out of the fashionable novel.

The fashionable novel was a more congenial form to Bulwer than to Disraeli. *Pelham* is a rather deliberate work, the result of conscious planning by an author who had already thrown off his earliest errors in *Falkland*. *Vivian Grey*, however, was the result of youthful audacity and lucky circumstance. What that circumstance was we have seen in the chapter on Plumer Ward. His novel *Tremaine* had been the publishing sensation of 1825, and discussion was rife as to the identity of the author. The Disraelis were acquainted with Austen, Ward's solicitor, through whom the negotiations with Colburn had been carried on, so that Disraeli knew the author's name, and knew, probably, what Colburn's terms were.

At that time, the Disraelis lived in Bloomsbury Square and the Austens close by in Guilford Street. In the autumn of 1825 the Disraeli family rented Hyde House, Ward's residence near Amersham, "and here Disraeli always said he wrote *Vivian Grey*, taking the idea from *Tremaine* and completing the book before he was twenty-one."[1] Whether he completed it there or not, there is little doubt that Disraeli's determination to write came from the success of *Tremaine*. The immediate incentive was his need of money to carry on his speculations during the inflation of 1825. The ensuing panic in December left the young financier saddled with a crushing debt. At the same time he saw the collapse of his ambitions in connection with *The Representative*, Murray's daily newspaper which was intended to rival *The Times* as a conservative organ. The contrast between the first and second parts of *Vivian Grey* may be attributed to the reverses which intervened and hurt Disraeli so severely.

Colburn again consented to accept an anonymous novel

[1] Monypenny and Buckle, *Life of Disraeli*, new and revised edition, London, 1929, 2 vols., I, 83.

through the Austens. Indeed, after his fortunate experience with *Tremaine*, he must have thought highly of their literary connections. To keep up the mystery, Mrs. Austen submitted the manuscript in her own handwriting. There seems to have been no reason for the anonymity except a love of mystification on Disraeli's part, or a desire to follow the authors of *Tremaine* and *Waverley*.

Colburn paid him two hundred pounds for Part One, and, a year later, five hundred for Part Two, a generous scale of remuneration which indicates Colburn's domination of the publishing field in the years immediately following the panic of 1825. His unconventional methods of advertising indirectly through columns of literary chat, rather than through customary announcements to the trade, were utilized to the full for *Vivian Grey*. Since Colburn himself did not know the author's name, he probably experienced an unusual glow of righteousness when he urged his puff-writers to concoct innumerable hints concerning the illustrious author of the "extremely satirical" book full of "portraits of living characters, sufficient to constitute a National Gallery."

Criticism was, for a time, stifled by the book's undeniable jauntiness, but the secret of the author's name leaked out through William Jerdan, editor of *The Literary Gazette*. Colburn had many and powerful enemies, and when it was learned that the author of *Vivian Grey* was no ex-cabinet Minister, but "a mere Jew boy," the game was up. Christopher North in *Blackwood's* denounced "the shameful and shameless puffery" by which the sale of the book had been effected, and dismissed it as "a paltry catchpenny" by "an obscure person for whom nobody cares a straw."[2] Such denunciatory criticism, however, served to keep up sales, and within two years three editions were called for. The critical outcry against his book hurt

[2] *Blackwood's*, July, 1826, p. 98.

Disraeli severely. He devoted a quarter century to efforts to suppress the novel, not yielding until 1853, when he issued a revised edition with a deprecatory preface.

Books written by boys, which pretend to give a picture of manners and to deal in knowledge of human nature, must necessarily be founded on affectation. They can be, at the best, but the results of imagination, acting upon knowledge not acquired by experience. Of such circumstances exaggeration is a necessary consequence, and false taste accompanies exaggeration. . . . Such productions should be exempt from criticism, and should be looked upon as a kind of literary lusus.

Monypenny loyally dismisses the book, claiming for it only biographical significance. It has more than that, however, in a study of the fashionable novel, for it remains, with *Pelham*, one of the chief examples of the type.

Vivian Grey is a smart and precocious youth, son of a man of letters partly modeled after Isaac D'Israeli. Vivian's education, like Benjamin's, is irregular, and gained more from private study than schools. Characterized by overwhelming ambition, Vivian contemplates many vocations before settling on politics. As influence is necessary for that, he picks the Marquis of Carabas, a retired party hack, for patron. Through the same adroitness that enabled Disraeli to ingratiate himself with the timorous Murray, Vivian easily revives disappointed political ambitions of the Marquis and is installed at his seat, Chateau Desir, as organizer-in-chief of a nebulous political faction. Vivian's astounding success, indicated by the jaunty motto on the title-page,

> Why, then the world's mine oyster,
> Which I with sword will open.

was both a prophecy and a challenge. Disraeli certainly was thinking of his own future struggles and at the same time drawing a comparison between himself and George Canning. In common with the young men of both parties he was fascinated by the brilliant leader whose rise to fame had met difficulties equal to Disraeli's own.

Part Two opens with another success when Vivian acquires Cleveland, a former member of Parliament, who had retired from politics in disgust after having been tricked by the Marquis. The political caucus thrives at Chateau Desir until Mrs. Felix Lorraine, formerly an intimate of Cleveland, inflames the weak mind of Carabas against Vivian, and the political scheme collapses. Vivian kills Cleveland in a duel, and sets out for Germany in an effort to forget. There he passes through his *Wanderjahre* in a series of adventures, of which the most amusing is a hilarious drinking bout with some Rhineland dukes, Niersteiner, Rudesheimer, and Johannisberg. In more serious vein he meets Beckendorf, prime minister of a petty kingdom, whose successful statemanship gives Vivian cause to reflect on his own failure. Some time later, Vivian is killed by an avalanche, and his death conveniently ends a book which was obviously outlasting the author's creative powers.

When it is remembered that the second part of *Vivian Grey* was written after his break with Murray over *The Representative*, the reason for the contrast between Parts One and Two is clear. Vivian's excursion into Wales to obtain Cleveland's aid is obviously a reflection of Disraeli's trip to Abbotsford and Chiefswood to secure the coöperation of Scott and Lockhart. Indeed, Murray, reading himself into Carabas's place, was so incensed by the parallel that he persisted in laying the blame for the collapse of the paper upon Disraeli. Yet while the circumstances are similar, no resemblance exists between Murray and Carabas.

Carried through the first volume by audacity and experience, Disraeli found the collapse of his hopes too grievous a burden. The book begins to deteriorate even during the Welsh trip, while from there on the story be-

comes more and more labored, its freshness lost in such
melodramatic incidents as those concerning Mrs. Felix
Lorraine and the duel with Cleveland. When he took
Vivian into Germany Disraeli virtually confessed his defeat. He threw himself doggedly back on the memories of
his trip there two years before and supplemented them
with half-digested incidents from *Wilhelm Meister*.

No doubt this German scene, particularly at the Court
of Reisenberg, and at the peasant *fête*, tends to imply a
greater debt to Goethe than really exists. It may be granted
without question that the *fête* is too closely modeled on
Goethe to be a coincidence. But the Court of Reisenberg
can hardly be Weimar, which Disraeli never visited, even
though there are certain resemblances between the grand
duke and Goethe's grand duke of Weimar. Beckendorf,
who started from the same point as Vivian, but succeeded
because he bided his time for thirty years, may well represent not only Disraeli's wisdom learned of experience, but
also some wisdom learned of Goethe. But the whole matter
of Reisenberg is probably a medley of small German courts,
chiefly Darmstadt, where, at the Opera, the young traveler
had seen the grand duke supervise a production of *Otello*.

To trace the connections between the first part of
Vivian Grey and various literary precedents is possible but
likely to be misleading, because the chief merit of the book
is derived from its personal flavor. The pattern for Vivian
Grey may have existed before, but he owes his appeal to
the fact that his author lived him. He is a picaresque hero
fitted to a new age, an intellectualized Tom Jones. The
simple virtues of the eighteenth-century *picaro* have been
discarded. Problems of material success are of chief importance in a new and acquisitive society. Disraeli had
presented this essentially modern creation with all the wit
and color that were in his own personality.

When Vivian, with his impetuous temperament, rushes

toward the goal with insufficient preparation, his chief
asset, colossal assurance, fails to sustain him. He retires
defeated and broken after the experience. His baptism of
fire is a powerful force that concentrates in a few weeks
enough emotional strain to last a lifetime. Here the connection with the Goethean worship of sorrow is apparently close, but the conception may be due rather more to
Byron. By 1826 Byronism consisted no longer of the
characteristics of one man, but was the current way of
looking at life. Novels like Lister's *Granby* and Ward's
Tremaine offer all the precedents needed to explain the self-
analysis of Vivian and the confessional quality of the book.

Edmund Gosse raises a curious objection to both *Vivian
Grey* and *The Young Duke*. "In either book," he says,
"what we feel today to be the great objection to our enjoyment is the lack of verisimilitude. Who can believe in
the existence of persons whose titles are the Earl of Fitz-
Pompey and Baron Deprivyseal, or whose names are Lady
Aphrodite and Sir Carte Blanche?"[3] This is rather captious
criticism. Certainly Disraeli was not the last of a long line
to use tag names for his characters, nor was he a reviver of
a defunct tradition. Dickens was yet to come. And it is just
as easy to believe in the existence of a Lady Aphrodite as
it is to believe in the reality of a Lady Erpingham, or a
Percy Godolphin, or a Clinton L'Estrange. Would Taper
and Tadpole become a whit more alive under the possible
appellations of Smith and Brown?

Closely allied to this objection is another to which
Disraeli lies far more open. That is the effort of the fashion-
able novel to achieve sales through the introduction of
public characters under little or no disguise. In *Vivian Grey*
Disraeli used a few transparent names; for example, the
Duke of Waterloo for Wellington, Lord Past-Century for

[3] Edmund Gosse, *Some Diversions of a Man of Letters*, "The Novels of
Benjamin Disraeli," New York, 1920, pp. 151–81.

Eldon, and Stanislaus Hoax for Theodore Hook. He also
sprinkled through the novel references to various books and
writers by name—Stewart Rose, Ward's *Tremaine*, Milman's
poem *Anne Boleyn*. By such devices the reader was certainly
led to search the novel for further originals. Then in the
seventh number of *The Star Chamber*[4] appeared a *Key to
Vivian Grey* which extended this list to most of the characters. The connection of Disraeli with this publication
appears to be much closer than is admitted in Monypenny's *Life*.[5] But whether or not Disraeli wrote the *Key*,
and whether or not he was deliberately trying to draw
recognizable portraits, the fact remains that neither his
skill nor his knowledge was equal to the task. Anyone
could do Wellington, Eldon, or Theodore Hook; few others
can be recognized even with the *Key*. The interest of the
Key, then, lies chiefly in its connection with Colburn's
advertising methods. When Colburn, who by the time of
issuance of the *Key* had learned that Disraeli was his
anonymous author, tried to learn whether the book pre-
tended to draw from living originals, Disraeli wrote a
noncommittal reply to Jerdan. Certainly his letter could
not serve to quiet enquiry or stifle sales.

More important to the reader than the mere introduction of names and the possible truthfulness of the
portraiture is the revelation they make of the author's
attitude. Disraeli, partly through his shameless handling
of great names, succeeds admirably in the first part of the
novel in establishing a spirit of make-believe. Vivian is
obviously a reflection of the author, but by some sort of
legerdemain Disraeli manages to evade his responsibility
and to cast a veil of fantasy over the whole action. This

---

[4] *The Star Chamber* was published weekly from April 19 to June 7, 1826.
[5] For a discussion of Disraeli's connection with *The Star Chamber* and
its principal satires, see *The Dunciad of Today, a Satire, and The Modern
Aesop*, published with an introduction by Michael Sadleir, London, 1928.

fantasy (or burlesque) is just what is needed to keep the novel from being a pompous failure. How else could a young writer with no knowledge of society except that which he had gained from books and the friends of his father write a novel in which the characters are lords, German adventuresses, parliamentarians, and country gentlemen, except by the assumption of the deft superiority of a showman displaying his wares before country yokels?

So Vivian assures a noble young poet that there is a magazine called *The Weimar Literary Gazette* which contains a review of his last volume by Goethe. "It is really delightful to see the oldest poet in Europe dilating on the brilliancy of a new star on the poetical horizon."[6]

And to a young lady sentimentally fond of autographs he presents a brand new autograph of Washington Irving. "Shall I write any more? One of Sir Walter's or Mr. Southey's or Mr. Milman's, or Mr. Disraeli's? or shall I sprawl a Byron?"[7]

In 1829, Disraeli conceived the idea of going to the East. Money was necessary, and his only resource was his pen. Like Bulwer, he wanted to write satire, but Colburn wanted his bright young men to continue in their early paths of profit. The result, after the labor of a few months, was *The Young Duke*. The author was completely convinced of his success, although Bulwer, to whom he showed it, counseled a thorough revision of many of his most highly valued scenes. "It is a series of scenes," Disraeli had boasted, "every one of which would make the fortune of a fashionable novelist."[8] Mrs. Austen was fairly well pleased, but when the publisher's readers joined Bulwer in counseling excision, Disraeli, considerably chastened in spirit, did a little toning down of the irritating egotism. The book appeared through Colburn in 1830.

[6] *Vivian Grey.*, p. 78.   [7] *Ibid.*, p. 80.
[8] Monypenny and Buckle, *op. cit.*, I, 127.

If it is difficult to treat *Vivian Grey* or *Falkland* wholly seriously, it is impossible to be ponderously grave about *The Young Duke*. Such a mad gallimaufry of extravagance had scarcely been seen since *The Arabian Nights*. Everything is superlative—gold plate, castles, fifty thousand a year, mistresses, gambling, balls, dancers—everything on the oriental palette of Disraeli is lavished on the book. The result is not so much just another fashionable novel as it is a fashionable novel to end fashionable novels.

"*The Young Duke!*" exclaimed old Isaac, "what does Ben know of Dukes?"[9] But the book has a great verisimilitude. It sounds as though it *ought* to be true of dukes. It satisfies in somewhat the same way Versailles satisfies the mental picture of a fairy princes' palace. If young dukes aren't like Disraeli's young duke, so much the worse for them. Anyway, it held the fee to the gorgeous East, for with the five hundred pounds in post-dated bills which Colburn paid for it, Disraeli and his friend Matthews set out on their travels.

The orphaned Duke of St. James's, released from the solicitous care of his guardian after college and foreign travel, returns to England and freedom. With wealth for the indulgence of every whim, life presents no imperative necessity for success in politics or literature. So the young duke's establishments, his balls, his racing studs, his mistresses become the sensation of London. He tries everything. At the height of his gambling mania he indulges in one thirty-six hour session which cures him by satiety and very nearly cripples his immense income.

Love for May Dacre, the Roman Catholic daughter of his guardian, proves his only lasting emotion, and after a hurriedly improvised speech in the House of Lords in favor of Catholic emancipation, his wild oats fail of harvest, the

[9] *Ibid.*, p. 132.

past drops away, and May Dacre becomes the Duchess of St. James's.

I have said that the book is not a genuine fashionable novel. Justification for such an assertion can come only from the book's extravagance. It is a caricature rather than an original specimen. It might have been written by Thackeray for his "Punch's Prize Novelists" series. Practically every successful feature of the fashionable novels is incorporated in it. The characters must be of high station—therefore, this one is about a duke. He ought to be in comfortable circumstances—this duke is as wealthy and well-born as Jocky Norfolk. The sins must be glamorous—this novel's sins include the latest dancer from the opera; the money gambled away is enough to impair fifty thousand a year; the new palace excels Belvoir or Blenheim. The extravagances must be heralded in *John Bull* or satirized in *The Age*—the young duke is the sole subject of a Sunday newspaper. There ought to be some politics—the young duke swings the House of Lords to Catholic Emancipation. Hackwork undoubtedly, but hackwork done with so much imagination that it almost takes on sublimity. With Disraeli the young duke becomes a veritable Caliph of Bagdad, the distillation of dukedom.

Fortunately the distillation was not too refined for a public which demanded soberness in handling serious subjects like dukes and dancers. The book sold moderately well,[10] and did not suffer too severely from any of the critical organs except *The Westminster Review*. And despite Disraeli's disavowal in the preface of personal portraiture,

[10] *The Young Duke* had a very large sale in the United States. *The North American Review*, July, 1842, p. 261, commented: "It is unfortunate, that the merchant's daughter and the farmer's boy should get their heads too full of the Young Duke and May Dacre; there is real danger, that, when such dreams are dreamed in every fifth or tenth house throughout the country, the affection with which our venerable frame of society ought to be regarded will be in some degree distracted or unsettled."

Colburn managed the advertising with his customary adroitness. At any rate, he deceived Sarah Disraeli. She wrote to Benjamin that the book was not being puffed to any extent.

To test the sincerity of Disraeli's desire not to be a hack, and to supply the materials for an interesting comparison with Bulwer, it will be necessary to go back a little in our chronological outline and consider his *Popanilla*. This was published in the late spring of 1828, and was the outgrowth of an earlier sketch, *The Voyage of Aylmer Popanilla*, which he had had hopes of publishing with John Murray's imprint. The break with the publisher had killed that hope, and the author had put the sketch aside for a few years. Finally he finished it for Colburn.

The short story (one might as well call it that) is interesting chiefly to political students of Disraeli because it shows his instinctive dislike of Utilitarianism and its "screw and lever" philosophy. Like Bulwer's enemies, Disraeli's early dislikes form strange groups. In *Popanilla* the future Tory premier conjures up a massive figure, the Aboriginal Inhabitant, to personify the iniquity of the Corn Laws, and the godfather of Imperialism jeers at the colonial policy.

Popanilla is a savage from a South Sea island, *Fantasia*, transported to Hubbabub, the chief city of Vraibleusia. His naïve reactions to English anomalies, the public debt, poor relief, competition, *laissez faire*, and society, furnish the material. Disraeli could not refrain from attacking the fashionable novel as indicative of the higher society, and it is this attack which shows the extent of his defection from principle when he wrote *The Young Duke*. The account of the fashionable novel's origin and rise hardly allows enough time because he attributes it entirely to the South American boom of 1822–25. As he puts it, the Vraibleusians became rich from the paper profits of their projected expedition to Fantasia, and the resulting flood of newly rich "determined to acquire in a day that which had hitherto been deemed the gradual consequence of tedious education."[11] When doubt arose as to the wisdom of raising all people to equal heights of fashion, the government took sides and determined to complete the work. It issued

an edict that a new literature should be invented, in order at once to complete the education of the millionaires and the triumph of the Romantic over the Classic school of Manners.

The most eminent writers were . . . in the pay of the Government, and "Burlington, a Tale of Fashionable Life," in three volumes, post octavo, was sent forth. Two or three similar works, bearing titles equally euphonious and aristocratic, were published daily; and so exquisite was the style of these productions, so naturally artificial the construction of their plots, and so admirably inventive the conception of their characters, that many who had been repulsed by the somewhat abstract matter and arid style of the treatises, seduced by the interest of a story, and by the dazzling delicacies of a charming style, really now picked up a considerable quantity of very useful knowledge; so that when the delighted students had eaten some fifty or sixty imaginary dinners in my lord's dining-room, and whirled some fifty or sixty imaginary waltzes in my lady's dancing-room, there was scarcely a brute left among the whole millionaires. But what produced the most beneficial effects on the new people, and excited the greatest indignation and despair among the old class, were some volumes which the Government, with shocking Machiavellism, bribed some needy scions of nobility to scribble, and which revealed certain secrets vainly believed to be quite sacred and inviolable.[12]

Despite this sneer at the fashionable novel, Disraeli's record for consistency suffered only one serious defection. That was at the publication of *The Young Duke*. His *Endymion*, appearing as late as 1880, is an attempt to recapture the glamor of the thirties. In two short pieces, *Ixion* and *The Infernal Marriage*, written in 1833 and 1834 for publication in Colburn's *New Monthly Magazine*, he attempted light

[11] *Popanilla*, New York, n.d., p. 412.   [12] *Ibid.*, pp. 414–15.

fashionable and political satire in the manner of Lucian.
His pictures of George IV as Jupiter, Byron as Apollo,
Talleyrand as Tiresias rank among his best, and show,
possibly, how satire of·this kind should be done.

But this irreverent vein was never for long the domi-
nating spirit in Disraeli. He chose to bring a greater seriousness to his work. We have seen, in the preceding chapter,
how much Bulwer owed to the apprenticeship novel of
Wilhelm Meister. Disraeli's understanding of it had a marked
influence upon his *Contarini Fleming*. Omitting such books
as *Alroy* and *Venetia*, which are entirely outside our field,
and passing over to the first of his greater novels, *Coningsby*,
we see that the natural development of Disraeli's novels
was toward the type with which his name is indissolubly
connected—the political novel.

The rise in political interest from *Vivian Grey* to *Coningsby* is by no means regular, but nearly all of the novels
show some concern with the subject. An unreal sort of
politics dominates the first part of *Vivian Grey*. There is
little actual understanding of the political art, but a
strenuous affectation of its motions. Vivian organizes a
party, and wins over doubtful men by the use of the
vaguest talk that even a politician ever used. In *The Young
Duke* political interest appears only once—when the re-
formed young lord rushes into a speech on the Catholic
question. Such an action is Disraeli's way of showing
complete conversion. Even in *Contarini Fleming* Disraeli
was unable to suppress altogether the expression of his
belief. that politics offers the highest vocation open to
anyone. "*The Psychological Romance* is a development of my
poetic character," he said in his diary. Yet the poetic hero
at the end of the book is left contemplating entering
politics.

Although *Popanilla* is general satire, its chief interest
lies in such political questions as arose out of Canning's

foreign policy, the Corn Laws, and the Utilitarian philosophy. "So in *The Infernal Marriage* there is a great deal of
the politics of the Duke of Wellington and Lord Grey's
government."[13]

By the time of *Coningsby*, ten years later than the last
of these works, much of the fashionable novel was still
discernible in the political novel. As Philip Guedalla puts
it, Disraeli's "social gusto was quite undiminished by experience of the great world."[14] To Thackeray, writing the
amusing burlesque, *Codlingsby*, what appeared most de-
serving of castigation was not the politics, but the extravagant settings.

I am tired of Schloss Schinkenstein; the Rhine bores me after
while. It is too hot for Florence; besides, they have not completed
the picture-gallery, and my place smells of putty. You wouldn't
have a man, *mon cher*, bury himself in his chateau in Normandy,
out of the hunting season? The Rugantino Palace stupefies me.
Those Titians are so gloomy, I shall have my Hobbemas and Ten-
iers, I think, from my house at the Hague hung over them . . .

The carpet was of white velvet (laid over several webs of Aubus-
son, Ispahan, and Axminster, so that your foot gave no more
sound as it trod upon the yielding plain than the shadow did
which followed you)—of white velvet, painted with flowers,
arabesques, and classic figures, by Sir William Ross, J. M. W.
Turner, R. A., Mrs. Mee, and Paul Delaroche . . .

Miriam, returning to the mother-of-pearl music stool, at a signal
from her brother, touched the silver and enamelled keys of the
ivory piano.[15]

It is interesting, and perhaps instructive, to note that

[13] Monypenny and Buckle, *op. cit.*, I, 459. Quoted letter to Mrs.
Brydges Williams. September 29, 1853.

[14] *Coningsby*, London (Bradenham Edition), 1927. Introduction by
Philip Guedalla.

[15] W. M. Thackeray, The Oxford *Miscellaneous Contributions to Punch*,
London, N.D., pp. 101–10. It may destroy Disraeli's reputation for possessing a luxurious imagination to note that the last paragraph above
contains an exact description of Prince Albert's piano now in the Bethnal
Green Museum.

Sir Robert Peel preferred the descriptions in *Coningsby* to the politics. Lord John Russell liked the love scenes best. And Disraeli wrote to his sister, "There is no particular news except that Bradshaw, the last of the school of Brummell, has read a book—and it is called *Coningsby*."[16]

Evidently, then, there is much in *Coningsby* that appeals to the inveterate reader of the most opulent fashionable novels. The settings in London mansion or on country estate differ not at all from those in *Pelham*, *Cecil*, or *Women as They Are*, except in the greater luxury. Disraeli in *Coningsby* is a more skillful architect than he was in *The Young Duke*, but the magnificent palaces of the Duke of St. James's are by the same hand that drew Coningsby Castle.

The people who throng the Palladian settings are unusually politically-minded. Such people are not unknown in the ordinary fashionable novel, but there they do not constitute such a large proportion of the whole. In *Coningsby* the members of the ruling-class are more interested in the government of their country than in general social gossip. Indeed, says Guedalla, "the real heroes and villains of *Coningsby* are political ideas."[17] But the people through whom these political ideas are expressed are familiar types. There is the great noble, the Marquis of Monmouth. There are dandies and men of fashion, the Prince Colonna and Mr. Melton. Coningsby himself at times seems to be drawn with the conscious desire to avoid a likeness to dandies like Pelham and Vivian Grey. "Not even the dancing-master had afforded his mechanical aid to Coningsby . . . No clever or refined woman . . . had ever given him the education that is more precious than Universities."[18]

[16] *Lord Beaconsfield's Correspondence with His Sister, 1832–52*, London, 1885, p. 145.

[17] *Coningsby, op. cit.*, p. xiii.   [18] *Ibid.*, p. 105.

There are women of the world—Lady Everingham and Lucretia. Lucretia in her statuesque beauty and eventual discomfiture is perhaps the more conventional, but Lady Everingham's administrations to the neglected Coningsby are more disinterested than is usual. Mrs. Guy Flouncey, an example of the always interesting social climber, is far less gross than most specimens of her class. Buckle thought her an anticipation of Becky Sharpe. She is more, perhaps, a copy of the Lady Harriett in Mrs. Gore's *Cecil* or of the Lady Harriett in the same writer's *Diary of a Désennuyée*.

When Disraeli is dealing with aristocrats his work at times reaches a note of lyrical rapture. At Eton, for example, the sight of "five hundred of the youth of England" leads him to compare them to a "band of heroes . . . marching from Athens, or Thebes, or Sparta, to some heroic deed. . . ." "And younger sons returned by family boroughs glowed in his fancy as figures of chivalry caparisoned for unknown quests." This attitude had not appeared so plainly in earlier books than *Coningsby*. For aristocrats going about their normal business of living, Disraeli had not the enthusiasm which leads to rapture. Political endeavor alone brought him to the requisite state of admiration and inspiration. In this truth lies the reason why *The Young Duke* is hackwork and *Coningsby* such a brilliant study of two political generations. Disraeli had finally learned to do what he wanted to do.

VI

MRS. GORE

Hardly rivaling the adaptability to the market that so distinguished Bulwer Lytton, Mrs. Gore, starting her career when the dominance of Scott's romances seemed unending, was slow to sense a change, and turned her prodigious energy to the manufacture of fashionable novels only after their popularity had slightly passed its crest. Her first essay at the new type was *Women as They Are, or, Manners of the Day*, published in 1830, a few years after the extraordinary success of Disraeli's *Vivian Grey*, 1826–27, and Bulwer's *Pelham*, 1828. She fully atoned for her tardiness in entering upon the composition of fashionable novels by continuing to write them for twenty-eight years. Before 1830 she had published three historical romances, *Theresa Marchmont, or, The Maid of Honour*, 1824,[1] *Richelieu, or, The Broken Heart*, 1826, and *The Lettre de cachet*, 1827; a volume of short stories, *Hungarian Tales*, 1829; a couple of short farces, and one dramatic poem, *The Bond*, 1824.

The arts of puffery practiced by her usual publisher, Henry Colburn, do not seem to have extended to publicity of her personal affairs; and she apparently held an artistic detachment from her work that forbade her justifying or defending it in any way, but there is a passage in *Women as They Are*, which may be taken as an apology for the sort of work that was so largely to engage her attention during the remainder of her life. " 'We have perhaps had more than enough of fashionable novels,' replied Lord Willers-

[1] This book was written in one week.—Her own statement in Add. Biog. MSS 28510, ff. 111. British Museum.

dale, 'but as the amber which serves to preserve the ephemeral modes and caprices of the passing day, they have their value.' "[2] Despite the danger of putting an author's voice into a character's speech, this fits in so well with what Mrs. Gore was doing that we may take it as her own.

Granted this conclusion, one observation from it is patent—that she knew exactly what she wanted to do. She was neither a Maria Edgeworth born to set the crooked straight by adherence to the latest and most approved methods, nor a Richardson seeking to bring back the age of innocence by following the dictates of Christian morality. Hers was a different, but not, perhaps, a lower aim— simply to be the "amber which seeks to preserve the ephemeral modes and caprices of the passing day."

Of the opportunities in her own life that enabled her to act as an interpreter of the upper ranks of society there is little enough evidence available. The writer of her obituary in *The Athenaeum* for February 9, 1861, considered her work "spoilt by too late an equality in the society of the persons, rich and magnificent, whom she partly courted, partly satirized." Yet Bulwer, possibly indulging his spleen toward Thackeray, could say that "she knew good society infinitely better" than Thackeray did.[3] Because of her retiring nature, and the surprising absence of references to her in the memoirs of the time, proof or disproof of *The Athenaeum's* statement can come only from stray pieces of information which may be gleaned in various places. The lack of biographical data is rather unfortunate, since one of the most insistent attacks that was made on the type of novel she wrote is based on the assertion that the people who wrote them were menials. *Blackwood's Magazine* published[4] an amusing dialogue between the Poet and the

[2] Mrs. Gore, *Women as They Are*, London, 1830, II, 233–34.
[3] Quoted, Michael Sadleir, *Edward and Rosina*, Boston, 1931, p. 277.
[4] *Blackwood's Magazine*, October, 1830, XXVIII, 623–27.

Squire which aptly serves to illustrate the prevailing attitude.

> Poet: Are there two of all the tribe
> Of would-be wits, who *know* what they describe?
> Lo! the fair laundress, perch'd in high St. Giles,
> Paints to one dimple how the Countess smiles;
> While Prince and Peer their wit and wisdom owe
> To pilfering valets housed in Rottenrow.

At any rate, the little that we do know of Mrs. Gore is sufficient to repel the insinuation that she and Jeames moved in the same social circles. Certainly after her marriage in 1823 she occupied a fairly assured social position, although there may be considerable doubt concerning her own family and birth. Her maiden name was Catherine Frances Moody.[5] Most reference books assert her birthplace to be East Retford, Nottinghamshire, where her father is considered to have been a wine merchant. A paper[6] in the British Museum which is marked, "Mrs. Gore encloses the paper corrected, and asks for a proof," definitely proves her to have been born in London in 1800.[7] She "received a careful education," and, according to the *Dictionary of National Biography*,[8] early exhibited poetical genius and was called "the Poetess" by her playmates. Her earliest juvenile productions were commended by Joanna Baillie, who was probably more kind than just. A letter of Mary Russell Mitford, while obviously written in jest, indicates how rapidly the young lady fulfilled her early promise.

[5] *Parish Register of St. George's, Hanover Square.—Publ. Harleian Soc.,* XXII, 1896. *The Athenaeum*, Feb. 9, 1861, p. 196, said: "We have heard that she was a Miss Nevenson." A. G. K. L'Estrange, editor of *The Life of Mary Russell Mitford*, New York, 1870, I, 297, says that she was the stepdaughter of a Dr. Nevinson.

[6] Add. Biog. MSS 28510, ff. 110, 111.

[7] Her marriage license describes her as coming from St. Marylebone. There is no baptismal record in the parish registers.

[8] The source of this account is *The New Monthly Magazine*, March, 1837, XLIX, 434-35.

Did I ever mention to you, or did you ever hear elsewhere of a
Miss Nevinson, poetess, novelist, essayist, and reviewer? I have
just been writing to her in answer to a very kind letter, but
writing in such alarm that I quivered and shook, and looked into
the dictionary to see how to spell *The*, and asked mamma if there
were two t's in tottering. You never saw anybody in such a
fright. It was like writing in chains, and now that I am writing
to you, for whom I don't care a pin, it's like a galley-slave let
loose from the oar . . . and so alarming a lady is Miss Nevinson,
so sure to put one on the defensive, even when she has no intention to attack. This is no great compliment to my fair correspondent, but it is the truth. Miss Nevinson is a very extraordinary
woman; her conversation (for I don't think very highly of her
writings) is perhaps the most dazzling and brilliant that can be
imagined.[9]

Her career begins to take on the definiteness of public
record with·her marriage on February 15, 1823, to Lieutenant Charles Arthur Gore[10] at the fashionable St. George's
Church, Hanover Square. Lieutenant Gore was a soldier of
a literary turn, apparently, for he made some of the translations which were published under his wife's name.[11] The
married life of the couple was probably pleasant, although
the excessive literary labor points towards straitened circumstances. In his will, after creating a trust fund for one
daughter, he named his "beloved wife" his trustee. Since
the will was made just before his death in 1846 one likes to
read into the phrase more, perhaps, than the conventional
wording will carry. There were ten children in all, only
two of whom survived Mrs. Gore. One of them, Cecilia
Anne Mary, became the second wife of Lord Edward
Thynne, M. P., a younger son of the second Marquis of

[9] A. G. K. L'Estrange, *op. cit.*, I, 297.

[10] He is usually called Captain Gore, but the Army List shows him to
have been a Lieutenant when he resigned in 1823. He had entered the 72
Reg. of Foot in 1817 as Ensign, was gazetted Cornet and Sub-Lieut. in
1822. The slowness of his advance points to lack of money and influence.

[11] Mrs. Oliphant, *William Blackwood and His Sons*, II, 348–49. Letter
of Mrs. Gore to Samuel Warren.

Bath. The other, Captain Augustus Wentworth Gore, became aide-de-camp to the Lord Lieutenant of Ireland and later distinguished himself in the Indian campaigns. For some time before her own death in 1861 at Linwood, Lyndhurst, Hampshire, Mrs. Gore was blind.

The *Dictionary of National Biography* states that her first published work was *The Two Broken Hearts*,[12] but since she approved a statement[13] declaring *Theresa Marchmont* to have been her first book, the *Dictionary* is probably in error, although possibly the reference is to periodical publishing. Her education must have included more real music than was usually the lot of young ladies of her day, because in 1827 she became fairly well known as the composer of several song hits. She wrote the music for a poem of Susannah Blamire's,[14] "And Ye Shall Walk in Silk Attire." For the words of "The Song of the Highland Chiefs,"[15] I have been unable to find an author. She perhaps wrote both the words and music for this, as she did for her last song, "'Tis Three Long Years."[16] This musical interlude forms a strange feature in her life. Apparently she was one of those versatile individuals who can do anything to which they turn their minds. In addition to her literary efforts in comedies, dramas, melodramas, farces, travel books, and garden manuals, beside several novels outside her sphere of fashionable life, she is said to have been a capable etcher.[17]

In 1832 she went with her husband to live in Paris for some years.[18] We get a glimpse of her here in the auto-

[12] This book is not in the British Museum.

[13] Add. Biog. MSS 28510, ff. 110–11.

[14] Susannah Blamire, "the muse of Cumberland" (1747–94), wrote simple lyrics that remind one of Burns and Bloomfield about the country folk she knew. London, C. Lonsdale, Musical Circulating Library, Guitar Songs, #2 Sola, 1827.   [15] London, J. Power, 1827.

[16] *Ibid.*   [17] *New Monthly Magazine*, XLIX, 1837, 434–35.

[18] This stay in Paris extended possibly to 1840. *Tait's Edinburgh Magazine*, November, 1841, VIII, 186, in a review of *Greville, or, A Season*

biography of Coventry Patmore, whose father, P. G. Patmore, was glad to have Coventry visit her on Sunday afternoons. For a time, at least, she presided at a *salon* in the Place Vendôme, visited by "the best literary and political society of Paris." She eventually returned to London, but we lose track of her except in the ever-recurrent announcements of new novels. She was living in Brussels when her husband died in 1846.[19] About 1850 she inherited a large sum at the death of a member of her mother's family.[20] This new affluence led her to relax her labors,[21] but in 1855 she suffered a severe loss when her bankers, Strahan, Paul, and Bates, failed for two-thirds of a million pounds. Her personal loss reached nearly £19,000, including £6,000 which she was holding as trustee for her daughter, Lady Mary Thynne. There is more than mere financial interest to this event, for, by a remarkable coincidence, Mrs. Gore had written a novel, *The Banker's Wife*, in 1843 which described the life of a dishonest banker, and, strangest of all, she had actually dedicated it to her Trustee and Banker, Sir John Dean Paul, Bart.

In this dedication to the edition of 1843 she was at pains to point out that she was not writing an attack upon a class but upon an individual. To the reviewer in *Tait's Edinburgh Magazine*, however, it seemed that the reader might "fancy that Mrs. Gore disliked the profession abstractly."[22] Banker Hamlyn, descendant of an old

---

in Paris, said that she has left "that gay capital for London." The inference is that the change was recent. Mr. Michael Sadleir, *The Strange Life of Lady Blessington*, Boston, 1933, p. 188, states that for a time her husband was in the diplomatic service.

[19] Her stay on the Continent was probably due to the cheapness of living there.   [20] *Gentleman's Magazine*, March, 1861, n.s., X, 345–46.

[21] She published only two full-length novels and one short tale between 1849 and 1855. Her only novel in 1855 was called *Mammon, or, The Hardships of a Heiress*, indicative of her state of mind, perhaps.

[22] *Tait's Edinburgh Magazine*, Edinburgh, Nov., 1843, X, 702.

Lombard Street banking family, has inherited a large
landed estate which the weakened bank cannot maintain.
He misappropriates funds in a desperate effort to save his
fortunes. After deserting his party in the Commons, he is
killed in a duel, and the bank's failure is disclosed. The
abstract dislike of banking which *Tait's* noted comes
from the remarks of an idealistic young widow who refuses to marry Hamlyn's son unless he will abandon his
intention to succeed his father at the bank.

What actually happened to Mrs. Gore twelve years
later is so close to the novel in general outline that if the
chronology were reversed, the commentator would be
forced to believe that the novel was founded on fact. The
banking house of Strahan, Paul, and Bates was an old one,
dating from the Restoration, highly respected in the City,
numbering among its clients some of the most eminent
people of the day. Through bad debts their affairs became
so involved that they sought frantically for funds, and
finally sold bonds and stocks held by them for depositors.
In 1847, Sir John Dean Paul proposed that Mrs. Gore lend
her funds to clients of the bank. She refused to do so, and
did not learn until the crash that her money, instead of
being secured in Exchequer bills or Consuls, was in fact,
hopelessly involved in the failure of the bank. The first
Baronet, her trustee, died in 1852, and was succeeded by
his son, Sir John Dean Paul, 2d Baronet. When the three
members of the firm were tried in 1856 for criminally di-
verting clients' funds to their own use, it was thus the son
of her trustee who was sentenced to fourteen years penal
servitude. There can be no doubt, however, that the elder
Paul was equally liable and dishonest.[23]

In an effort, excusable enough, to recoup some of her
losses, Mrs. Gore allowed the reprinting in 1858 of her

[23] This material is taken from the papers on file at the Court of Bank-
ruptcy in Carey Street, London. File 1239.

novel. She canceled her earlier preface, however, and substituted another in which she remarked that in her novel of
fifteen years ago she "was far from foreseeing that her own
fortune would become partially involved in a catastrophe
similar to the one described in its pages." She went on,
"To his [Sir John Dean Paul's] conduct . . . or to certain
extraordinary coincidences connected with the story, it
would be ungenerous now to advert, further than to
justify myself for having cancelled the dedication."

The biographical interest of *The Banker's Wife*, however,
has diverted us far out of our chronology. Mrs. Gore's life
was so regular and laborious that the few actual details we
do know of her must be given.

We have seen that in the 1820's she was actively
engaged in the writing of plays, historical tales, and romances, and in the composition of songs. In 1830 she began
what was to be her lifelong work, the writing of fashionable novels. Her first, *Women as They Are, or, The Manners of
the Day*, suffers from dullness, the one fault unforgivable
in a light transcript of manners. True, George IV said[24] of
it that it was the best bred and most amusing novel published in his remembrance, but then, by 1830 George was a
dying man. Later in her career, with many books behind
her, when invention began to flag or exhaustion to set in,
she also achieved dullness, but never again quite such a
mixture of woodenness in character creation and stiffness
in manipulation. The plot itself, though conventional, has
many possibilities, and apparently Mrs. Gore thought so
too, for she used it with variations in other novels. One
measure of Mrs. Gore's modernity may be seen in the observation that the heroine here, and often elsewhere, starts
as a married woman.

An eighteen-year-old country girl entered upon her
apprenticeship when she married Lord Willersdale, aged

[24] *The New Monthly Magazine*, XLIX (March, 1837), 434-35.

forty, and a member of the Cabinet. Taken from the simple and wholesome environment of a country home to the drawing rooms of Mayfair, married to a man twice her age and occupied with the cares of State, exposed to the machinations of his fashionable sister, Lady Willersdale triumphs only with the greatest difficulty. Naïve mistakes, social blunders, mutual misunderstandings, and even the suicide of the sister mark her London life. Endless pages of talk revolve about love matches versus *marriages de convenance*, younger sons and eldest sons, entails and inheritances, until one is thoroughly convinced that the boasted English romantic way of marriage is only an illusion.

What Mrs. Gore has done in this novel is to reproduce in the story of Lady Willersdale the journey towards adjustment taken by so many characters before—Fanny Burney's Evelina, Maria Edgeworth's Belinda, Bulwer's Pelham, Disraeli's Vivian Grey. We have seen in the chapter on Bulwer that the picaresque romance, made thoroughly English by Fielding and Smollett, was changed by the influence of Goethe's *Wilhelm Meister*. While Mrs. Gore, in *The Manners of the Day*, hardly approached even *Vivian Grey* in solidity and psychological insight, certain of her novels to come, such as *Mothers and Daughters*, and *Cecil*, found her vastly improved. Although she never became capable of delving much below the surface, she seldom strained her art by attempting more. Bulwer might render his predecessors obsolete with his "metaphysical" subtleties;[25] Mrs. Gore was content to tell the old, old story of man's adjustment to his environment, satisfied if

---

[25] In *Pin Money*, London, 1831, II, 53, she declared: "A few long sentences, sufficiently complex and ungrammatical to perplex the mind of a booby, impart a wondrously philosophical character to a work of fiction; while a little high-flying touch of metaphysics ensures from the lesser fry of critics a plausibility or two . . ."

she could render the environment as elegant as a tea at Gunther's.

The book did not attract much attention upon its appearance, or some young Benthamite would have been sure to annihilate it as the work of a laundress. Mrs. Gore rashly anticipated in part this hypothetical critic. In the course of the conversation between Lord Willersdale and others, of which part has been quoted, one of the speakers objects to the lack of naturalness caused by a writer's looking up to high life and regarding it as something unique, governed by different laws from those that obtain among ordinary people. As an illustration of what he means, he gives the classical instance of Richardson's fine gentlemen, Lovelace in particular. *Mais nous avons changé tous cela!* In books like *Tremaine*, *Granby*, and *Pelham*, he goes on, there is a prevailing air of reality; the characters are distinguished from other people only by their individual characteristics. It is a pity that Mrs. Gore should have ventured on such ground when the very words in which she does it bear witness to her own failure in achievement.

Take Lord Willersdale, for example. Modeled on the pattern of the pompous statesmen (compare Disraeli's Marquis of Carabas), he never discards his starched toga, and speaks only in measured accents. But it is clear that Mrs. Gore does not wish to make him the ass that Susan Ferrier's Lord Rossdale is, although at times the portraiture comes dangerously near to caricature. In this early book, Mrs. Gore's failure is not due to awe of her fine gentlemen, but to lack of skill.

She followed *Women as They Are* with another novel of the contemporary period which she found more congenial to her taste, and throughout a writing career which extended over four decades, she returned to it again and again. At the beginning of her career her usual setting was the time she was living in; in 1836 *The Diary of a Désennuyée* is slightly historical, covering the last ten years. In 1841, in *Cecil*, she goes back to 1800, and brings the coxcomb actually into the reign of Victoria, but even after a quarter century of the Victorian *milieu*, Mrs. Gore is emphatically of the "twenties," that important and neglected transitional period when most of the Romantics were dying and their successors had not yet appeared. It is likewise the decade when England partially responded to the impulse toward democracy which the Industrial Revolution had brought about. The English are a politically-minded people but perhaps never before or since has popular interest in politics been so tremendous as in the years preceding the Reform Bill. Thus in her new novel, *The Hamiltons, or, Official Life in 1830*, 1831, Mrs. Gore was directly appealing to a twofold interest in her audience—fashionable life and politics.

The plot of the novel is another version of the married life theme of *Women as They Are*. Augustus Hamilton, the son of a Tory member of Parliament, marries a young girl. He is a heartlessly cynical dandy, whose inconsiderable abilities are devoted chiefly to staying in office. Susan Hamilton soon learns that she has been cheated, but remains loyal to her husband until evidence is forthcoming that he has had a mistress. The mistress' husband kills Hamilton in a duel. Susan then marries a faithful lover, Lord Claneustace. By dint of never appearing to take sides, while stressing the frantic efforts of Hamilton and his Tory colleagues to stay in office, Mrs. Gore betrays her bias toward the Whig, or rather Reform, side of the struggle. As a picture of the class of office holders, *The Hamiltons* has considerable merit, their selfish, tightly-knotted little souls being skillfully dissected. The excessive interest displayed by the characters in mere office holding, however, partly disqualifies the book as a society novel, although because of its lack of creative political theory, it remains equally remote from the true political novel.

The year 1831 was a prolific one, as Mrs. Gore published some thirteen volumes—*The Hamiltons, Mothers and Daughters*, and *Pin Money*, each in three volumes; *The Tuileries, a Tale*, and *The Historical Traveller*, "comprising narratives connected with European History, etc.," each in two. It is interesting to note that she produced some two hundred volumes during a writing career of thirty-five years, with an average annual production of six volumes running to about three hundred pages apiece. This reduces itself to six pages a day, Sundays and holidays omitted, for a third of a century. Is it any wonder that some of her books seem to have been written with her left hand, especially when we remember that she bore ten children during a period of twenty-three years?

Pin Money shows, however, that she had come into capable grasp of her materials. She began to attract an attention hitherto denied her, and even received semi-favorable notice from the *Westminster*. Because Mrs. Gore was not addicted to the writing of prefaces setting forth her views on life and art, the presence of even a page-long introduction to *Pin Money* offers us one of our opportunities to get a glimpse of her theory.

She disclaims, as did most of the fashionable novelists just then, any attempt at describing real people. Writers were forced into such denials largely because of the unscrupulous methods with which publishers advertised their wares, but so common was the denial that there is reason for assuming it was a legal fiction.

More interesting than this conventional denial of living originals for her characters is her description of the book:

Exhibiting an attempt to transfer the familiar narrative of Miss Austen to a higher sphere of society, it is, in fact, a novel of the

simplest kind, addressed by a woman to readers of her own sex;—
by whom, as well as by the professional critics, its predecessor,
The Manners of the Day, was received with too much indulgence
not to encourage a further appeal to their favor.

If Mrs. Gore's estimate of her debt to Jane Austen is a just
one, then apparently in seeking to establish her connection
with Bulwer, Ward, and Burney we have been off the right
track. There is some truth in her remarks. Jane Austen's
"familiar narrative" deals with provincial society in quiet
country houses or in centers like Bath, while Mrs. Gore's
more elaborate treatises deal with London society. Both
get their effects with the sharp weapon of irony, and both
manage to achieve more memorable character sketches
when a little vindictiveness drives their pens. Yet one
feels a difference in their work not to be atoned for by any
amount of similarity in aim or subject. The delicate clarity
of an Austen novel is as remote as can be from the prolix
cumbrousness of a Gore novel. When Disraeli described
Mrs. Gore as "a sumptuous personage—looking like a
full-blown rose," we feel that he should have met Jane
Austen in order to give us a simile for her derived from
some more retiring plant. An easy transference of similes
from authors to books would then have indicated some of
the differences. The over-elaborateness of Mrs. Gore's
style, her resolute insistence on verbal ornament, utterly
obscure a perhaps fundamental resemblance in outlook
upon society. Would Jane Austen ever have called, for
example, a stuffy boudoir, "a reeking sudatorium, past the
ascertainment of Réaumur or Fahrenheit"?[26]

The modesty with which Mrs. Gore restricts her
message to women is probably due to her ostentatious in-
sertion of the names of fashionable shops in the narrative.
The Westminster Review, indeed, called *Pin Money* a London
Directory, and suggested that it be taxed as an advertising

[26] *Mothers and Daughters*, London, 1831, I, 8.

medium.[27] The novelist who writes for a group restricted
by sex or age, does so at his own peril, and in so far as he
succeeds, robs his work of universal appeal. Mrs. Gore's
use of shop names, partly a device to further realism, became chiefly a method of interesting women readers. She
strove so earnestly for the coveted placard "By Appointment," that she definitely aligned herself with the trades-
men, and did her reputation much harm. It is the evident
surrender of Mrs. Gore to the practices of the silver-fork
school that forces us to consider her in the line of descent
from Hook rather than from Jane Austen. She probably felt
an intellectual kinship which blinded her to the immense
differences between Jane Austen's understanding of provincial society and her own conception of Regency gilt.

Pin Money, dealing with the possible complications in a
wife's independent income, is a slight reshuffling of the
plot of *Women as They Are. The Westminster*, fairly enough,
described it as "a novel which shows, in three volumes,
the danger of a married lady's possessing four hundred a
year independent of her husband."[28] Lady Rawleigh,
younger than Sir Brooke, lacks sufficient balance to handle
her funds wisely, and not until the closing chapters are
the difficulties solved.

The surface quality of Mrs. Gore's art is nowhere displayed more strongly than in a comparison of her male and
female characters. Knowing men only outwardly, she
usually achieved a clear, if not profound picture of them.
She attempted more with women, but often achieved less.

The perennial interest of the marrying mother theme
furnished Mrs. Gore with the subject for her third fashionable novel in 1831, *Mothers and Daughters, a Tale of the Year
1830*. There was nothing new to be said on the subject, and
true to form, the daughter who marries for love wins the
happiness denied her more calculating sisters.

[27] *The Westminster Review*, XV (Oct., 1831), 433.
[28] *The Westminster Review*, XV (Oct., 1831), 433.

The Fair of Mayfair, a three-volume collection of short tales published by Colburn and Bentley in 1832, hardly advanced her reputation. Some of the tales, like "The Flirt of Ten Seasons" and "The Divorcée," sound like parodies of Lady Charlotte Bury, having her special mixture of pretentious morality and awkward prose. Others, like "Hearts and Diamonds," are a reworking of the society lady's remorse-and-suicide theme of *Belinda*. "My Granddaughter" has a paragraph describing the fashionable lady in a manner strongly prophetic of Thackeray's asides.

The most eminent of our light novelists has depicted with great success "the hard parboiled look of fashion" characteristic of an Almack's belle. But neither he nor any other chronicler of fashionable small beer (that flattest of beverages, which the reading public so greedily yet so grumblingly drains to the dregs), has ever analyzed the hieroglyphics of the occult science of worldliness; which have their only permanent inscription among the wrinkles of a well-worn dowager, and may be traced in their first faint shadowing on the hollow brow of many a fading beauty . . . the rouged, scornful, attenuated, dissipation-seethed cheek of an habitual woman of fashion.[29]

This book was the occasion of correspondence with Bulwer. *The New Monthly* for June, 1832, had reviewed the work and quarreled with her use of *embêtee*, saying it was "a word no decent French-woman could even hear without embarrassment." She wrote to Bulwer, then editor, defending the word, and reproaching him with his prejudice against fashionable novels.[30]

. . . I will not attempt a defence of fashionable novels. I leave it to *Grandison, Clarissa, Belinda, Ennui, The Absentee, Vivian Grey*, etc., to plead their cause, and entrench myself in the obstinacy of a woman's opinion that every picture of passing manners, if accurate, is valuable from the drawing-room to the ale-house and

[29] *The Fair of Mayfair*, London, 1832, III, 191.
[30] Quoted Michael Sadleir, *Edward and Rosina*, Boston, 1931, pp. 276–77.

that every writer does best who paints the scene more immediately before him. I could not have written *Eugene Aram*. Why attempt it? I *could* write the *Divorcée* and if you were not a doctrinaire you would admit it has far more truth, tenderness and power and passion. I am not sure that if you were not very hardened against fashionable novels, it might not draw an iron tear or two down your cheek.

. . . I think I shall write another fashionable novel in order that you may abuse it, and I may show how indifferent I am to criticism, when satisfied it does not arise from a spirit personally hostile.

The correspondence thus started was kept up for many years. Bulwer had not written the review to which she objected. The letters which she wrote to him he endorsed after her death with one of his "usual portrait-paragraphs," more revealing, perhaps, of his own suspicious resentments than of the subject.

It would seem from the later letters that I appeased her resentment . . . though I doubt if she did not secretly seek to injure me through the channel of certain scurrilous periodicals. She was a remarkably clever woman, and her novels have a merit that has never been sufficiently appreciated. She preceded Thackeray, and as she knew good society infinitely better than he did, her satire makes his look like caricature.

The next few years, during her sojourn in France, were not years of active publishing. One might suppose that preoccupation with family affairs, or a possible desire to recuperate from the active work of composition is responsible. A letter of hers to C. W. Dilke, the editor of *The Athenaeum*, however, reveals that the poor critical reception of *The Fair of Mayfair* (some reviewers had hinted at exhaustion) temporarily dissuaded her from writing.

You will receive in a day or two a novel of mine, called *The Sketch Book of Fashion*. I should feel greatly obliged if you would *not notice it at all*, unless, indeed, you find that it contains something demanding reprobation. As you may imagine there is something mysterious in this Medea-like proceeding towards my offspring, I ought to add that general condemnation has rendered me somewhat ashamed of my sickly progeniture of fashionable novels, and that I have now in the press a series of stories founded on the history of Poland, which I hope will prove more worthy of attention.[31]

Between *Polish Tales*, *The Sketch Book of Fashion*, of 1833, and *The Diary of a Désennuyée*, of 1836, she refrained from publishing anything, although the large number of works printed in 1836 and 1837, most of which were probably composed at this time, shows that the period was not one of entire relaxation. The French sojourn also bore fruit in an increased knowledge and use of French material, both in *Cecil* and in *Greville, or, A Season in Paris*.

The Diary of a Désennuyée[32] is Mrs. Gore's first striking accomplishment in what may be described as a "diary novel." All the action revolves about the chief character, the *désennuyée*, with a concentration of interest that heightens the effect of the story. *Pelham* and *Vivian Grey* were of this description, and Mrs. Gore's later *Cecil* was to extend her effort to a masculine society. In the *Diary*, however, even the love affair is not permitted to intrude on the purely feminine material of the tale.

Mrs. Harriett Amelia Delaval (Mrs. Gore had Bulwer's weakness for high sounding names) is a widow of twenty-five, with £6,000 a year, firmly resolved not to be bored and to keep her freedom. She does not become *blasé* but in the end marries a Byronic politician. Mrs. Delaval finds that in the rigor of the social game there is no time to be jaded, and in demonstrating that, Mrs. Gore has accomplished her aim. The book is light, scintillating, and brief. It deals with most of the trivial pastimes of the

[31] *Papers of a Critic*, selected from the writings of Chas. Wentworth Dilke, London, 1875, pp. 34-35.

[32] The title, though not the material, was doubtlessly suggested by Mrs. Jameson's *Diary of an Ennuyée*.

society woman, and even includes a humanitarian lament
of the hard life of milliners' apprentices.[33]

The five years from 1836 to 1841 were the apex of Mrs.
Gore's literary life. During this time she produced twelve
novels,[34] among them all of her best. The vogue for fashionable novels obviously did not collapse with the passing of
the Reform Bill, even if the society which produced them
did pass. To continue in the drying stream, she was forced
to become increasingly historical, and her next novel, *The
Cabinet Minister*, ends with the reign of William IV.

In *The Cabinet Minister*, young Frank Grenfell is dependent on the bounty of a wealthy baronet with whom he
has been educated. To achieve independence, Grenfell becomes a student in the Middle Temple, but the lure of
society proves too much for him, and he soon neglects his
studies. Gradually working himself into political circles,
he becomes a member of the Carleton House group and a
friend of Sheridan. After years of idling he returns to law,
and begins to take politics as other than a mere adventure
and marries his boyhood sweetheart.

It is evident that *The Cabinet Minister* is a restatement of
a familiar formula. The young wit playing with politics,
making himself useful to a party by the composition of
pamphlets and the execution of political tasks, and
eventually frustrated in his ambitions because of the
ingratitude of ministers was a pattern created by Disraeli
both in *Vivian Grey* and in real life. With Disraeli's future
yet hidden, it is hardly possible that Mrs. Gore had him
in mind, although she had known him personally since

[33] Short and casual as the mention of the apprentice is, this is very
early use of such material, and especially noteworthy for coming from a
fashionable novelist.

[34] Three of the novels were not fashionable: *Mrs. Armytage, or, Female
Domination*, 1836 (said by some critics to be her best book); *Stokehill
Place, or, The Man of Business*, 1837; *The Heir of Selwood, or, The Epochs of a
Life*, 1838, a study of a mixed Protestant and Roman Catholic marriage.

1832. Disraeli described his introduction to her in a letter to Sarah:

... We had a very brilliant *réunion* at Bulwer's last night ... there was a large sprinkling of blues—Lady Morgan, Mrs. Norton, L. E. L., etc. Bulwer came up to me, said, "There is one blue who insists upon an introduction," "Oh, my dear fellow, I cannot really; the power of repartee has deserted me." "I have pledged myself, you must come"; so he led me up to a very sumptuous personage, looking like a full-blown rose, Mrs. Gore.[35]

Through Lord Lyndhurst and the Wyndham Lewises, the acquaintance was at least kept up, since in 1836 we find Mrs. Gore lending Lord Lyndhurst her copy of *Henrietta Temple*. "She says it is the best thing you have written since *Vivian Grey*."[36] On August 4, 1837, he dines at the Wyndham Lewises', the party composed of the Clarendons, Prince and Princess Poniatowski, Mrs. C. Gore, Lady Floyd; Mrs. Dawson, Parnther, Beauclerk.[37] When Mrs. Lewis had become Mrs. Disraeli, she and her husband dine at the Gores' in Paris.[38]

But whether or not the hero of *The Cabinet Minister* was modeled on Disraeli, the connection between it and *Vivian Grey* is close enough. Starting in politics with only the motive of personal aggrandizement, Grenfell comes at last, largely through disillusionment with the fribbledoms of society, to some honest political convictions. His zeal never reaches the lyrical heights of Disraeli's exaltation; if it had reached those heights, Mrs. Gore, instead of Disraeli, might have been the parent of the political novel. She was merely the passive satirist with a deft touch. Most of the writers of political novels, from Disraeli to H. G. Wells, have been people with stronger convictions. One can infer her sympathies from the fact that Grenfell is a Whig, while the villain in *The Hamiltons* is a Tory. Samuel Warren, who

[35] Monypenny and Buckle, *Life of Disraeli, ed. cit.*, I, 207.
[36] *Ibid.*, I, 340.   [37] *Ibid.*, I, 381.
[38] *Home Letters*, London, 1928, p. 211.

had hopes of getting her work for *Blackwood's*, wrote, "By the way, remember the Tory character of *Blackwood's*, and do not give your Whig friends too many flattering representations in your characters."[39]

Abandoning politics in order to vary and widen her appeal, according to the custom so common with large-scale producers of fiction, Mrs. Gore decided to essay a study in patronage. To distinguish it from Edgeworth's novel, she called hers *Preferment, or, My Uncle the Earl*, 1840.

The same year she produced a three-decker entitled *The Dowager, or, The New School for Scandal*, a remarkably confused novel based on a clear plot. An old gossip of seventy-three, living in a London square, imperils the peace of all her neighbors by scandal mongering. The modern reader cannot stand three volumes of vacuous scandal, yet *The Athenaeum* considered the novel as reproducing[40] "not merely the conventional forms and conventional jargon of a particular society . . . but a faithful copy of its ideas and feelings." The eager world called for three editions in all: the second in 1854 became part of the "Railway Library" (the book apparently being useful as a soporific on rough roadbeds); the third in 1876, consisted of the unsold remnant of the second with a new title-page.

To her lengthening list of dandies, true-wits and false-wits, she added Greville among the former, and Fred Massingberd among the latter, in *Greville, or, A Season in Paris*, 1841. Earl Greville, only son of a widowed countess, goes to Paris accompanied by a friend of limited income and unlimited coxcombry.

He [Massingberd] was, in fact, one of those useless excrescences of the present highly artificial state of society, which may be compared with the newly-acquired race of orchidaceous plants; —curious weeds, the growth of a noxious climate, and requiring

---

[39] Mrs. Oliphant, *op. cit.*, II, 348–49.
[40] *The Athenaeum*, Nov. 4, 1840, pp. 899–900.

the waste of a fortune to maintain the factitious state of atmosphere essential to their existence.[41]

Of course, the manly good sense of Greville triumphs over the false standards of Massingberd; it was getting too late in the century for a dandy to receive sympathetic treatment. Massingberd was a "cutter," and middle-class democracy had no use for cutters.

Mrs. Gore is undoubtedly at her best in *Cecil, or, The Adventures of a Coxcomb*, and its sequel, *Cecil, The Peer*. In these books she summed up all she had to say about her favorite era—1800 to the Reform Act, the period which saw the virtual rise and fall of the phenomena known as Dandyism and Byronism; saw the last flourish of English Aristocracy, slowly collapsing before the rise of the middle class. Consider Mrs. Gore's splendid (if ironic) apostrophe to the aristocracy and its social butterflies:

"Away with such triflers!" cries the sage, flinging aside our pages into the depths of his gloomy library, as if the grubbers among the dry bones of history did more to expedite the progress of the times, than those fluttering butterflies who oppose, at least, no dead weight to the general impetus. The truth is that, like a straw thrown up to determine the course of the wind, the triflers of any epoch are an invaluable evidence of the bent of the public mind. *They* are always floating on the surface,—always ostensible!—*They* are a mark for general observation. Statesmen and beaus are the only *really* public men. Posterity will see, in Brummell and Castlereagh, the leading characters of the Regency, —of the gilded, not the golden age![42]

Mrs. Gore had already written a novel, *The Diary of a Désenuyée*, which deals with these social flutterers, but she had greatly increased her scope between the early and late versions. The first book is a woman's for women; *Cecil* is concerned with men mainly, the sort of novel Jane Austen would never have attempted. That Mrs. Gore succeeded in writing about men like a man is evident from the mystifica-

[41] *Greville*, London, 1841, p. 33.   [42] *Cecil*, 1840, I, 103.

tion caused by her anonymous publication of it. Even Disraeli was taken in. On February 23, 1841, he wrote

I am spoken of with great *kudos* in *Cecil* (le livre du jour), which indeed was given to me for some time and is an imitation of the *Vivian Grey* school. But Lord Howden is now universally understood to be the author, with the exception of myself, for I am not credulous, and think the writer is nearer home; but I shan't whisper my suspicions.

To maintain the illusion, Mrs. Gore even denied outright to Samuel Warren that she had written it.[43] Richard Hengist Horne in his *The New Spirit of the Age*, speaking of "that clever, but surprisingly impudent book *Cecil*," said "We believe she has never avowed it."

This refusal to own books she wrote was her common practice. When negotiating for the sale of *Adventures in Borneo*, she wrote to F. Shoberl:

But as it would destroy the authenticity of the narrative if the name of a novelist were attached to it, I mean to publish it anonymously, though *in the end* I shall be proud to acknowledge it . . . I have not offered it to Fisher's successor, nor mentioned it *even in my own family*, as I consider a strict incognito essential to its success. If, therefore, Mr. Colburn does not wish to purchase it, I rely upon you not to allude to the authorship to any one . . .[44]

What was one to do else? The public has always demanded a certain kind of book from a given writer, let us say, and he wants to write another kind. Like Bulwer he puts out an anonymous trial balloon. Or, he wants to profit from the scandal value of an ostensibly libellous book dealing with well-known personages. To put one's own name to it would be fatuous; Presto! anonymity will make the public regard it as the work of an amateur. In a similar

---

[43] She wrote to Warren later, Nov. 6, 1842: "The mystery of my denial arose from the fact that my name (having been appended to numerous translations of my husband's) is more hackneyed than my pen. The only three successful books I have produced—*Mothers and Daughters*, *The Peeress*, and *Cecil*—appeared anonymously."—Oliphant, *op. cit.*, II, 348–49.   [44] *Notes and Queries*, Series 10, IV, July, 1905, 7.

situation to that presented by *Adventures in Borneo*, Defoe put down his name as editor; Mrs. Gore did not dare to go even so far.

But to return to *Cecil*. The book is autobiographical in manner, and starts as all proper stories do with the writer's earliest memories. These, with Cecil, are of nothing more domestic or boyish than his mother's boudoir. Little Cecil has long curls, and he knows what a mirror is for. As the years pass, school beckons, and the curls fall, but the mirror retains its charm. He is "rusticated" from Oxford after a year, much to his mother's horror, until she learns that the word has nothing to do with agricultural pursuits. Back in London, Cecil drops all collegiate habits and is assigned some sort of sinecure in the Foreign Office. His copious talents open to him the gates of Carleton House.

Carleton House (at the period of which I [Cecil] treat) had not yet put on its judge's condemning cap.—It was the Carleton House of the Prince, not of the Regent; it was the Carleton House of the Whigs, not of the Tories;—the bivouac of the Opposition, not the tabernacle of Church and State.—To me there was nothing very striking in its aspect; for the same degenerate passion for trinketry and Lilliputian *vertu*, encumbered its *consoles* with china and its chimney-pieces with fanciful *pendules*, that rendered my mother's drawing-room a Daedalian mystery. Elegance, however, was there, though over-gauded with superficial refinement. Even gold may be degraded by super-gilding, or attenuated to too fine a thread.[45]

Dressing is an art, and in it Cecil is an irreproachable artist. He is a virtuoso in knotting ties, for example.

It is not every man who can wear a white waistcoat and cravat, without looking either insipid as a boiled chicken, or dingy as a Spanish olive. But for those qualified by nature, by clear complexions and well-planted whiskers to surmount the difficulty, nothing like it to mark the inborn distinction between a gentleman and a butler.[46]

[45] *Cecil*, pp. 104–5. [46] *Cecil*, p. 105.

Cecil's artistry, however, did not operate in affairs of
the heart. The girl is the visiting daughter of an English
merchant in Spain. When Cecil meets her she is the guest
of a mere attorney, her father's and Lord Ormington's man
of business. Her doubtful social status causes Cecil to
bungle his approach rather badly, but for a while he
carries it off well enough. "Fine sentiment was not the
order of the day. The pallid muse of Byron, in her black-
crepe weepers, had not yet brought despair and anguish
into fashion. There was no encouragement to turn Octa-
vian, or let grow one's beard."[47]
Fashion or no fashion, however, when she returns to
Spain, he follows her, using a convenient diplomatic errand
as an excuse. Unfortunately, before he can recover from a
fever, she dies of a Byronic broken heart. Thoroughly
stricken, Cecil seeks death on Peninsular battlefields, but
it evades his grasp. A report of his death precedes him to
England, and his arrival rather upsets his family's sense of
the appropriate. He is at loose ends now; his former position is out of the question, and despising politics, he
drifts back into the circumscribed dandyism of a younger
son. Later, through the death of his elder brother's child,
Cecil becomes heir apparent to his father's title, but the
unfortunate accident of the boy's death, in which Cecil
was involved, drives him into the army and the battle of
Waterloo. As his mother lies dying, she confesses that
Cecil is not Lord Ormington's child. Solicitude for the
family honor induces all concerned to keep the secret.
The successive shocks to which Cecil has been exposed
make a change of scene imperative. He enters upon a delayed Grand Tour, and Mrs. Gore, in order to achieve a
sense of contemporaneity, makes Byron his traveling companion in Switzerland and Italy. After Cecil and Byron
part, Germany and the Rhine provide a setting for Cecil's

[47] *Ibid.*, p. 147.

passion for Wilhelmina, wife of the Herr Bau-, Berg-, und Weg-Inspector von Schwanenfeldt.

Gott in Himmel!—to see the idol of one's soul fill the lips that Leonardo would have delighted to paint, lips like the half-open bud of a Boursault rose,—lips that seemed formed only to emit a murmur of tenderness and joy,—the plaint of Margaret,—the song of Thekla,—to see those lips dilate to receive a vile, circumferential slice of Braunsweiger Bratwurst.—Oh! Tommy Moore,—oh! Johannes Secundus,—oh! Lord Stangford!—oh! Camoens! oh, everybody else who has ever versified upon those ruby portals of the Temple of Beauty,—feel for me! Es rührt mich der Schlag auf der Stelle![48]

When Cecil's travels are ended, he accepts a position with his old friend, the Prince Regent, now George IV, and idles away his days in the stupid somnolence of court life. Another love affair ends much like the first; the girl dies from the broken heart he has inflicted, and there is no war for him to run off to. Thereafter he remains a confirmed bachelor.

The second book, *Cecil, a Peer*, takes up the story from this point. After the deaths of his half brother and his supposed father, Cecil succeeds to the estates and the title. He makes few changes in his mode of life. Upon the death of the King, he retires from the court and lives for indolent pleasure, a somewhat cynical commentator on the life that passes before him. Catholic Emancipation, the Reform Bill, and even the arrival of the pretty young Queen in 1837 make up the spectacle of his existence.

The narrative style of the book, presented as the reminiscences of an old dandy, is a happy choice for Mrs. Gore enabling her to carry on a chorus of philosophical cogitations on the social comedy that forms the staple of the fashionable novel.

Unable always to weave refractory historical material directly into her plots, she does perhaps the next best

[48] *Cecil*, II, 73-74.

thing by putting into the mouths of her characters running commentaries on contemporary events.

Cecil's career is coexistent with the rise of dandyism; to him dandyism could have had no connection with economics or history. His relation to it was entirely sartorial and personal, and his apology, perhaps, is superficial, but it does give a witty account of how dandyism appeared to a contemporary.

The creation of Dandyism—(pshaw not, ye critics! nor exclaim "hold, enough!"—for the thing is obsolete, "*et il n'y a rien de nouveau que ce qui est oublie*") the creation, I say, of Dandyism afforded the first indication to the public, that, in spite of Stultz and Truefitt, the portraits of Sir Thomas and the certificates of Sir Henry,—the Prince was growing old!—Had we written the word then, it must have been this,—, or at worst, O-d; for no one presumed to approach more definitely that fatal hint. . . .

Nature, however, was no courtier. Nature began to hint that liqueurs were an unsafer beverage than sherry,—that jollity was a plebeian effervescence,—wit a more princely thing than humor, superciliousness than noise.—And, lo! dandyism "rose like an exhalation"—stole in on tiptoe;—and the vulgar began to record the prowess of George Brummell, as they now enlarge upon the feats of Sir Robert Sale.[49]

After dandyism, the next most important phase of manners that comes under Cecil's observation is its translation into the feminine world with the rise of Exclusivism. What that meant to Cecil when he was active in society we are not told. At a distance of ten years or more he is fluent about it.

People are beginning to forget the Exclusives; I believe because they were written out of fashion by a remarkably bad novel [*The Exclusives*, Lady Charlotte Bury, 1830]. It is now a thing of tradition! Exclusivism, fashionable novelism, Nashism, and fifty other fribbleisms of the West-End, were utterly extinguished by the Reform Bill.[50]

. . . mob-assemblies went out with George the Fourth . . . an

---

[49] *Ibid.*, p. 102.   [50] *Cecil, the Peer*, p. 23.

enormous schism arose in society, at the epoch of the Reform
Bill . . . The Capulets and Montagues of the great world would
scarcely meet in the same room . . . Even the insulting term
"Exclusives," applied to those who were desirous in inviting
their friends, to secure them from having their ribs broken and
their dresses torn from their backs, did not avail to frighten the
grande monde into a renewal of the exploded system of the bear-
garden.[51]

The impression of first-hand knowledge left by these
vivacious and shrewd descriptions is completely suited to a
light novel of manners. A duller novelist might have
labored over the material—historical novelists at the time
were doing that very thing—but Cecil's reminiscences
have a delightful aerial quality. In *Pin Money* she had declared:

. . . it becomes necessary from time to time to throw a heavy
lump of marl on the surface, where it must lie for ever in inaffini-
tive disunion, in order to deceive the dunces into a belief that
some mysterious process of improvement is carrying on for their
advantage.[52]

There is exceedingly little marl to be found in *Cecil*.

For the curious there is appended in the Bibliography a
fairly complete list of Mrs. Gore's books; to mention
separately all of the novels she wrote would double the
length of this chapter. She had completed all that was
important when she finished *Cecil* in 1841.[53] After 1841 she
went on mechanically turning out copy for the printers,
a character study like *Modern Chivalry, or, A New Orlando
Furioso*, 1843,[54] or a deceptively titled book like *The Story*

---

[51] *Cecil*, pp. 333-34.   [52] *Pin Money*, London, 1831, II, 53-54.

[53] *Self*, 1845, had an address to the Public by Cecil Cecilizeth, ". . . in
the following pages you shall find the pen of the coxcomb flourished with
all of its original grace and spirit, by the unique and solely competent
hand of—The Author of Cecil."—p. viii.

[54] In 1843, *Modern Chivalry*, "edited by William Harrison Ainsworth,"
appeared in *The New Monthly* of which he was editor. Later in the year
when published anonymously in book form, the preface was signed
C.F.G. S. H. Ellis, *W. H. Ainsworth and His Friends*, London, 1911, thinks
that each had an equal share in the work.

of a Royal Favorite, 1845. Her name was getting to be in such favor with the public that publishers were anxious to put her name on the title-pages of books with which she had only the slightest connection. It is extremely unlikely that she read Danish, yet she is put down as editor of *The Queen of Denmark*, translated from the Danish of T. C. Heiberg, 1846. This was probably the work of her husband, however, and her name may have been used at his desire, not the publishers'. From time to time she wrote what her youth had known as fashionable novels—*The Débutante, or, The London Season*, 1846, and *Castles in the Air*, 1847. In the latter she again found space to justify the species by claiming for it the credit of having killed by ridicule and "reiterated exposure," the exclusivism and dandyism of the Court of George IV. *The Dean's Daughter, or, The Days We Live In*, 1853, is slightly anticipative of the Barchester novels; if it had been more concerned with the gloomy, hypochondriac dean than with his daughter, the resemblance would have been closer, but the daughter associates with so many lords and ladies that the church group gets crowded out. *The Two Aristocracies*, 1857, is a social novel, and appeared two years after Mrs. Gaskell's *North and South*, which it resembles. Mrs. Gore's story is a study of the relationships between the representatives of two powerful groups, an iron-founder and his daughters, and the family of a landed gentleman.[55] She ended her long career with *Heckington*, 1858, dealing with the upper class characters so dear to her.

Although nothing has been said heretofore about Mrs. Gore's style, the reader has perhaps drawn some conclu-

---

[55] *The Athenaeum*, July 4, 1857, thought it "by many degrees the best and pleasantest of Mrs. Gore's later novels. There is the old cunning . . . Mrs. Gore cannot draw manufacturers and their establishments like one who is to the manner born, but she does it well enough for the purposes of a novel."

sions of his own from the quotations. These may not have been extensive enough to allow him to note what is her most irritating characteristic—the use of foreign tags. In a review of her first fashionable novel, *The Edinburgh Review* had protested against her "excessive introduction of French," but the habit grew rather than diminished. One can hardly discuss, for instance, the habits of gourmands without calling upon the phrases of that race of famous cooks, but one wonders, sometimes, why they must all eat *coquilles de volaille à la financière*. German is more sparingly used, being mostly confined to *Cecil*, where its appropriateness is unquestioned. Italian is still rarer. She astonished the critics with her use of Latin and Greek in *Cecil*, for she had hitherto displayed no signs of a classical education beyond the use of a few standard quotations easily dug out of a dictionary. R. H. Horne, in his *New Spirit of the Age*, attributed this knowledge of hers to William Beckford, who thus stands responsible for two such widely separated subjects as a knowledge of clubland and a knowledge of Greek and Latin. It is only fair to say that Mrs. Gore used her French with as much unction as did her contemporaries. Her weakness gave great glee to Thackeray, who seized upon it in his parody, *Lords and Liveries, by the Authoress of Dukes and Déjeuners, Hearts and Diamonds, Marchionesses and Milliners*.[56]

Another of her edifying frailties is the love of the long word. She speaks, for instance, of "orchidaceous plants" when she means orchids, of "innoxious" when she means harmless. And by an excessive use of punctuation, particularly the dash and exclamation point, she achieves a certain artificial quickness and emphasis that impose on one for a while, but soon become narcotic in effect. Her style at its best, however, is such a happy blend of quick-

[56] One of the "Novels by Eminent Hands,"—*Punch*, June 12, 21, 1847; *Miscellanies*, II (1856).

ness, ease, and wit that one regrets that she did not write
less and polish more.

Any absolute comparison of Mrs. Gore with the great
masters of English fiction is inappropriate, but in the historical study of the novel she deserves a place larger than
she has. In her own time she was a rival of Thackeray;
today hardly a recollection exists that her novels treat of
the same people at very nearly the same time. Fecundity
alone is a poor claim to immortality, but it is at least true
that the two hundred volumes in which she described her
age cannot be entirely neglected by the historian of manners or literature, except at his own risk. Seen in her proper
place as a chief member of that group of novelists who
belong to the interregnum between Scott, Galt, Austen,
and Edgeworth, and the Victorians, Dickens, Thackeray,
and Trollope, she is sufficiently important to merit considerable attention. She does not have the cocky insolence
that distinguishes *Vivian Grey*, nor does she consistently
rival Bulwer's *Pelham*, "with its sparkling conceits, that
blind one, as though the pages were dried with diamond
dust."[57] But on the other hand, neither does she stoop to
the vapid mouthings or rhapsodical flights of Lady Charlotte Bury. Her chief quality is a strain of common sense
that redeems her pages from the sentimentalism of the
"Annual" school and enables her to see as steadily as anyone, perhaps, the chief actors in that gilded age which
she made so peculiarly her own.

[57] Gore, *Women as They Are*, p. 234.

VII

LADY CHARLOTTE BURY

How I long for a well-written romance! It would be so refreshing to get off the beaten track of modern novels, away from the
lords, and ladies, and fashionables, and would-be representatives
of the beau monde, such as the rage for scandal, renders the idol,
the Moloch idol of most publishers, and many novel readers
of the day . . . But I know *not of one publisher* who will with-
draw the veil of obscurity from before such a work. . . .[1]

LADY Charlotte Susan Maria Campbell Bury, who is
responsible for the admirable sentiments voiced at the
head of this chapter, had, before the enunciation of her
doctrine, published several novels, among them *Flirtation,
A Marriage in High Life,* and *The Separation;* afterwards she
published many more, *The Exclusives, The Ensnared, The
Divorced, Love, The History of a Flirt, The Maneuvering Mother,*
and *The Lady of Fashion.* If this were a text on literary
geometry, one could write Q. E. D., and rest from one's
labors, but criticism more resembles a trial, and the de-
fendant must be given a chance at rebuttal.

She began as a poet, but since the desire to be a poet
was stronger than her need for expression, there is not
the slightest trace of merit in her verses. Her prize volume
was called *Poems on Several Occasions,* by a Lady, and it
was privately printed in Edinburgh in 1797, when she was
twenty-two years old. The book is slim, forty-eight pages,
and the range of her lyre is narrow also. There is an "Ode
to Evening"; a set of verses called simply "Evening";
others called "On Seeing Some Withered Roses Thrown
Away," "On Being Accused of Levity and Insensibility,"

[1] Bury, *Journal of the Heart,* London, 1830, 89–93.

and so on. The last title displays a singular obtuseness on the part of her companions, for insensibility was the last fault of which one could accuse her. The book is hardly of any importance to us except as it may help to throw light on her later work. She never outgrew it. On December 28, 1831, she gave a copy to the Viscountess Kirkwall, on which she wrote, "Printed but not published— The Girlish Lays of one who has sung since but almost always to a Lyre of Sorrow."[2] It will have served its purpose if it help us to understand the basic tendency in Lady Charlotte's character towards an incurable sentimentality.

She was of excellent family, the youngest daughter of John Campbell, fifth Duke of Argyll. Consequently, her marriage in 1796, to her almost penniless cousin, John Campbell, the eldest of a family of fourteen children, was opposed by her friends and family. But her romanticism never showed itself more genuine than in both her marriages to comparatively poor and obscure men. Known as the beauty of the Argyll family, after her marriage she continued to do the honors of Edinburgh to distinguished literary visitors. It was at one of her parties that Walter Scott met Monk Lewis. In 1803 she and her husband moved to Hartwell, Buckinghamshire, but frequent and long visits in Edinburgh kept her active in its social life. Mr. Campbell died in 1809; at the time he was Member of Parliament for Ayr. Lady Charlotte had borne him nine children in thirteen years, and the literary impulses she may have had were very effectively stifled for the time. The year of his death she accepted an appointment as Lady-in-Waiting to the Princess of Wales. It will be recalled that the Prince of Wales had left his wife shortly after the birth of the Princess Charlotte in 1796. Caroline had necessarily established her own court, which she still maintained after her husband's ascendancy to the regentship. The position

[2] This particular volume is in the British Museum.

of Lady-in-Waiting Lady Charlotte kept until 1814, partly because she needed the money and partly out of a sense of loyalty to the Princess. By 1814, however, the favoritism shown by Caroline to her excourier, Bartolomeo Bergami, forced Lady Charlotte to leave. Her servitude temporarily concluded, she went abroad, only to meet the Princess at Geneva and travel with her for another month before leaving her for good and all at Milan. Upon Charlotte's return to England, Susan Ferrier, her intimate friend since the days when Mr. Ferrier had been the agent for the Argyll estates, reported in a letter to Miss Clavering: "Lady Charlotte seems more eat up with sentiment than ever; all *her* sayings and doings are delightful, to be sure, in her, but how odd they would seem in the ugly part of creation!"[3]

This unregenerate sentimentalism was only a prelude to another act when she again threw family counsel to the winds, and married at Florence in 1818 the Rev. John Bury, an unbeneficed clergyman traveling in Italy for the love of art. The happy couple stayed abroad until they were forced to return to England because she was needed in the trial of Queen Charlotte in 1820. Shortly afterward, she resumed her writing, since her husband coupled a love of art with a love of living beyond his means. He died in 1832. Her own death occurred in 1861, the same year as Mrs. Gore's, when she was eighty-six years old.

We shall pass quickly over her first books, since, coming before the development of the fashionable novel, they are not exactly to our purpose. *Self Indulgence, a Tale of the Nineteenth Century*, written during her first period of poverty after the death of Mr. Campbell, appeared anonymously in 1812; she revamped it in 1830 and sold it to Colburn and Bentley as a new work, calling it *The Separation. Conduct Is*

[3] *Memoir and Correspondence of Susan Ferrier*, edited by J. A. Doyle, London, 1898, p. 132.

Fate, 1822, was handled for publication by Susan Ferrier, who had a connection with Blackwood through his publication of her novel, *Marriage*. Poor Blackwood was shocked at Lady Charlotte's count and countess, for he wrote to Miss Ferrier,

At the same time I hope the author will pardon me for the liberty I take in hinting that I feel confident that she could very greatly improve the first volume so as, in my humble opinion, to make it acceptable to British readers, who are not accustomed to a husband knocking down his wife, nor yet to some other traits of Continental manners. Of all this, however, an author, and not a bookseller, is the best judge.[4]

The years spent by Lady Charlotte in the none too refined circles of the court of the Princess had obviously qualified her to describe certain "traits of Continental manners." Then, too, the little group of Miss Ferrier, Miss Clavering, and Lady Charlotte was a forum for theories on the proper relationship between the sexes. At a dinner which Miss Ferrier once gave to Lady Charlotte and John Wilson, the question arose as to whether a lady in her right mind would prefer as a husband a stabber or a kicker. "I [writes Susan] am for a stabber, but I dare say you will be for putting up with a kicker. It was talking of Lord Byron brought on the question. I maintain there is but one crime a woman could never forgive in her husband, and that is a *kicking*."[5]

Lady Charlotte's travels in Italy left other identifiable traces in her books. In 1826 she published anonymously *Alla giornata, or, To the Day*, an Italian story of the last crusade. In the same year she also published a series of prayers, *Suspirium sanctorum, or, Holy Breathing*, which incurred the honor of a parody review by Thackeray. The prayers were serious enough; Miss Ferrier thought them "far superior to her novels, and highly creditable both as compositions and as showing so much Biblical research."[6]

[4] *Ibid.*, p. 156.   [5] *Ibid.*, p. 131.   [6] *Ibid.*, p. 168.

But Thackeray, whose instinctive dislike of snobbery was aroused by titled authors, thought the prayers were rubbish. In his paper, "The Fashionable Authoress," he proposed to review a volume, *Heavenly Chords, a Collection of Sacred Strains, selected, composed, and edited by the Lady Frances Juliana Flummery.* Thackeray probably considered Lady Charlotte too small game, or he might have added a parody of her to his collection of Disraeli, Bulwer, and Mrs. Gore. A really good parody might have prevented a somewhat similar and later effusion with a still more resounding title. This was Lady Charlotte's *The Three Great Sanctuaries of Tuscany, Valombrosa, Camoldoli, Laverna, a poem, with historical and legendary notices,* 1833. The exceptionally *de luxe* volume was partially redeemed by her husband's drawings, which were much better than the poems. But all of this work, including prayers, historical romance, and early novels, was amateurish. Not until she devoted her energies to the production of fashionable novels did she become a professional writer and achieve any success.

Flirtation, 1828, her first, was very well received by the public, running through three editions in its first year. She apparently determined upon developing this popularity, for the third edition contained the advertisement of the forthcoming, *A Marriage in High Life,* by the author of *Flirtation.*

In the titles of these and later books one senses the hand of Colburn, who in his expert capitalization of the sex theme, was certainly born out of his due time. *Flirtation* is the story of two nieces of a General Montgomery, Lady Frances and Lady Emily. Lady Frances is haughty, high-strung, and stylish. Her life is consequently selfish and miserable. Lady Emily is gentle, kind, and self-effacing; her marriage comes as the crowning blessing of a life spent in doing good for others. Owing far more to Plumer Ward and Maria Edgeworth than to Hook and Disraeli, *Flirta-*

tion was hardly contemporary in tone. The comparatively late age—fifty-three—at which Lady Charlotte Bury entered upon the composition of fashionable novels kept her work always definitely old-fashioned.

Marriage in High Life, 1828, is another illustration of Lady Charlotte's skill in applying a fashionable title to sentimental novels of the vintage of 1810. She was willing enough to profit from the increased sale which such a title would give, while solacing her conscience with the reflection that she was really doing good. In this tale, Lord Fitzheury marries Emmeline Benson, whose father is a wealthy banker. It was an affair arranged by the parents of the couple in their childhood without reckoning on possible complications. Lady Florence Mostyn is the complication. Lord Fitzheury informs his unsuspecting bride that he doesn't intend to live with her intimately, since he considers himself allied to the woman he really loves. Only when the book is nearly finished does he awake to the sterling character of his wife and the falseness of Lady Florence. Then, of course, it is too late; he is dying of tuberculosis. Lady Fitzheury had at one time tried to suppress the pain she felt at her husband's perfidy by a temporary devotion to Almack's. Thus Lady Charlotte was able to include this very popular feature and yet keep tight hold of the moral issues involved by presenting that exclusive resort as an anodyne for the unhappy. One is frequently forced to admire her ingenious and perhaps self-deceiving shifts.

The struggle to be didactic and to be fashionable must have been too much even for her, however, what with the pressure of Colburn and the desire for greater returns. Finally she wrote and published "a remarkably bad novel," *The Exclusives*, 1830, which is avowedly and consistently nothing but a fashionable novel. But could she do that frankly and honestly? Here is her defense:

There is an indulgence in spleen, a silly, gossiping espionage, which delights in prying into the faults of others, without any motive but that of gratification of its own mean nature—but there is an investigation into the habits and manners of the actors in the scene of fashionable folly, which, by dispelling the illusion, may preserve others from being heedlessly drawn into the vortex of so dangerous a career. A sermon would not, could not, descend from its sacred dignity to affect this.[7]

Lady Charlotte was endeavoring to convey the impression that she was giving the inside story of the patronesses of Almack's. The Countess Leinsingen of the novel was meant to be the Princess de Lieven, Lady Tenderden, Lady Cowper. As portraits of the persons involved there was probably sufficient surface resemblance to enable the contemporary reader to make the necessary associations.

Her chief exclusive is conceived satirically enough to please any hardened reader. Lady de Chere "even carried the perfection of induration so far, as to boast of having cut her own mother." Thus she was an eminently suitable member of the group formed to control society in the interests of good manners, and to demonstrate "that mysterious quality known as *ton*."

Qualifications for membership in the coterie are stated explicitly:

The first requisite for a newly-initiated member to know is, how to cut all friends and relatives who are not deemed worthy of being of a certain coterie; the next, is to dress after a particular fashion, talk a particular species of language, not know anything or any person who does not carry the mark of the coterie, and to speak in a peculiar tone of voice. To hold any conversation which deserves that name is called being prosy; to understand anything beyond the costume of life, pedantry.[8]

Lady Charlotte's novels present a society devoid of any virtues that would justify its policy of exclusion. Not content, however, with simply offering her comments, in her *Journal of the Heart*, she was at pains to disparage competitors.

[7] *The Exclusives*, London, 1830, p. 17.   [8] *Ibid.*, p. 199.

... of others, it may be said, the nonentity of their pages is their best claim to being a true portraiture of the most confined circle which they depict . . . The fact is, that most of the things calling themselves pictures of *ton* and high life, have been either written by persons who never could have opportunities . . . even of seeing or mixing, at whatever distance, and under whatever circumstances, with those they intend to represent; and others, again, by persons who have only *achieved their station* among *the race apart*, and are not of that indigenous stock which can alone enable anyone to write of the arcana of *ton*. Pitiful prerogative! if unsupported by better stuff.[9]

But what does she, to the manner born, tell us of society's satellites? That they are infinitely silly, and often of almost criminally insane tendencies. The one writer, presumably, who is in a position to know, brings back worse reports than the people whom she attacks as vulgar or insipid. The truth is that it is impossible to take the novels of Lady Charlotte as legitimate pictures of the aristocracy. Her failure to convince arises partly from her inability to write well, and partly from her evident surrender to the demands of the literary market. The suspicion inevitably arises that she was not gifted with much sense. Her novels, while they were seldom best sellers, did sell. Their significance lies only in the indication that they give of the sort of books people read in those days, and from that we can infer a great deal.

The criticisms just made concerning *The Exclusives* apply as well to *Love*, 1837. Mabel Elton, a charming and exemplary heiress, marries Lord Herbert. He is of commoner clay, and gradually slips into the path of a drunkard. One night when she attempts to get into bed, he strikes her violently. She remonstrates rather timidly, whereupon he says:

"What, you, madam! you—you will dare to arraign me and my behaviour! Turn out, madam, out of my bed for ever."

9 *Journal of the Heart*, London, 1830, pp. 89–93.

And he rudely hurled her on the floor. She wept bitterly.[10]

Thackeray reviewed this *opus* sardonically in the *Times*, January 11, 1838.

If this is exclusive love, it should be a lesson to all men never to marry a woman beyond the rank of a milkmaid and *vice-versa*. But may we venture humbly to ask, are exclusives, fashionables, lords, or whatever they are called, so continually drunk? . . . Do they kick their ladies out of bed? Do they, after having so ejected them, proceed to flog them as they lie on the floor?

Through Susan Ferrier and John Wilson, we can perhaps trace the genesis of this book back to Lord Byron.

The Divorced, published by Colburn in 1837, was the first novel to which Lady Charlotte put her name. Hitherto she had relied on anonymity to protect her against critical reproach. *The Divorced* is a description of the status in society of the divorcée, and may have reference to Lady Holland. Lady Howard leaves her husband for another man, thus deserting her only child. Eventually she marries again and gives birth to more children. When the children by the two marriages grow up and learn about their mother the tragedy is complete. At Lady Howard's home no lady ever calls, for according to the code of the day, such women were taboo. The veracity of this picture is borne out by the actual occurrences at Holland House. The book leaves an impression of sincerity and tempts one to rate it as her best work.

By the publication in 1838 of her *Diary of a Lady-in-Waiting* at the Court of George IV, Lady Charlotte made her surest bid for immortality, but realization of that could hardly have been a comfort to her during the furor of publication. The *Diary* was fashionable gossip, anonymous, and bandying great names around under only the thinnest disguises. An eighteen-year separation from the trial of the Queen had served only to increase the desire to come at last

[10] *Love*, London, 1837, Book II, p. 283.

to the true account. Colburn's undeniable skill at advertising was hardly needed to produce an immense sale.

There are conflicting stories of its publication. One account claimed that her husband had secretly abstracted from her desk a manuscript not intended for publication and had sold it to a bookseller. But since the Rev. Bury died in 1832, while the *Diary* did not appear until 1838, the story is hardly credible. The truth is, one may be sure, that Lady Charlotte, who was perennially hard up, found the prospects of Colburn's thousands so welcome that she betrayed, and not for the first time, all her splendid professions of morality in her *Journal of the Heart*. She trusted to occasional third-person references to herself to lead astray people who might remember her former position. In this she was mistaken. Hardly a review failed to mention her in connection with the authorship of the book; in fact, one can question Colburn's good faith in the matter, since his *Literary Gazette* reviewed it immediately after publication, and first hinted, and then asserted, that Lady Charlotte was the author. She never issued a denial. *The Edinburgh Review*, after saying more disagreeable things about both King George and Queen Caroline than even Lady Charlotte had, denounced her vigorously, and lamented (curiously enough) the present lamentable breakdown in the enforcement of the laws of libel. *The Quarterly*, finding its Tory toes stepped on, denounced her with equal gusto. Thackeray, in his alias of Charles Yellowplush, wrote of it in *Fraser's:*

Most suttnly a femail wrote this *Diary* . . . A thousand pound! nonsince! it's a phigment! a base lible! . . . there is in this book more welgarity than ever I displayed, more nastiness than ever I would dare *to think on*, and more bad grammar than ever I wrote since I was a boy at school.

. . . *O trumpery! O morris!* as Homer says: this is a higeous pictur of manners, such as I weap to think of . . . As for believing that Lady Sharlot had any hand in this book, Heaven forbid! she is all gratitude, pure gratitude,—depend upon it.

But Thackeray, despite this expressed contempt, used the *Diary* as a source in his history, *The Four Georges*.

Altogether, Lady Charlotte must have sat shuddering in her library at the denunciation poured out upon her memoirs. All her enemies, all her friends, apparently joined in the chase. Charles Kirkpatrick Sharpe was particularly horrified to find letters reprinted which he had written in confidence to the daughter of a duke.

Yet the consensus of opinion today seems to be that the *Diary* is a fairly authentic account of a disreputable period in English court history. While favorable to the pretensions of the Queen, so far as they apply to the grounds upon which George sought a divorce, Lady Charlotte makes no effort to disguise the innate levity and carelessness of Caroline's conduct. Any unfavorable notions that may be drawn of George himself are, of course, hardly to be questioned. She is not to be relied upon for absolute accuracy; she doubtless printed as truth what was at best only hearsay. An instance is the garbled account of the early life of Lady Holland, over which a dispute waged in *The Times* and *The Literary Gazette*.

Looked at in this way, the *Diary* forms the best defense that Lady Charlotte could have put forth regarding the general truth of her novels. Granted that it is "a higeous pictur of manners," neither *Conduct Is Fate*, nor *Love* surpasses it in this respect. Lady Charlotte had spent about five years in a court of doubtful standing; is it any wonder that her view of society was warped? The result of long exposure to such disgraceful behaviour must have inevitably led to a belief in strong contrasts, in jet blacks and glaring whites, that left no room for the even gray of more normal existence.

The next three novels [11] and their surprising successor,

[11] *The History of a Flirt*, 1840; *Family Records, or, The Sisters*, 1841; *The Maneuvering Mother*, 1842.

a cookbook,[12] show the straits to which Lady Charlotte was reduced. For a woman of her birth and social position, there must have been something positively revolting in being forced to write hackwork like *The History of a Flirt* when she was sixty-five, or a cookbook at sixty-nine. Her last two works—one posthumous—are a little better. *The Lady of Fashion*, 1856, a study of Brighton society versus the old county family, deals quite adequately with the contrasts between the old and the new society. *The Two Baronets, a Novel of Fashionable Life*, 1864, was another member of that large group of publications forming "The Railway Library." Lady Amelia Seagrave has an invalid husband and many lovers. Lady Charlotte's final message to society was a gesture of contempt.

The impression which the reader carries away after a study of Lady Charlotte's life and works is one of futility. One cannot do better than recall Susan Ferrier's remarks, "all her sayings and doings are delightful, to be sure, in her, but how odd they would seem in the ugly part of creation!" At this distance, when whatever she may have had of personal charm is evaporated, there is nothing left but the conclusions of Thackeray on Lady Frances Juliana Flummery, "Her poetry is mere wind; her novels, stark naught; her philosophy, sheer vacancy." The almost universal report of her when she was young and beautiful in Edinburgh is of a kind that would lead us to expect, if not a high achievement in the world of letters, at least a successful career as the leader of a *salon*. When she was twenty-three

---

[12] *The Lady's Own Cookery Book*, and new dinner-table directory; in which will be found a large collection of original receipts, including not only the results of the authoress's many years observation, experience, and research, but also the contributions of an extensive circle of acquaintance: adapted to the use of Persons living in the highest style, as well as those of moderate Fortune. 3d ed., Colburn, 1844. No one but Colburn could so skillfully work the fashionable appeal into so prosaic a work as a cookbook.

she had already, in bringing Scott and Lewis together, done more for creative literature than she was ever to do again. But the *salonière* in her was frustrated after marriage. Her removal to Buckinghamshire, where comparative poverty deprived her of the sort of background she had enjoyed at Edinburgh, and frequent childbearing, were the principal elements in turning this charming and witty fine lady into the shallow and rather silly writer of bad novels. If she had maintained her social and financial position, occasional essays in verse might have continued to satisfy her vanity. By a coincidence, fortunate for her, the type of literature that was most in demand when she began writing was the very type she was best fitted to produce. And since the system of puffery thrived on hints (not too obscure) thrown out in public prints about authors' social rank, even the dullest copywriter could turn out thrilling advance paragraphs with Lady Charlotte as the subject.

According to N. P. Willis, Lady Charlotte received about £200 a novel. This was not a high rate of compensation; in fact, the figure represents for the 1820's and 1830's the sum which Colburn was accustomed to pay tyros. There was, therefore, recognition by the publishers and the public (which did not buy her books in great numbers) that she was not successful; that she had a wretched command of language; that she constantly mutilated her all too frequent quotations from other languages; and that her character creation does not deserve serious mention.

In the more important qualities of the novelist's craft, she was unbelievably defective. She had no ability in plot construction. Her novels move awkwardly and joltingly to an end which does not have the slightest inevitability. More than any other of the female writers, she justified Thackeray's attacks by showing just how bad a fashionable novel could be.

VIII

THE COUNTESS OF BLESSINGTON

THE quality of Lady Blessington's work does not entitle her to an important place in a literary study. Her novels are no longer read, and the *Books of Beauty* and *Keepsakes* which she edited have little value save as the sources of supply of steel engravings. But because of her manifold activities as novelist, essayist, poet, editor, and leader of a *salon*, she touches upon more kinds of literary activity than better writers. Her fashionable novels, because of the sensational nature of her personal history, have what might be described as curiosity value. After the death of Lord Blessington, Lady Blessington's income was derived largely from continuous writing, and it is hardly doing her books a critical injustice to say that their sale was possible mainly because of their author's position in the Bohemian fringe of London's Mayfair. Most of her work would never have been published if she had been untitled and obscure. Our study of Lady Blessington will therefore deal more with her life and editorial activity than has been thought necessary in the case of writers of greater literary merit.

Margaret Power, the homely little Irish girl who was to become the beautiful Lady Blessington, was born September 1, 1789, at Knockbrit, near Clonmel, County Tipperary. Her father, at one time a magistrate, at another a newspaper publisher, was always dissolute, a dandy resplendent in buckskins and topboots, lace ruffles, and white cravat. He was known as Shiver-the-Frills or Beau Power. Fit mate for the Irish squireen was the weak, romantic mother, rapt in contemplation of the lost glories of her ancestors, the royal Desmonds. With such parents, it is not surprising that Margaret was neglected. She might not have received any education had not a friend of her mother's encouraged the girl in her independent reading. The drunkenness of the father led to brutality, which the mother was powerless or unwilling to stop. One refuge from the miseries of her home Sally found in weaving tales for the entertainment of her brother and sister.

Even this wholesome exercise of her talents was not long permitted. In 1804, when she was fifteen, her parents forced her to marry a Captain Maurice St. Leger Farmer. The bridgegroom was a man of beastly and ungovernable temper—some say he was insane.[1] Three months of intolerable horror to the young girl followed, and Margaret, badly shocked by the experience,[2] returned to her father's house. Power, his worst nature aroused by the collapse of his scheming, made her position a difficult one. But Margaret had no other refuge, and she endured his indignation for three years until her slowly ripening beauty offered a means of escape. An army officer, Captain Thomas Jenkins, with a small estate in England and great expectations, offered to take her with him. She accepted, and although the exact story of her life at this time is obscure, she apparently lived with him in Ireland and England for about six years.

A chance visit of the Earl of Blessington to Captain Jenkins renewed an acquaintance with Mrs. Farmer began years before. Blessington was an Irish peer with an annual income reaching thirty thousand pounds which he was

[1] Samuel Carter Hall, *A Book of Memories*, London, 1871, p. 400.

[2] Michael Sadleir, in *The Strange Life of Lady Blessington* (Boston, 1933) suggests that the girl was so terribly affected by this marriage that she became incapable of physical love. Both Jenkins and Blessington, according to this belief, sought only the witty companionship of a beautiful woman. Further, Count D'Orsay, Mr. Sadleir thinks, was sexually impotent. While there may seem to be too much assumption in all this, the theory does go far to account for many facts otherwise difficult to explain.

rapidly impairing by fantastic extravagances. On the death
of his first wife, for example, he spent three or four thousand for a funeral procession which startled Paris, London,
and Dublin. Completely recovered from his grief, he was
fascinated by the winsome Mrs. Farmer, and soon proposed
that she obtain a divorce and marry him. Since Captain
Jenkins, when consulted, gallantly offered to forego his
slight claims in the face of the Earl's superior resources,
Blessington engaged a house in Manchester Square, London,
where he installed Margaret under the protection of her
brother, Robert. As a delicate discharge of obligations, he
sent Jenkins a draft for ten thousand pounds to cover his
expenditure on jewelry and dress. Probable difficulties in
the way of Mrs. Farmer's being granted a divorce were
saved when her husband was accidentally killed in October,
1817. Four months later Margaret Farmer became Marguer-
ite, Countess of Blessington.

The couple, after a short visit in Ireland, engaged a
mansion in St. James's Square, and entered upon a lavish
course of entertainment. Despite obvious social handicaps,
Lady Blessington found success not too difficult in a society
avid for the latest sensation. The Earl, however, tired of
the social struggle as he tired of everything else, and in
August, 1822, the Blessingtons set out for the Continent.
They were accompanied by Lady Blessington's sister, Mary
Anne Power, and were joined later by Charles Mathews, a
student architect, son of the comedian, and by Count
D'Orsay. Their regal progress over France and Itlay has
been recorded both by Lady Blessington and by Mathews.
They were in Genoa during April and May, 1823, in daily
contact with Lord Byron. Most of their sojourn abroad was
spent in Naples. It was there in 1827 that D'Orsay married
Harriet, a daughter of Lord Blessington by his first wife.
From Naples they began to work their way homeward, but
at Paris, May 23, 1829, the Earl died of apoplexy. Lady

Blessington did not return to London until driven from Paris by the Revolution of 1830. Then she leased the St. James's Square house and went to Seamore Place, Mayfair. The death of her husband had cut her income to about two thousand pounds a year, and retrenchment was necessary.

The numerous references in memoirs and journals to Lady Blessington during her five years in Seamore Place and her thirteen in Gore House, Kensington, testify to the extent of her acquaintance among men of letters and affairs. But her attempt to win a place in London female society was made impossible by slander. Charles Molloy West-macott, editor of *The Age*, the "Sneak" of Bulwer's *England and the English*, started to blackmail her as early as August, 1829. The difficulties of her position were not entirely new, of course, but heretofore Lord Blessington's presence had served partly to disarm criticism and partly to make her indifferent to public opinion. Samuel Carter Hall, who met her about 1831 when he was Bulwer's assistant on *The New Monthly Magazine*, said, "Her visitors were all, or nearly all, men. Ladies were rarely seen at her receptions. Mrs. Hall never accompanied me to her evenings, although she was a frequent day caller."[3]

But whether women visited her in the thirties or not, she ruled a *salon* in Seamore Place as brilliant as the earlier one in St. James's Square. "Everybody goes to Lady Blessington's," said Haydon in 1833.[4] "She is the center of more talent and gaiety than any other woman of fashion in London." And Tom Moore "Dined at Lady Blessington's; company, D'Orsay (as master of the house), John Ponsonby, Willis the American, Count Pahlen . . . Fonblanque."[5]

Gore House, to which she went in 1835, though farther removed from Parliament and the clubs than her other

[3] S. C. Hall, *A Book of Memories*, London, 1871, p. 367.
[4] Benjamin R. Haydon, *Journal*, Feb. 27, 1835.
[5] Thomas Moore, *Diary*, Aug. 11, 1834.

homes, permitted of entertainment on a larger scale. The
charm of its hostess continued to attract men of wit and
intellect, some of whom were willing to pay poetical
tribute. James Smith's verses are, at least, sincere, and
unlike Byron's "Impromptu," amusing.

> Gore House: An Impromptu
> Mild Wilberforce, by all beloved,
> Once owned this hallowed spot,
> Whose zealous eloquence improved
> The fettered Negro's lot;
> Yet here still Slavery attacks,
> When Blessington invites,
> The chains from which *he* freed the Blacks,
> *She* rivets on the Whites.[6]

There is more than one reason, however, for wondering
at the position Lady Blessington held in the society with
which she surrounded herself. There are the books she
wrote, her sensational conduct, her gaudy carriages and
ostentatious equipage. The faults in her writing and in her
personal accouterments are similar. Her novels are too long
—at least for her inventive powers. Time and again a supply
of incident adequate for one volume is forced to do duty in
three volumes. Her ability to improvise on a theme, to
spin words endlessly to no purpose, betrayed her into a
verbosity that is her besetting sin. Even in her own time
readers revolted against this looseness of construction, and
she had no chance whatever of achieving a permanent
reputation.

Although Lady Blessington is not greatly superior to
Lady Charlotte Bury as a novelist, she was a much better
hand at bargaining with publishers, for she earned two or
three thousand pounds annually for several years.[7] Her

---

[6] Quoted in *The Maclise Portrait Gallery*, London, 1898, p. 160. Composed Nov. 10, 1836.

[7] She was in a position, as well, to assist Landor in finding a publisher
for his *Examination of William Shakespeare*.

novels were not even the chief source of this income. It was due mostly to her annuals, notably Heath's *Book of Beauty*, and, later, *The Keepsake*, gigantic publishing ventures which provided a commensurate income.[8] Her labors in composing, editing, and selling must have been prodigious. Charming as she was, she could not wheedle money out of publishers without giving some return.

Her earliest adventures in print had not the excuse of poverty, for she began writing in 1822 when the Earl was still alive and the financial skies clear. The urge for self-expression apparently seized her, and her pen was employed from time to time in the composition of various snatches of sweetness and light. Possibly she had some sort of easy-going connection with Longman, Hurst, Rees, and Company, whereby she endorsed their checks for charity; for that is what she did with the royalties received from her first three volumes.

Eleven years were to elapse before she added another volume to the three of 1822. Life was too full of joyous living during the years in Italy and France to leave time, or furnish the mood, for writing. A short experience of the comparatively narrow allowance of her widowhood, however, induced a changed attitude toward the art. Forgotten was her urge for self-expression as writing became almost an economic necessity. A real search for material this time led her back to the scene of her unhappy childhood. Since the day when Mrs. Farmer had left Ireland with Captain Jenkins, she had never set foot there again except on the occasion of her marriage to the Earl of Blessington. Then she stayed only a short time. Nevertheless, her first professional novel, *The Repealers*, 1833, is on the subject of Irish absentees, much in the manner of Miss Edgeworth. It had a limited sale, and did not do nearly so much to

[8] S. C. Hall estimated that the public paid £100,000 a year for annuals during the height of the fad.

establish her fame as the serial publication in 1832-33 of her *Conversations with Lord Byron* in *The New Monthly Magazine* under Bulwer.

The Irish novel was much better practiced at that time by William Carleton, the Banim Brothers, and Gerald Griffin. The Byron material was special literary property dependent on timeliness for appeal. It was inevitable that Lady Blessington should come to the writing after that of fashionable novels. The scent for publicity found in every successful actress was hers, and even the most hardened copy writers needed no artificial enthusiasms to puff her books. The existing rumors concerning her early years, her premarital relations with the Earl of Blessington, and now her intimate connection with Count D'Orsay, Prince and last of the Dandies, however much they may have hurt her reputation, were priceless assets to publishers on the hunt for sensational copy. She had the éclat of a royal mistress; she was the goddess of fashion herself to the circulating library readers. Her name on the title-page of a fashionable novel meant far more than the quality of the novel itself. And so, about a year after she had assumed the editorship of the *Book of Beauty*, she published her first fashionable tale, *The Two Friends*, 1835.

If Mrs. Gore was worrying about the possible effect which competition from this new and startlingly authentic source was going to have on her sales, she was soon disabused. For *The Two Friends* totally lacked Mrs. Gore's wit, and seriously rivaled only Lady Charlotte Bury. I propose, as the most effective criticism, to quote the two opening paragraphs.

"You are late this morning, my dear Desbrow," said Lord Arlington, as he entered the dressing-room of his friend, who had not yet exchanged his robe-de-chambre for his morning toilette.— "How jaded you look; but no wonder, for I dare be sworn you have passed the night in the House of Commons."

"You are correct in your surmise," replied Mr. Desbrow. "I

did not get away until six o'clock this morning, and had the mortification to find myself in a most discouraging minority, and to have lost sleep, breath, and time, for no purpose.''

There are two volumes of two hundred pages each in this soporific manner. As James Scarlett, Lord Chief Baron of the Exchequer, wrote her, ''the composition occasionally rises into great elegance, and is always marked by correct feeling.''[9] Time, however, has tarnished the elegance.

Mr. Desbrow is a sober, wealthy Member of Parliament; Lord Arlington is a giddy young man who gambles and borrows from Jews. Both of them have chequered love stories, Arlington's complicated by an affair with a married Lady Walmer and Desbrow's made difficult by the Paris Revolution of 1830. ''The Friends returned to England blessed with wives, whose virtues render them an ornament to society, and a source of the purest happiness to their domestic circles.''[10]

The book is incredibly awkward, inept, and stilted. She worried about the novel's stiffness and lack of passion, but Bulwer, to whom she confessed her misgivings, answered (before reading it) that lack of passion did not matter. ''Miss Edgeworth has no passion—and who in her line excels her?''[11]

By this time her hand was well in, and book followed book so fast that the sedentary laborer grew stout from lack of exercise. She wrote to Landor: ''The truth is, the numerous family of father, mother, sister, brother, and his six children that I have to provide for, compels me to write when my health would demand a total repose from literary exertion, and this throws me back.''[12]

---

[9] Quoted by J. F. Molloy, *The Most Gorgeous Lady Blessington*, London, 1897, p. 306.

[10] Lady Blessington, *The Two Friends*, London, 1835, Vol. II, last page.

[11] Quoted by J. F. Molloy, *The Most Gorgeous Lady Blessington*, London, 1897, pp. 306–7.

[12] *Ibid.*, p. 337.

And behind the interminable stream of books one can feel the driving pressure of a need no less real because it sat amid the glories of Gore House.

The next effort to stave off the creditors was *The Confessions of an Elderly Gentleman*, 1836, in which a retired Don Juan relives his memories of six ladies. As if to counteract the unhappy impression left by the stories of the six, Ackerman and Company, publishers of the first English annual, brought out the same year, *Flowers of Loveliness*, *Twelve Groups of Female Figures Emblematic of Flowers*, designed by E. T. Parris, Esq., with poetical illustrations by the Countess of Blessington. Strictly *de luxe* in binding, paper, engravings, the format of this effort was worthy of its title, and the verses matched the format in their parade of learning, their use of Latin, Greek, and French, their display of charming flower legends. This occasional volume was simply a variant of her annual *Book of Beauty*. Its success led to another annual, *Gems of Beauty*, upon which she ventured in 1836. In this short-lived publication, lasting for only four issues, female beauty was symbolized by jewels instead of flowers. During 1840 she took over *The Keepsake*, and published still another sumptuous poem, *The Belle of a Season*, illustrated by A. E. Chalon, R.A., and engraved by Heath. In octavo couplets, the débutante sweeps on to a good marriage in her first season, becoming the very euphonious Lady Mary Deloraine.

Lady Blessington's years of writing and dealing with publishers had taught her the use of adroit introductions and prefaces. The title-page of her novel, *The Victims of Society*, 1837, promised scandal:

> 'Tis you that say it, not I; you do the deeds,
> And your ungodly deeds find me the words.

The preface disclaimed any allusions to living people. Recognizing that she could no longer bait the public with anonymity, she boldly signed the novel,[13] and offered her signature as warrant of the absence of personal portraiture. That no one in the book was so well drawn that he could be identified with certainty did not matter. She, or her publisher, was shrewd enough to realize that the public would not believe the denial. This apparent frankness was a variant of a customary method of advertising used by Henry Colburn. He loved to contradict the obviously untrue. To puzzle and amaze readers, and to achieve a *succès de scandale*, was his way of running up sales.

Probably to avoid certain difficulties in construction, Lady Blessington chose the epistolary method for *The Victims of Society*. The principal correspondents are Lady Mary Howard and Lady Augusta Vernon, who discuss marriage in long philosophical communications. Both are married early, Lady Mary wisely to Lord Delaward, and Lady Augusta unwisely to Lord Annandale. A friend, Caroline Montressor, who has acquired wordly notions of expediency from her French ancestry and residence, is the insidious counsellor responsible for Lady Augusta's misfortunes. With the arrival of a villainous ex-suitor of Caroline's, the plot becomes frankly melodramatic. Lord Annandale deserts his wife, who soon dies; the ex-suitor commits a murder or two, and Caroline marries Annandale. Tardy justice catches up, when Caroline, conscience-stricken, dies of a broken heart.

The story is too fantastic to bear the weight of much social argument. By the end of the first volume, however, Lady Blessington's need for direct utterance had become so acute that she dropped all pretense at writing a novel and plunged into a dissertation on English society. Caroline Montressor, in the course of a long letter to a sophisticated friend in Paris, analyzes London society with consider-

[13] Lady Charlotte Bury's novel, *The Divorced*, the first to which she put her name, was also published in 1837 by Colburn.

able ill will. This subterfuge was convenient to the author, who could claim immunity for the sentiments of her characters. Fifty-seven pages enables Lady Blessington to touch upon most of the conventional reproaches laid to fashion, and to give them occasionally a personal flavor which reanimated the stale arraignment.

As we have seen, her position in society was such a difficult one that a defense would seem well-nigh impossible. Yet she establishes a case of considerable merit.

So few women in fashionable society here can afford to be merciful to others, that they are often led to a severity they are far from feeling to avoid incurring the imputation of impropriety. It is never the guilt or innocence of the accused that it made the point of debate as to her reception; it is, simply whether Lady So-and-So, and a certain *clique*, will countenance her. As it is only the perfectly virtuous and irreproachable that can risk being lenient, you may conclude that, in the exclusive circle, few are the examples of mercy: but, *en revanche*, innumerable are the instances of forbearance towards those whose amatory adventures furnish the daily topic, and who are blessed with husbands whose charity covereth a multitude of sins.[14]

Nothing is more usual than to hear, in a morning visit, reports the most injurious to female honor, of divers ladies, and yet meet these very persons, in the most fashionable society at night, as well received as if no such rumors had ever existed.[15]

Comment on these paragraphs must start by recognizing the cleverness of Lady Blessington's assumption that guilt or innocence is not the question. Admission that it was the question, would, of course, have left her without a case at all. The curious convention by which ladies contracted left-handed friendships while remaining ostensible "non-callers" shows the question was purely one of countenance. Samuel Carter Hall, in accounting for Mrs. Hall's informal day-time calls and formal evening absences, said, "We were not of rank high enough to be indifferent to public opinion."[16]

[14] *The Victims of Society*, London, 1837, II, 39-40.   [15] *Ibid.*, p. 31.
[16] S. C. Hall, *A Book of Memories*, London, 1871, p. 367.

As for "husbands whose charity covereth a multitude of sins," well, there was Lord Holland. "Another reason for the toleration shown Lady Holland," says Frances Kemble, "was the universal esteem and affectionate respect felt for her husband, whose friends accepted her and her peculiarities for his sake."[17] Lady Conyngham, mistress of George IV, found that the possession of a complaisant husband smoothed her social path. At least, his existence enabled censorious ladies to enter court with a better grace.

Lady Blessington's charity was extended to cover other unfortunates as well as herself. She and Bulwer were stanch friends of the unfortunate Letitia E. Landon, who, in 1830, became involved in a scandal caused by the circulation of scurrilous, anonymous letters. "In London," says Lady Blessington,[18] "any woman in a brilliant position may lose her reputation in a week, without even having imagined a dereliction from honor." A recollection of L. E. L.'s affair may be responsible for this assertion.

Any discussion of the social status of scandal in the thirties inevitably brought about reference to one or two of the newspapers of the day. "This peculiar taste for scandal in my compatriots is so well known, that it has become a staple commodity of traffic; journals have been established to retail it; and the more pungent the satire they contain, the more extensive is their sale."[19]

Such an allusion to *John Bull*, or *The Age*, considered as an attack, sounds like a studied understatement. Lady Blessington and D'Orsay were not the only ones who had suffered from the scandalmongers. Male victims usually fought back with a horsewhip or a challenge, but far more effective than either the horsewhip or Lady Blessington's bland remarks is Disraeli's clever burlesque of such papers in *The Young Duke*.

[17] Frances Kemble, *Records of a Later Life*, London, 1882, I, 98.
[18] *The Victims of Society*, p. 35.   [19] *Ibid.*, p. 34.

When *The Victims of Society* was written there were only two *salons* which enjoyed an equality with Gore House.[20] One was still Holland House, and the other, Lady Charleville's in Cavendish Square. Lesser assemblages like Miss Spence's and Miss Benger's where literary men went in search of conversation and tea, were supplanting the more formal *salons*. A certain amount of rivalry, intensified by personal causes, naturally existed among the partisans of the old order, but Lady Blessington permitted herself only one gibe at a rival. "A few of the houses with the most pretentions to literary taste have their tame poets and *petits litterateurs* who run about as docile, and more parasitical, than lap-dogs: and, like them, are equally well-fed, ay, and certainly equally spoiled."[21]

The reference to houses with tame poets would seem to have but one subject—Holland House and Samuel Rogers. Lady Caroline Lamb had drawn in *Glenarvon* a picture of the poet at "Barbary House" inspired by malice, but a similar feeling, while justifiable, is not displayed by Lady Blessington. Indeed, Dr. John Allen, Sydney Smith, Tom Moore, and a host of other poets and wits who flourished at Holland House were likewise friends of Lady Blessington. D'Orsay himself was a frequent caller at Holland House.

With a citation of the besetting sin of the age we may end our quotations from *The Victims of Society*. "The English fashionables are the only people who unshrinkingly display their mental diseases, though they carefully conceal their physical ones. I refer again to that epidemic malady, ennui."[22]

Ennui was hardly the keynote of Restoration comedy, nor was the "spleen," a closely related disease of the eighteenth century, a dominant note in the sentimental comedy.

---

[20] Lady Cork's *salon* should perhaps be included, but the old lady was over ninety and very eccentric.

[21] *Ibid.*, p. 19.   [22] *Ibid.*, p. 18.

But ennui had grown ominous with Maria Edgeworth, and was to run its course like a pestilence through the fashionable novel. Hook, Lister, and Ward knew it, but it disappeared in the happy vivacity of Disraeli and Bulwer, only to reappear with renewed vigor in the pages of the female novelists. Mrs. Gore only scotched it with her witty *The Diary of a Désennuyée*, and something of the spirit of Lady Blessington's remark appeared again in Samuel Butler's *Erewhon*.

The only interest of *The Victims of Society* lies in these well-mannered comments and remonstrances which show how guardedly Lady Blessington fought back at the feminine society which banned her. The novel was, in a real sense, written by a victim of society. Bulwer, who had criticized the manuscript, even thought her very severe, though truthful. That the victim chose to do her fighting in this impersonal way is indicative of her real nature, and goes far to justify the enthusiasm for her displayed by so many men of talent and position. Contrast her restrained statement of the case for the defense with lurid attacks written by Lady Caroline Lamb and Lady Lytton Bulwer. The former's *Glenarvon*, and the latter's *Cheveley, or, The Man of Honor*, 1839, fairly abound with personalities drawn with the most offensive explicitness. What contemporary reader could fail to recognize Lady Holland in the Princess of Madagascar, or Bulwer-Lytton in Lord de Clifford? Lady Blessington simply did not possess the driving malice which animated the other noble ladies. In a sense this is understandable, for their grievances were against individuals, Lady Blessington's against a system. Although unkind critics might remark that the gorgeous lady lived in a glass house, so did many of her contemporaries who were less than kind. And while she does not complain, she must have felt the inconsistency when the same society which ostracized her gladly received D'Orsay.

Her novel of 1836, *The Confessions of an Elderly Gentleman*, called for a counterpart, *The Confessions of an Elderly Lady*, which appeared in 1838. Lady Blessington did not dare, what Thackeray later attempted, write a novel with a female *picaro* as the heroine. That the book purports to tell the story leading up to a "good" marriage means nothing more than that it points the moral of real love missed for wealth. But the book's faintly genial taste is due, perhaps, to the fact that the separated lovers do not die of the customary broken hearts. The quondam lover of the lady appears at the end of the story, gouty and decrepit, and the disillusioned Lady Windermere returns to her favorite occupation of nagging her paid companion. Lady Blessington was endeavoring to show that death from blighted love was not the only way out. Life goes on and develops into the indifference and narrow selfishness of old age, and this may be just as tragic as death. Because of her inability to create really convincing characters, her laudable attempt failed.

Lady Blessington, like every other writer except, possibly, Mrs. Gore, was feeling the exhaustion of the fashionable novel. Her novel output decreased, and in those she did write, fashionable material took a diminishing place. She desperately sought other ways of interesting readers, trying now a thesis novel, now an adventure story, and even resorting again to her Irish memories. But so scanty was her inspiration that in the next four years she published only one novel, and had to fall back on her journals to supply failing subject matter.

By 1842 she had written enough short stories and sketches to make up a volume, *The Lottery of Life*. Most of the tales are worthless, but one, "Scenes in the Life of a Portrait Painter," is of fair quality. Another, "The Parvenu," deserves mention because it exploits the conventional prejudices of the aristocrat against the newly rich.

But neither *The Lottery of Life* nor *Meredith*, her 1843 novel, an adventure story combined with a limited amount of fashionable paraphernalia, served to rescue the sales of Lady Blessington's books from an alarming slump. *Meredith* had sold only 384 copies in five months.[23] Determined, apparently, to stun the public into acceptance, Lady Blessington presented them two years later with a four-volume novel of 1,229 pages, *Strathern, or, Life at Home and Abroad, a Story of the Present Day*. From her point of view the book was a huge success, since she earned £600 by it. What proportion of this sum came from serialization in the Sunday *Times* and what from its appearance in book form, is not known. Colburn wrote her dolefully that he had sold only 400 copies and thereby lost forty pounds.[24] He declined to consider any more of her novels. J. Cordy Jeaffreson, writing in 1858,[25] remarked about *Strathern's* failure to sell, "It is something to say for the taste and intelligence of the readers of fashionable novels that they declined to patronize Lady Blessington, and that in the later years of her career she found it difficult to get a publisher to publish a novel from her pen at his own risk." Jeaffreson's comment is biased by his low opinion of her morality.[26] More probably the sales were low because the fashionable novel, according to Lady Blessington's formula, was outmoded. She did not make Lord Strathern a dandy, but did present a high-minded young nobleman of international background exactly like Ward's Tremaine.

"And this is called society," said Strathern to himself, "Better, far better, would solitude be, where freed from the puerile shackles

[23] Letter of Messrs. Longman, Nov. 3, 1843. *The Blessington Papers*, 2d series, privately printed, London, 1895.

[24] J. F. Molloy, *op. cit.*, p. 417.

[25] J. C. Jeaffreson, *Novels and Novelists from Elizabeth to Victoria*, London, 1858, II, 175–76.

[26] Jeaffreson may never have read her novels. He thought them coarse, whereas they are offensively genteel.

imposed by this heartless and artificial mode of life, one could indulge the love of rural scenery, and hold communion with those choice spirits whose lucubrations, too seldom resorted to, fill the shelves of our libraries."[27]

Strathern's love affair with Louisa Sydney offers the author opportunity for more sprightly comment than usual. The style throughout this interminable book is light and readable, especially when customary English solemnity is exchanged for humorous excursions into Irish circles. Part of the action is laid in a sculptor's studio—the original is Westmacott's—and an impression of authenticity is given. But the book is interesting only as a curious survival of a form which had vitality in the two previous decades.

The failure of *Strathern* in book form would seem to indicate that its serial appearance had also been unsuccessful. Nevertheless, Lady Blessington's name seems to have retained its power in newspaper circles, for in January, 1846, she established a profitable connection with *The Daily News*, a paper started in 1845 by Bradbury and Evans with Charles Dickens as editor. She was asked in confidence for "any sort of intelligence she might like to communicate of the sayings, doings, memoirs, or movements of the fashionable world."[28] The salary was to be four or five hundred pounds a year. The new editor who succeeded Dickens and Forster, however, refused to renew her contract after the six-month trial period was over.

As we have seen, Lady Blessington's income from her novels was not limited to returns from publication in book form. If there had been such limitation, the chances are that none would have been written after 1840. She exploited the profitable Sunday newspapers through the serial publication of her long novels. Additional returns came from the sale of advance sheets to American publishers whose

[27] *Strathern*, Tauchnitz edition, Leipzig, 1844, I, 22–23.
[28] Quoted by J. F. Molloy, *op. cit.*, p. 402.

democratic public relished such heady diet as she provided. Mrs. Sigourney wrote her a flattering note in 1841. "Your ladyship's writings, and some of the splendid works which you have occasionally edited, are known in this country."[29] Poor Lady Blessington probably grimaced over these congratulations when she remembered the slim returns she was getting from Lee and Blanchard in Philadelphia.[30] However, in the absence of copyright law, any returns at all were a testimony to a publisher's honor. Other Americans were not so honest. Her next novel, *Memoirs of a femme de chambre* appeared in Philadelphia, n. d., as *Ella Stratford, or, The Orphan Child, a Thrilling Novel Founded on Facts*. The pirate's hand surely is revealed in that switch from French to explicit English. Then, too, the Continental editions of Baudry and Tauchnitz[31] began to pour their share into her coffers. Her *Lottery of Life* was published in 1842 in Baudry's "European Library, Collection of Ancient and Modern British Authors." In American libraries today what few of her books survive are sure to be Philadelphia printings or Tauchnitz. Both *Meredith* and *Strathern* were reprinted by Tauchnitz. My copy of her next book, *Memoirs of a femme de chambre*, is from Leipzig, and bears the date 1846, the same year it appeared in London.

The promise that was implicit in Lady Blessington's undertaking to write fashionable novels was never fulfilled. From her gilded eminence in society and her success as the leader of a *salon*, more might legitimately have been expected than the production of two or three novels of slight merit amid a mass of inferior work. Although she was the

[29] R. R. Madden, *A Memoir of the Literary Life and Correspondence of the Countess of Blessington*, London, 1855, II, 83.

[30] Lee and Blanchard offered five pounds for the sheets of *Meredith.—Blessington Papers*, letter of Longman's.

[31] Another letter of Longman's, July 18, 1843, discusses ways of preventing the importation of Tauchnitz editions.—*Blessington Papers*.

friend of Disraeli and the counsellor of Bulwer, her own novels show no understanding of the distinguishing features of *Vivian Grey* or *Pelham*. Her satire is seldom fresh, but continues to ring the changes on themes which were hardly new to Fanny Burney. And although her publishers paid dearly for her name, they might have got better novels from some hack in a garret whose nearest approach to Mayfair was a glimpse of Lady Blessington in her carriage.

IX

HENRY COLBURN

Colburn:—"I need hardly say that, to use no more ambitious phrase, it was allotted to me to be the instrument by which a signal revolution was effected in our literature. I it was who first gave you delineations of the most refined society, by its most refined members. I—excuse this necessary egotism—I it was who rescued the annals of Polite life from the Swiss, the valet, and the lady's-maid, the rip, the roué, and the blackleg."[1]

THE history of any publishing house, touching as it does both the business and artistic sides of literature, affords a valuable glimpse into a side of literary history too often neglected. Supply and demand, which influence literary products quite as much as they do commodities, may best be studied through the publisher, that necessary middleman between genius and its audience. Fashionable novels, at least nine-tenths of which bear the imprint of Henry Colburn, are especially susceptible of treatment from the business side, for perhaps more than any other fad in literature, they were the result of a single publisher's enthusiasm.

Luckily for Colburn, he came into maturity when Constable and Murray were hardly in a state to offer competition. Constable had gone down with Scott, and Murray was curtailing his activity during the panic of 1825–26. Colburn, by a series of fortunate financial and literary speculations, had been steadily expanding, and the panic, while it forced him to admit his printer, Richard Bentley, into partnership, was not able to curb him seriously. With considerable shrewdness he tied his balloon to fiction, which,

[1] *The Court Journal*, May 23, 1829. "H—— C——, a Colloquy on the Progress and Prospects of the Court Journal."

while largely of one type, the fashionable novel, was still sufficiently diversified to enable him to take advantage of any best seller vogue which might develop. Through his numerous magazines, a direct source of income, he nursed and cultivated writers and public. Despite such notable publishing successes as the Pepys and Evelyn diaries, *The Literary Gazette*, and the historical romance, his name has become inseparably attached to the fashionable novel. There have been other publishers who dominated their fields because they were linked with a Byron or a Scott; there are no others who have controlled so many best sellers over so long a period of time.

The publisher of Burke's *Peerage* was himself born no one seems to know where, or when, or to whom. He died in 1855, and he may have been twenty-five or thirty in 1814, when he started *The New Monthly Magazine and Universal Register*. Samuel Carter Hall speaks of him in 1830 as "somewhat aged,"[2] and newly married. He lived to marry again, however, and Hall's term is not very exact. Surmises as to his parentage are much more romantic, so romantic, indeed, that they sound inspired. To the gentleman who made press-agentry a fine art, the securing of a few flattering allusions to his own birth must have been child's play. In any case, Hall wrote, "No one ever knew his history, but it was said that he was a natural son of old Lord Lansdowne."[3] William Carew Hazlitt, sometimes an unreliable gossip, brought Colburn (perhaps in jest) right back to royalty. He had heard that Colburn was a son of the military chieftain, the Duke of York, by one of numerous mistresses.[4] With this we may leave the question— royal bastard or guttersnipe matters little.

His apprenticeship in business was begun in the shop of

[2] S. C. Hall, *Retrospect of a Long Life*, New York, 1883, p. 182.   [3] *Ibid*.
[4] W. C. Hazlitt, *Four Generations of a Literary Family*, London and New York, 1897, I, 168–73.

William Earle, a bookseller in Albemarle Street. Later he worked for Morgan's Circulating Library in Conduit Street. Then, apparently, came a sudden accession of capital from an unknown source. Frederic Shoberl, with whom he started *The New Monthly Magazine*, does not seem to have provided it, judging by his subsequent publishing career, which tended to the editorial rather than the proprietary.

There was already a *Monthly Magazine* run by Sir Richard Phillips which furnished the incentive to Colburn and Shoberl. Sir Richard's magazine was radical in a day when radicalism was a bugbear to respectable folk. *The New Monthly* sought even in its title to supplant the old, and like it, was largely political in its content, although it stood for Tory conservatism and the *status quo*. By 1820 Colburn wearied of fighting the Jacobins, and *The New Monthly* was converted to literary and general interests. John "Dictionary" Watkins was the first editor, to be succeeded later by Alaric A. Watts.

For a time Colburn seems to have combined pietistic publishing with his general bookselling, but the fortunes of a semi-religious press rise, but too slowly, and the experiment was dropped. By 1816, he had acquired the proprietorship of Morgan's Circulating Library. For some time he had been interested in the publishing of general literature, taking a book on shares with another publisher to lessen the risks. Constable and Blackwood started in the same way. Individual success first came to Colburn in 1817 when Lady Morgan's *France*, damned by Gifford in the *Quarterly*, sold rapidly to the Whigs.

The political nature of *The New Monthly* was so pronounced that the rising publisher felt the need of a literary organ. He started *The Literary Gazette*, designed to fill this need, on January 25, 1817. This weekly at a shilling set a new standard in periodical publishing. Literary reviews up to the time of the *Gazette's* appearance had been rather ponderous affairs appearing monthly or quarterly. Their style was likely to be pontifical and their contents dreary. The *Gazette* aimed at lightness and readability, while naturally its low price made it available to a far larger body of readers than could be reached by reviews selling at seven-and-six. H. E. Lloyd, a clerk in the post office, a Miss Ross, and William Paulet Cary were the first editors. After twenty-six numbers William Jerdan bought one-third control; Longman acquired a share formerly held by the publishing firm of Pinnock and Maunders, and Jerdan became sole editor. With the accession of Jerdan to the editorship, the magazine gradually ceased to be a mere collection of articles, and assumed a definite character. After a quarter of a century, Jerdan bought complete control, urged on, no doubt, by the desire to free himself from the reproach of handling Colburn's books too favorably.[5] His position had never been an easy one, for Colburn was insatiable in his demands for publicity. Jerdan always maintained his impartiality, and in his autobiography was at pains to establish the right of the *Gazette* to be considered a reliable source book for future scholars. Because it was, as A. A. Watts declared, "the best advertising medium for books,"[6] *The Literary Gazette* is a most useful source of publishing dates.

Colburn was one of the most sensitive of men when his self-love was affronted, or his advertising schemes thwarted. Much less than adequate cause would lead him into the spending of sums at which his ordinary caution would have balked. When Jerdan discovered that Lady Morgan's *The O'Briens and the O'Flaherties* was an improper book for ladies to read and told the world so in the *Gazette*, Colburn may

[5] *Fraser's* went so far as to buy space in the *Gazette* itself to attack Colburn's novels and the magazine. It quoted the *Aberdeen Magazine's* description of the *Gazette* as "the common sewer of the vilest bibliopolical corruption."—*The Literary Gazette*, Oct. 30, 1831.

[6] Oliphant, *op. cit.*, I, 498.

be forgiven his wrath. He declared that Jerdan's action had cost him £500.[7] Not content with that loss, however, he promptly decided to purchase a half share in the *Athenaeum*, a new magazine contemplated by James Silk Buckingham. Buckingham was a traveler, an amateur archaeologist, and a restless publisher who had already been connected with two or three periodicals.

Colburn found himself in the awkward position of partially owning but not controlling two magazines on opposite sides of the political fence. He announced his purchase in a letter to Jerdan and Longman:

At the same time I may state, that the step I am now taking does not seem to me likely to injure the sale of the "L. G." The "Athenaeum" will be published on another day of the week; it will address persons of other politics, and, *when likely to be treated with impartiality* in the "L. G." early copies shall be supplied to both publications on the same day, leaving it to chance which shall anticipate the other in its notice of them.

Buckingham, for his part, had the extremely delicate revelation to make to his readers that he was associating himself with Henry Colburn. He announced the connection in small type on the last page of the first issue. Readers would have naught to fear from partiality, he was sure, because Colburn did not own more than he did, and he, J. S. Buckingham, was editor.

It would be an insult to the understandings of that class [readers] to suppose they could believe for a moment that so ignoble a phantom as the fear of any author's or publisher's displeasure would make me shrink from the stern and honest performance of my duty. My own heart answers—NEVER!

The high-falutin language thought necessary on this occasion did not augur well for the permanence of the connection, nor did it last very long. Since the *Athenaeum* was not a financial success, the *London Literary Chronicle* was

[7] *Ibid.*, I, 519–20. Letter of Crofton Croker to Blackwood, January, 1828. See also W. J. Fitzgerald, *The Friends, Foes, and Adventures of Lady Morgan*, Dublin, 1859, p. 115.

united with it in July, 1828, and Frederic Denison Maurice, editor of the *Chronicle*, became editor and part proprietor of the united magazines. Associated with him was John Sterling. By November of that same year, Sterling wrote to R. C. Trench, "Are you inclined to buy my share in the *Athenaeum?* It will cost you, if I remember right, a little more than a hundred pounds."[8] Maurice resigned in May, 1830, and another group, the chief of whom was Charles Wentworth Dilke, took it over. Just when Colburn withdrew is not known; he may have sold when Buckingham did, July, 1828, or he may have held on until Dilke's time. Reviews of Colburn books, usually occupying a place next to the leader, were favorable up to the middle of 1830.

Colburn was in no way discouraged over the failure of this periodical enterprise, for no sooner had it proved unprofitable than he persuaded one of its numerous backers, a printer named James Holmes, to venture with him on *The Court Journal*. This appeared on May 2, 1829. Within three weeks Colburn permitted the *Journal* to publish an article called "H—— C——, a Colloquy on the Progress and Prospects of the Court Journal." It was probably written by P. G. Patmore, the editor, and in its delightful exaggeration represents the buoyant nature of Colburn. The successes of *Tremaine*, *Vivian Grey*, and *Pelham* offered sufficient cause for the braggadocio.[9] The same year he started *The United Service Journal and Naval and Military Magazine*, while still later he acquired a large share in the *Sunday Times*.

This expansion into general magazine ownership and speculation had been prefaced by quieter expansion of his book-publishing business two or three years earlier. A few successes like Lady Morgan's *France*, in 1817, enabled him to move from Conduit Street to larger quarters in New

[8] R. C. Trench, *Letters and Memories*, London, 1888, I, 17.
[9] See the quotation at the head of this chapter.

Burlington Street by 1823. The two famous diaries, Evelyn's, in 1818, and Pepys's, in 1825, although they had most gratifying critical response, were not immediately profitable. "Indeed so far from realizing a fortune, when . . . the crisis of 1826 paralyzed trade, and swept away two-thirds of the publishing houses of the time, Colburn himself talked of disposing of his business."[10]

Because he needed help, not because he wanted to expand, Colburn, in September, 1829, took into partnership Richard Bentley, one of the brothers in his printing firm of Samuel and Richard Bentley. Colburn's quarrels with his editors show that he frequently had trouble with associates, and the affairs of the new firm did not go too smoothly. The fault seems chiefly to have been his, although the account of the quarrels may be biased, since it comes entirely from Bentley.

One of the main causes of dispute was the value of the copyrights. Colburn was inclined to take advantage of his partner's inexperience by valuing them too highly. Several new ventures, "The National Library," the "Family Classical Library," and the "Juvenile Library," did not succeed very well. Strained relations came to a break in August, 1832, when an agreement to dissolve the partnership was signed. Colburn sold the business to Bentley (retaining his magazine holdings), and as part of the terms agreed not to set up in business again within twenty miles of London, Edinburgh, or Dublin. This peculiar condition, of course, was meant to prohibit his ever becoming a rival, but Colburn chose to interpret the terms literally, and at Windsor, twenty-one miles from London, took a place of business. Restless, he tried to persuade Bentley to allow him to set up in London again. Bentley was furious at being

[10] Richard Bentley, *Some Leaves from the Past Swept together by R. B.*, Privately printed, 1896, pp. 88–92. Written by the grandson of Colburn's partner.

tricked, but realizing that he had been outwitted, he accepted a sum of money to release Colburn before some other ingenious evasion was perfected. Colburn reopened in Great Marlborough Street.

One series of reprints which Colburn and Bentley had started in 1831, their "Standard Novels," was a highly successful venture.[11] The first volume was Cooper's *Pilot*, then seven years old. The aim was not to make the series a cheap edition of current novels, so much as "an attempt to register the permanent value of certain novels written since the great period of eighteenth century novel writing, but not hitherto fittingly represented in handy and cheap form." Later, however, the firm used the series to reprint their own best sellers. "Nowadays," complained Samuel Rogers, "as soon as a novel has had its run and is beginning to be forgotten, out comes an edition of it as a 'standard novel.'"[12]

Authors were required to revise, or write a preface. If the author was not available, the publishers provided notes in order that their boast, "the only genuine edition extant of the works in question," should not be an idle one. The first nineteen volumes were the firm's; from the twentieth on, the series was Bentley's.

Colburn started a similar series of fictional reprints in 1835, "Colburn's Modern Standard Novelists." The authors were much the same as those in Bentley's series, since Bentley naturally kept such books as the joint firm had published. Thus of the nineteen volumes between 1835 and 1841 many were fashionable novels by Bulwer, R. P. Ward, T. H. Lister, and Theodore Hook. There were also novels by Lady Morgan, Horace Smith, Captain Marryat, G.P.R. James, G. R. Gleig, and others.

[11] *The Colophon*, Part X, 1932. Michael Sadleir, "Bentley's Standard Novel Series; Its History and Achievement."
[12] Samuel Rogers, *Table Talk*, p. 138.

It is to this period of intense rivalry between the separated partners that Thackeray's picture in *Pendennis* belongs. Bacon is Bentley, and Bungay, Colburn.

Since they have separated, it is a furious war between the two
publishers, and no sooner does one bring out a book of travels or
poems, a magazine, or a periodical, quarterly, or monthly, or
weekly, or annual, but the rival is in the field with something
similar.

When Bungay engaged your celebrated friend Mr. Wagg [Hook]
to edit the *Londoner*, Bacon straightway rushed off and secured
Mr. Grindle to give his name to the *Westminster Magazine*.[13]

So bitter and irrational was the enmity between the two
that Colburn engaged Hook at £400 a year to edit a magazine not even planned in order to prevent Bentley's engaging him for the projected *Bentley's Miscellany*. Ultimately
dissuaded from his rashness, but resolved to get value
received for the money Hook had already spent, Colburn
made him editor of *The New Monthly*, and thereby dis-
gruntled Hall, the subeditor.[14]

Mrs. Gore, who had more obligations to the partners
than Thackeray did, contented herself with calling them
"the Scylla and Charybdis of the novel craft."[15] Harriet
Martineau, who had just returned from the United States,
compared their relations with authors to the methods of
auctioneers selling slaves in the South. She was waited upon
by Bentley, Colburn, and Saunders, each anxious for the
account of her travels. Bentley offered extravagant terms
for the travel book and £1,000 for a novel. Saunders offered
£900 for a first edition and all American profits. Colburn
came armed with an introduction from Thomas Campbell
and offered her £2,000 for so many copies of the American
book, and £1,000 for a novel. "He pathetically complained
of having raised up rivals to himself in the assistants he

[13] *Pendennis*, chap. xxxi.
[14] S. C. Hall, *Retrospect of a Long Life*, New York, 1883, pp. 182–83.
[15] Mrs. Oliphant, *op. cit.*, II, 348–49.

had trained.''[16] Saunders and Otley got the book, and
Colburn always after that declared himself to have been
too late.[17]

Increasing age finally led to his retirement from active
publishing, and although he kept his name on a few standard books until the end, Hurst and Blackett purchased
everything else. On his death in Bryanstone Square,
August 16, 1857, seven of his copyrights realized £14,000
when sold at auction. He had kept Warburton's *The Crescent
and the Cross*, Evelyn's *Diary*, Pepys's *Diary*, Strickland's
Lives of the Queens, and three forms of Burke's *Peerage and
Baronetage.*[18]

So widespread had a literate public become, and so
cheap the processes of papermaking and printing, that
Constable planned to sell a book a month to the very
butcher boys. Colburn's aim was hardly that of Constable's—fashionable, not cheap literature was to be his
contribution to the spread of reading. He succeeded, however, in distributing his fashionable and expensive books in
immense quantities. Hardly any books of the day except
the cheapest tracts surpassed in circulation the guinea or
guinea-and-a-half, three-volume Colburn novels.

The Athenaeum, September 17, 1828, examined Colburn's
list for the season and discovered that he was publishing
65 *new* books. There were books by Mrs. Shelley, Hazlitt,
Horace Smith, Disraeli, Lister, Godwin, Normanby,
Landor, Thomas Roscoe, Ward, Lady Dacre, Hood, the
Banims, Bulwer, Cooper, Campbell, Colley, Grattan, Lady
Morgan, Leigh Hunt, Hook, Lady Charlotte Bury, and

[16] The only Colburn-trained rival I can trace is William Shoberl, son
of Frederic Shoberl, who was an assistant of Colburn's before he set up in
Great Marlborough Street. Colburn probably included Richard Bentley
in his reproach, despite the fact that his former partner had been a successful printer before engaging with him.

[17] Harriet Martineau, *Autobiography*, Boston, 1877, pp. 402-3.

[18] *Notes and Queries*, 2d series, III, 458.

George Croly. Shortly after there were books by Marryat
and G. P. R. James. By far the largest part of the list
(seventy-four volumes) was "high life literature." Only
four volumes were poetry. In short, there were thirty
pounds worth of novels and only four-and-six-pence worth
of poetry. *The Athenaeum* concluded regretfully, "Mr.
Colburn is a fashionable publisher, and, perhaps, is the
best gauger of the public taste in existence."

Just how good Colburn was as a gauger may be inferred
from the assertion of the Rev. George Croly in 1827.[19] He
declared that Colburn had cleared £20,000 a year for the
last three years. The sums he paid his authors were commensurate with his profits. For Hook's *Sayings and Doings*,
first series, admittedly an experiment in public taste, he
paid £600; for the second series he paid one thousand
guineas, a sum later increased by £200 and £150. Hook's
regular scale was £1,000 for a novel like *Maxwell*. To Lady
Morgan for her *Florence MacCarthy* he paid £2,000.[20] Ainsworth, in writing to his friend Crossley that at any time he
could get £500 for a fashionable novel, was in no way
exaggerating.[21] Colburn paid Robert Gillies £200 for his
Sir Basil Barrington. We have seen what he paid Disraeli for
Vivian Grey, £200 for the first part, and £600 for the second.
Five hundred pounds was the first payment for *Tremaine*,
and much more was added when the book proved profitable.[22] He agreed to pay Horace Smith £500 for a first
novel. Smith wrote it, but burned the manuscript when a
friend told him it was no good. Then Smith wrote *Bramble-
tye House*, and Colburn added £100 to the original sum.[23]
When Lady Morgan demanded more money for her first

[19] Mrs. Oliphant, *op, cit.*, I, 481.
[20] Lady Morgan, *Passages from My Autobiography*, New York, 1859,
p. 16.   [21] S. M. Ellis, *op. cit.*, I, 160.
[22] P. G. Patmore, *My Friends and Acquaintance*, London, 1854, II, 11.
[23] A. H. Beavan, *James and Horace Smith*, London, 1899, p. 261.

novel as it entered upon a second edition, he gave it to her without demur, and agreed to pay her £1,000 outright for *France*. He added more later when edition after edition was called for.

For magazine contributors he relied on a lavish purse. He offered Maginn £30 a sheet, Horace Smith £20, and he offered to "give Talfourd his weight in gold rather than part with him."[24] His terms to Campbell for *The New Monthly* were princely, £500 a year, to include twelve articles, half verse and half prose. The copyrights were to revert to Campbell. Not only that, but Colburn agreed to provide a working editor, and to pay extra for any other contributions.[25]

Maginn closes his novel, *Whitehall, or, The Days of George IV*, with a lively description of Colburn's purchasing methods. Apsely, in charge of the historical novel department, is speaking to Smithers, the hero of the novel:

"I beg pardon if I am troublesome, but master bade me to be sure not to let your honor quit the shop without asking you to give us your adventures since you've been in town. Oh! do, Sir,— fifty—a hundred—a hundred and fifty—O, Lord, Sir! you're a knowing one—well, you shall have the cool two hundred— done?"

"Done," said Smithers; "done!" and he disappeared amidst the windings of the street.

"Done!" echoed Apsely,—"Done—done!"

The master manufacturer at that instant returned and with electrical rapidity comprehending the state of affairs, slapped his brawny thigh and re-echoed "Done, done,
DONE!"

But the long list of books published and the prices paid for them are perhaps second in interest to the extraordinary efficiency of his advertising, the attractive side of which is seldom mentioned. *The London Magazine*, however, once saw fit to give him his due.

[24] G. K. L'Estrange, *op. cit.*, I, pp. 351-52.
[25] Wm. Beattie, *Life and Letters of Thos. Campbell*, London, 1849, II, 357.

Colburn seems to have succeeded to his [Murray's] place as a publisher. He sometimes publishes trash, but his last list of works in the press contains many works of the first importance and I must say, for the honor of Colburn, that by extensively circulating the praises of his penmen, he has acquired a just title to the name of a patron of literature, which Dr. Johnson said the booksellers alone deserved.[26]

Two months before, in an article entitled "The Art of Advertising Made Easy," this same magazine had awarded Colburn's advertising copy an equal degree of merit with that employed on Prince's Russia Oil, Rowland's Macassar, and Wright's Cape-Madeira.[27] This attitude was the customary one. Colburn was, said Mrs. Oliphant, "supposed to be the inventor of an extra-ordinary new system of puffery, and was the butt of all the wits."[28] Assertions as to the novelty of any commercial system are rash, however, and we may presume to doubt that Colburn actually invented literary inflation. Undeniably he was the most resourceful publisher of his day, and the systematic zeal with which he sought to advance the sales of his authors should endear him to this generation. Colburn and puffery become synonymous terms and the hand of the press agent was seen in every act he did.

Once when Lady Morgan arrived in London from Ireland, she wrote to a friend of hers, "Colburn, as usual, has indulged his puffing vocation by sending our arrival to the 'papers,' as if anybody cared about it."[29] We have traveled far in the art of literary advertising since then. No modern author would have such scruples.

Writers, especially those whose books were not published by Colburn, loved to make slighting references to his

[26] *The London Magazine*, April, 1825, pp. 618–26.

[27] *Ibid.*, February, 1825, pp. 246–53. Macaulay in his essay on Satan Montgomery, *Edinburgh Review*, LI (April, 1830), 101, made the same comparison.

[28] Mrs. Oliphant, *op. cit.*, I, pp. 395–96.

[29] Lady Morgan, *op. cit.*, p. 38.

puffery. The reader could then infer that the book he was
reading had been circulated purely on its merits. Even
Robert Montgomery, in his *The Age Reviewed, a Satire*,
London, 1827, speaks of his own book,

> Thus patronless, oh! dars't thou hope to please,
> Will Colburn puff, or Murray purchase thee?[30]

And he adds a footnote of advice,

Let but the smile of Colburn suavity, illuminate the MS. and
your forthcoming prodigy will wander through all the papers in
the full tide of paragraphic celebrity.

In Maginn's *Whitehall, or, The Days of George IV*, there
are several hits at Colburn's salesmanship as well as at his
buying of manuscripts. One of the numerous pseudo-
scholarly footnotes reads: "See 'De Arte Puffandi Indirecte,
vel per Head-and Sholderos,' Autore Henrico Colburn. In
newspaper folio, 3591 volumes."[31] A lengthy description of
Colburn's place of business includes a receipt for a historical
novel, "Serve up, hot and hot, with puffs; them you manufacture yourself, or you hire a regular baker."

The shrewdness of Maginn's last hit—for who should
know more about the details of puffing?—is borne out by a
letter of Hood's. In his capacity as editor of the *New
Monthly*, he wrote to a correspondent seeking books to
review,

I undertook to review all books except Colburn's own, with the
puffery of which I of course desired to have no concern. They are
done by the persons of the establishment—Patmore, Williams, or
Shoberl. If you see the Mag. you will know what wretched
things these reviews are . . . I am ashamed of them at present or
should be were it not pretty well known that I have no hand in
them.[32]

From time to time in *Blackwood's*, North took shots at
Colburn. We have already seen his opinion of the handling
of *Vivian Grey*.

[30] *Ibid.*, p. 33.   [31] Maginn, *op. cit.*, pp. 139, 316.
[32] Walter Jerrold, *Thos. Hood, His Life and Times*, London, 1907, p. 370.

Colburn, James, must have sent puffs of V. G. to all the news-papers, fastening the authorship on various gentlemen, either by name or innuendo.

But if he persists in that shameful and shameless puffery which he has too long practised, the public will turn away with nausea from every volume that issues from his shop . . .[33]

Yet North says elsewhere in the *Noctes*,

Sir . . . if I were a novelist, I am by no means sure that I should have any objections to deal with Mr. Colburn, for I hear the man's a civil man, and an economical, and an exact, and a thriving.[34]

Crofton Croker, whom Colburn hated, wrote to Black-wood in June, 1828, proposing an article on Colburn's puffery.[35]

The idea would be, stating C. N.'s happiness at no longer having the trouble of reading new books for the purpose of criticizing them; that two very respectable and talented gentlemen had been for some time past retained by the best publisher of the day to review all his important publications and to acquaint the public with their opinion thereon before the appearance of the works.

Colburn's business staff irritated his enemies. *Fraser's* even went so far as to accuse him of having an advertising department!

Does he not keep clerks and writers whose exclusive employ is, as he says, "solely to look after the papers and advertisements?" And does not the little man boast of being able to stuff his in-conceivable trash down the reluctant maws of the public in spite of magazines and newspapers and critics?[36]

He was popularly credited with spending £9,000 a year on advertising. North conjectured that he spent £100 a month on the *New Monthly* alone.

Alaric A. Watts, who had offered himself to Blackwood

---

[33] *Blackwood's Magazine*, July, 1826, p. 98.
[34] Quoted, A. S. Collins, *The Profession of Letters*, London, 1928, p. 243.
[35] Mrs. Oliphant, *op. cit.*, I, 519-20.
[36] *Fraser's Magazine*, April, 1830, p. 319.

as a sort of literary agent and business spy in London, sent
his employer a bit of verse which duly appeared in the
Noctes.

> Colburn, Campbell, and Co. write rather so so,
> But atone for't by puff and profession—
> Every month gives us scope for the *Pleasures of Hope*,
> But all ends in the Pains of Possession.[37]

But no anthology of squibs against Colburn's puffery
can give an adequate idea of how widespread was the
opinion of contemporaries that Colburn owed most of his
success to his advertising gifts. He himself was not loath
to take credit for his labor. Writing to persuade Lady
Morgan, in 1817, to make him her publisher, he said,[38]
"No one bookseller, I am certain, takes a tenth part of the
pains I do in advertising, and in *other* respects I do not think
any one will *in future*, cope with me, since from January
next, I shall have under my sole control *two journals*."

"Colburn had always more faith in his own advertisements for the success of a work than in the genius of the
author," she says elsewhere.[39] This obviously irked the
brilliant Irishwoman, who was accustomed to set values
on her work which tried even Colburn's generosity. He had
offered her £1,000 for *France*, and she had tried, unsuccessfully, to get Blackwood to raise the offer.

A perusal of these testimonies to Colburn's powers may
prepare the reader for revelations of the marvellous in the
art of advertising. Such expectations, however, will not be
fulfilled, for judged by comparison with present-day men-
dacity, Colburn's is unbelievably crude. His most lavish
announcements consist of hardly more than a mere statement of the name of a book, the name of the author,
and possibly a quotation from some real or imaginary
notice from the press. He devoted less care to the writing

[37] Mrs. Oliphant, *op. cit.*, I, 498.
[38] Lady Morgan, *Memoirs*, II, 145.   [39] *Ibid.*, II, 74.

of the advertisements themselves than to their placement. This was done in order that the way might be opened for those anticipatory notes which journals published when suitably rewarded. All his real art was expended on the careful cultivation of the news value of his books and authors. The proper place to look for Colburn's advertiseing genius is not in the ostensibly paid-for sections of a paper, but in the news columns. "Brilliant extracts," said A. A. Watts, "speak to the intellect of the newspaper reader if he happens to have any; and since the accession of Colburn to the throne of imperial supremacy, people have begun to decide for themselves, and will no longer rely on mere advertisements."[40] Colburn was aware of this last fact. He pushed log-rolling to artistic heights.

Doctor Maginn, when scouting for *Maga* and Blackwood in London, wrote, June 25, 1823, "As for 'Bull' [*John Bull*], I have *carte blanche* to do as I like. But puffs in the inner page must not exceed a quarter, or at most half, a column."[41]

Odoherty comments in the *Noctes*, "The art of puffing has made great progress of late. Devil a book comes out without some dirty buttering in it, either of you, North, or the Edinburgh, or the Quarterly, or some other periodical the author wishes to conciliate."[42]

John Bull was perhaps more venal than other magazines, yet Macaulay, in a letter to Macvey Napier, asserted that Brougham's speeches were puffed in the number of the *Edinburgh Review* which followed their appearance.[43] *Fraser's* had asserted that Colburn planted his paragraphs in every newspaper but two, the *Times* and *Morning Herald*.[44] The truth is that few journals were free from the taint until

[40] Mrs. Oliphant, *op. cit.*, I, 501-2.   [41] *Ibid.*, I, 398.
[42] *Noctes Ambrosianae*, Phila., 1843, I, 149.
[43] *Selections from the Correspondence of Macvey Napier*, edited by his son, London, 1879, p. 110.   [44] *Fraser's Magazine*, April, 1830, p. 318.

C. W. Dilke succeeded in establishing the independence of
the *Athenaeum*. Puffery in return for favors had become
standard business practice.

Harriet Martineau puts the custom in the least unfavorable light. When her book on the American trip was about
to appear, Saunders asked her to "write the notes." "What
notes?" "The notes for the Reviews, you know, Ma'am."
He was surprised at being obliged to explain that authors
wrote notes to friends and acquaintances connected with
periodicals "to request favorable notices of the work."[45]

Then, too, such matter was cheap, costing nothing more
than scissors and paste. A. A. Watts, advising Blackwood
to advertise in the *Literary Gazette* and to stand well with
Jerdan, said, "the country papers mostly exchange with
him, and consequently quote numerous extracts from the
Gazette. These are copied from one to another, and thus
you have useful paragraphs without expense. I have
known twenty provincials quote anecdotes from the same
article."[46]

But most important of all, puffery paid, either directly
or indirectly. Even in quite respectable papers, the placing
of an advertisement seems to have been a direct bid for
favorable reviewing and advance notices. G. B. Whittaker
complained to Jerdan that the *Gazette* treated his authors
unfairly and if this did not cease he would discontinue his
advertising.[47] Colburn wrote with great satisfaction to
Lady Morgan to tell her that the *Examiner*, the *New Times*,
and *John Bull* had abstained from saying anything against
her latest work [*Italy*], adding realistically, "I am intimately acquainted with the editors, and *advertising with them
a great deal, keeps them in check*."[48] And again, in 1821, he
writes, "The *Times* has acted the part of a traitor, after

[45] H. Martineau, *Autobiography, ed. cit.*, p. 404.
[46] Mrs. Oliphant, *op. cit.*, I, 498.   [47] Jerdan, *op. cit.*, IV, 21.
[48] Lady Morgan, *Memoirs*, II, 145.

getting two copies from me."[49] Modern newspaper ethics have fallen no lower.

When he was puffing *Vivian Grey*, the following notice appeared in *John Bull*, March 18, 1827: ". . . a prose Don Juan . . . much more properly regarded as a new Anastasius . . . and if Mr. Hope be really not the author of *Vivian Grey*, as well as of A., the latter novel has met with a formidable rival."

The same issue carried a notice of Bulwer's *Falkland:* "A novel, reported to be one of real eloquence and passion is on the eve of publication, entitled *Falkland*. Its plot is founded on a melancholy fact, of recent occurrence, in elevated life."

The *New Monthly* version was: "A novel of great eloquence and passion, is in the press, to be entitled *Falkland*. Its plot is founded on a melancholy fact, of recent occurrence in elevated life."[50]

These may have been copied by one from the other, but the chances are that both notices came directly from Colburn.

The notice in *John Bull* for Ward's *De Vere* is still more suggestive.[51] Hearsay and gossip are employed with fine effect.

We hear that this new work, by the celebrated author of *Tremaine*, embraces . . . affairs of the most elevated . . . nature . . . Indeed, none but the author in question, who is generally suspected to be an individual of political consequence, could detail the scenes and events . . . which form prominent accompaniments to the fable of De Vere; such for example, as the high affairs of the Court, the mysteries of the Cabinet, the secret intrigue of administration, etc.—Quoted from *Morning Chronicle* of July 20, 1828.

In contrast with what was achieved for *De Vere*, the notices for *Pelham*, one of which we have already quoted, are indeed restrained.

[49] *Ibid.*, p. 146. [50] *The New Monthly*, March, 1827.
[51] *John Bull*, March 25, 1827.

These notices are typical, but they fail to give an adequate idea of the scale and continuity of Colburn's methods. An article in *Fraser's* for February, 1831, called "The Novels of the Season," contained an interesting statistical summary of Colburn and Bentley's list. The total number of books was fifty-two.

18 books were puffed in the *Court Journal*
11 books were puffed in the *Literary Gazette*
—
29
  8 books were not published yet
  4 books were reprints
  4 books did not need puffing
  —
45
  7 books were unpuffed in C. & B. papers
  —
52

Books published, books projected, books whose titles only yet existed, were exploited in all the columns of all the papers, just as they are today.

Colburn got into surprisingly few scrapes over his publicity, but once, at least, he was attacked by enemies who had found a real opening. The discovery was made that Lady Charlotte Bury's novel, *The Separation*, was a revision of one published a score of years before as *Self Indulgence*. The *Athenaeum* commented [52] "The real fraud practised, was *upon the public*, and not by rewriting and improving an old novel, but by puffing paragraphs and criticisms that preceded the publication."

A review in the *Court Journal* a month earlier was the first to call attention to the book's literary history, and should be cited as evidence of the firm's innocence. The *Journal* said,[53] ". . . it strikes us that we can trace a resem-

[52] *The Athenaeum*, Oct. 30, 1831, pp. 680.
[53] *The Court Journal*, Sept. 18, 1830.

blance to a novel called *Self Indulgence*, published some fifteen years ago and attributed at the time to the same noble authoress."

The Athenaeum then proceeded to quote *The Literary Gazette*, which had rushed to the defense of Colburn and Bentley, not by denying the facts, but by asserting that the firm was not aware of the deception.

"We are convinced," says the Editor of the *Literary Gazette*, "that Mr. Colburn must have been unconscious of the trick, for we find the following preparatory announcement in *The New Monthly Magazine*, for August, *which is also his publication, and would not have sanctioned the utterance of such a paragraph had he been aware of the truth*" . . . Here is the admission of the Editor of the *Literary Gazette* that Mr. Colburn is in the habit of *sanctioning and approving* (of inserting, for that is the plain English) paragraphs in *his own papers* and *the newspapers*, which are so worded as to pass for the honest judgment of the Editor of the work;—and the editor of the *Literary Gazette* speaks with authority, seeing that *Colburn is a large shareholder in his own paper*.

After this revelation of the age of the novel, a study of of the paragraphs from *The New Monthly* ought to be illuminating. The July, 1830, release was:

The Novel so often announced under the piquant title of *The Separation*, and which has been, by peculiar circumstances, so long delayed, is now positively about to appear. Separation is the natural consequence of Flirtation. [Her last novel].

In August the report was amplified:

The report which has gone abroad regarding the work entitled *The Separation*,—namely, that the story is connected with the noble Authoress's former tale of *Flirtation*, is not correct . . . its incidents are said to be, in themselves strictly true, not merely *founded* in fact; and the cause of the peculiar interest which it is understood Lady Charlotte Bury has imparted to the work, is to be traced to a "certain case" in the "great world," which took place a few years ago, and which was more industriously than successfully attempted to be concealed.

These two paragraphs display the art of the puffing para-

grapher at its supremest. The attempt to float truth and
fiction in the boat of public favor has never been bettered.

Advertising, as conceived by Colburn, did not begin
with the delivery of a completed manuscript. Books which
he had not commissioned directly might take their chance,
but whenever his connection with the author permitted,
Colburn could be very helpful. He had his fingers on the
public pulse, and writers who deferred to his judgment
usually had their rewards in sales. Cyrus Redding, subeditor of *The New Monthly* under Thomas Campbell, said,
"Colburn always regarded, in publishing, the fashionable
taste, no matter how absurd, for the fashionable was a
buying taste, and no Lintot looks further."[54]

Curiously enough, this man who was such a creature of
indecision in so many matters, knew pretty well what he
wanted when it came to satisfying the public. A story is
told of him and Sydney Smith which demonstrates his
power of decision. Smith had recently lost money, and
Colburn, hearing of it, and thinking it a good chance to
secure a story, made an offer.

The canon thought he would test him, so he said he liked the
proposal much; that he would have an Arch-deacon for a hero,
and make him intrigue with the Pew-opener, and that under the
Hassock would be a good place for depositing the love letters.
"Oh," says Colburn, "we will leave all that to your well-known
taste and judgment," and came away quite cock-a-hoop.[55]

Colburn was not only the publisher of books, but the
progenitor of them in the sense that he commissioned
authors to write books deliberately made-to-measure.
Frederic Shoberl, then a reader for Colburn, was very doubtful about the possibilities in *Pelham* when the manuscript
first arrived. Charles Collier was skeptical, but though
there might be something in it. Colburn skimmed it hurriedly, and announced that it would be the hit of the year.

[54] Cyrus Redding, *Fifty Years Recollections*, London, 1858, II, 322.
[55] Oliphant, *op. cit.*, II, 356–57.

It was. Naturally enough, when Bulwer threatened to satirize the fashionable taste so unmistakably in the planned *Greville*, Colburn would have none of it. That was remarkably short-sighted of him, no doubt, for *Greville* would probably have become a best seller, but Colburn feared that it would destroy the market for dozens of other books. And so, as we have seen, Bulwer abandoned *Greville* and wrote *Devereux*. Perhaps not just the book that Colburn wanted, *Devereux* effectively staved off its dangerous predecessor. The refusal of *Greville*, was, however, the least of three serious mistakes in judgment which Colburn made.

Despite the fact that "tempting mother Colburn" urged Disraeli to write what became *The Young Duke*, the ungrateful author proffered it first to Murray. Disraeli always submitted his books to Murray hoping that he would accept them as a symbol of his forgiveness in the affair of *The Representative*. But Murray did no more than offer to read the manuscript, which he refused. So Colburn, after all, got the fruits of his planning. With *Henrietta Temple* the coöperation between author and publisher was whole-hearted. Colburn watched over the composition of his best sellers as a chef watches an underling mix a favorite sauce. "I hope," Colburn writes while the book is in preparation, "you will have a dozen more originals to draw from beside old Lady C[ork]; an exhibition of two or three leading political characters would not be amiss." In another letter he "wants to know all he can that he may say something about it in the papers to excite curiosity and expectation without in the least gratifying it." [56] And after all his coaching, Colburn was in high spirits about *Henrietta Temple*. "He says he shall not be content unless he works it up like Pelham."

Colburn was at his best when scheming with authors to copy recent events, to throw a thin veil of fiction over

[56] Monypenny and Buckle, *Life of Disraeli*, I, 348.

particularly juicy news items or over celebrated personages.
He spent as much care on titles as Hollywood. He thought
himself a virtuoso at fashioning a title or a paragraph of
advertising. R. P. Ward had named his second novel
Bardolphe, or, The Decayed Gentleman. P. G. Patmore suggested *Clifford;* Colburn added the *De*.[57] The particle was as
aristocratic an improvement over Patmore's title as his had
been over Ward's. Colburn seems often to have chosen the
names for the books he sponsored, as for instance, Horace
Smith's *Zillah*.[58]

As befits an alert publisher, Colburn was quick to take
advantage of a novelty. Sir Charles Morgan wrote to his
wife, Lady Morgan, May 29, 1826, "I have just opened a
new mine for magazine writing; but this is a secret. Colburn
wants me to write a *political* novel—for God's sake make
me out a *canevas*, and I shall try my hand at it."[59] Unless
the resulting political novel was anonymous, as the magazine articles referred to evidently were, Sir Charles did not
write his novel. However, Colburn's demand for a political
novel as early as 1826 is interesting. Part One of *Vivian
Grey* had appeared the previous April, and Colburn was
apparently exercising his prophetic vision about the
popularity and fashionableness of the form.

Colburn was generous enough to Leigh Hunt, yet the
publisher got from him just what he wanted. Hunt was
stranded in Italy after the death of Byron. To get necessary
funds, he arranged with Colburn to write a book, and to
provide £150 worth a year of prose and verse for *The New
Monthly*. The publisher paid in advance, and poor Hunt's
heart was filled with gratitude. "I shall set him down as the
most *engaging* of publishers. What I mean to do for him is
infinite."[60] However, Hunt's biographer, Edmund Blunden,

[57] P. G. Patmore, *op. cit.*, 120.   [58] A. H. Beavan, *op. cit.*, 262.
[59] Lady Morgan, *Memoirs*, II, 227–29.
[60] E. Blunden, *Leigh Hunt*, London, 1930, p. 220.

regards Colburn's generosity coldly. "Colburn's rescue was to be paid for in a sensational work which Hunt could neither refuse to supply, nor write without injustice and danger to himself."[61] Hunt appears to have promised a volume or two on Italy, a selection from his own writings, and a memoir of himself. This promise was modified under Colburn's skillful handling into the production of an autobiography filled with Byronic material. The result was a *succès de scandale* which reached a second edition the first year.

When Hunt was writing *Sir Ralph Esher*, Colburn paid twenty pounds weekly as installments of copy were delivered.[62] The novel, announced in *The New Monthly* for April, 1830, was postponed until the passage of the Reform Bill once more made the name of Libertas acceptable. The anonymity of *Esher* would not have protected it against Hunt's milignant enemies. Here, Colburn's handling of Hunt seems to have been unreservedly generous but also profitable to himself.

Colburn's revenge on authors who mistreated him or offended his vanity could take grotesque forms. Lady Morgan had provided him with many best sellers, and she had always been his favorite author. When she was in Italy engaged on her life of Salvator Rosa, he went so far as to entreat her to take care of her eyes, and begged her to ensure their health by the use of a green cloth on the table when she wrote.[63] When she was ready to sell her second book on France, in 1830, Colburn naturally assumed it would be his. She, however, thought he was not running after it fast enough, and sold it to Saunders and Otley. Colburn's rage knew no bounds. On the day the book was to appear he inserted an advertisement in the papers, LADY MORGAN

[61] *Ibid.*, p. 220.
[62] *The Bookman's Journal*, Series 3, XVIII, (1930), 15–17.
[63] Lady Morgan, *op. cit.*, II, 304–9.   [64] *Ibid.*, II, 152–53.

AT HALF PRICE. He said that on account of losses on former works he had declined Lady Morgan's new book, and that he was liquidating his stock of her novels in anticipation of a falling market. He behaved, she said, "like an angry lover seeking a reconciliation with his mistress."[64] Formal peace with Saunders and Otley was only reached through court action in 1831.

The story of Colburn's connection with Thomas Hood also displays the less generous side of the publisher's nature. Hook, editor of *The New Monthly*, died in 1841, and Colburn offered the job to Hood. He wanted to pay £200, while Hook had been getting £300. Hood, poor and ill, nevertheless refused to come for less than Hook had been getting and Colburn finally gave in. By September, 1843, Hood had had enough of Colburn, and consulted Dickens about the matter. Dickens's verdict was, "there can be no doubt in the mind of any honorable man that the circumstances under which you signed your agreement are of the most disgraceful kind in so far as Mr. Colburn is concerned. There can be no doubt that he took a money-lending, bill-broking, Jew-clothes-buying, Saturday-night-pawnbroking advantage of your temporary situation."[65] Colburn was so affronted when Hood resigned to start *Hood's Magazine* that he endorsed three letters addressed to him at the magazine office, "Not known to Mr. Colburn."

An eagerness to get books talked about at all costs, occasionally led him to flirt seriously with the laws of libel. The circumstances surrounding the publication of Lady Charlotte Bury's *Diary* furnish an example of this. He actually wrote, "It is a fact that, without having the opportunity of seeing more than a few pages of its contents, I paid £1,000 for the copyright of the entire manuscript." One is reminded of the story told of Jerdan,—that he cut the pages of a book and smelled the paper knife for matter

[65] Jerrold, *Thomas Hood, His Life and Times*, London, 1907, p. 364.

on which to base a review. Consequently when Henry
Webster, son of Sir Godfrey Webster and the future Lady
Holland, offended by reflections on Lady Holland, sought
through Colburn to convey a challenge to the diarist,
Colburn was forced to apologize for printing, and to assure
him that the diarist was a woman.

He had precisely the same apology to make to Lady
Morgan. A passage in the *Diary* mentioned her unfavorably.
She refused any compensation or adjustment, but she did
take pleasure in telling him that ever since he and she had
parted company he had been declining in reputation.

He made another error—not against the libel laws, but
against public opinion—when he published a pirated edition of Jared Sparks's *Washington* in 1839. The American
edition in some eight volumes was being imported at £10.
Colburn had an English editor supply notes to an abridged
biography and to one volume of selected letters. These two
volumes he offered at twenty-eight shillings. He succeeded
very poorly, finding it necessary to redate the edition in
1842. A public outcry in the journals was perhaps directed
as much against the deed because it was Colburn's as for any
other reason. Certainly the Americans themselves who were
pirating Colburn's authors like Bulwer, Massie, Disraeli,
and Gore, had no right to object.[66]

Occasionally his discretion was equal to his lust for
sales. When Harriette Wilson consulted Westmacott, editor
of *The Age*, about publishing her *Memoirs*, he recommended
her to Colburn "as the universal speculator in paper and
print."[67] But Colburn refused, warned perhaps, by the
unsavory stories afloat concerning her blackmailing habits.
The publication was finally, the story goes, paid for by
threatening blackmail on proposed victims.

[66] Herbert B. Adams, *The Life and Writings of Jared Sparks*, Boston,
1893, II, 318-19. *The North American Review*, July, 1842, pp. 257-58.
[67] Charles Molloy Westmacott, Bernard Blackmantle, *pseud. The
English Spy* . . . London, 1825, II, 60.

Whether a publisher's sins of omission are worse than his sins of commission is debatable. A bad book is evidence of poor taste or judgment, but the story of the rejected manuscript may last longer, if, as occasionally happens, the book becomes immortal. Colburn's failures in publishing are dead these many years, but the two books which he refused will always remain to darken his reputation for sagacity. They were *Wuthering Heights* and *Vanity Fair*.

For a publisher like Colburn to refuse the former is hardly strange. The curious thing is, perhaps, that a book so far out of his usual line should ever have been submitted to him. But for the godfather of the fashionable novel to fail to recognize the merit of *Vanity Fair* has always seemed evidence either of Colburn's fatuity when confronted by real genius or of declining business sense. After a lifetime spent in developing and cherishing novels about London society, he declined the one book of indubitable genius which had come his way. That he did refuse it is unquestionable. Thackeray wrote to Professor Aytoun, January 2, 1847, just when *Vanity Fair* was beginning to appear, "Colburn refused the present 'Novel without a Hero.'"[68]

But Colburn's refusal was not of the complete manuscript of *Vanity Fair;* indeed, it was not of such a title at all. When Thackeray began his attempt to place his new work he had not as yet written more than a small number of opening pages, nor had he given them the famous title. It was *Pencil Sketches of English Society*, the introduction to a volume of undetermined length, which Colburn saw and rejected for his *New Monthly Magazine*. The late development of Thackeray's art is a commonplace of criticism. He was thirty-six when *Mrs. Perkin's Ball* and *Vanity Fair* began to bring him even a share of the fame which had been Dickens's at twenty-four. He was known chiefly as a competent writer of magazine articles for *Fraser's* and *Punch*,

[68] Lewis Melville, *William Makepeace Thackeray*, London, 1910, I, 216.

and *Fraser's* had even cut short the serial publication of his *The Great Hoggarty Diamond*. What little he had contributed to Colburn's *New Monthly* was definitely not his best work. Therefore, when Colburn was presented with a chapter or two of a manuscript by his not over-valued contributor, he can hardly be blamed for not being eager about it. He must have felt that he was playing second fiddle to Thackeray's more usual publishers.

Colburn's reputation has been harmed by the rejection. If he could have crowned his list with the work which represents the culmination of the fashionable novel, he would have made unquestionable his preëminence as a publisher of society novels.

X

EPILOGUE

WHEN in 1837 a prim young lady ascended the throne occupied until recently by her wicked uncles, the fashionable novel might legitimately have expired, but because two old ladies hung determinedly on to life and their pens, it lived almost to witness the second Reform Act. Indeed, the dandies and ladies of 1830 moved ceremoniously once more in the mellow light of wax candles, as an ex-Prime Minister of England, who fifty years before had written *Vivian Grey*, labored in the bright mornings at Hughenden to regale his readers with *Endymion*. The warm sun of France split itself on a pyramid of stone at Chambourcy; the end of the masquerade did not point too obvious a moral, for these two were together again, with the wagging tongues across the Channel silenced at last.

The nineteenth century asserted its belief in progress (which was its substitute for the permanence of the eighteenth), although a few alert souls were wrestling with doubts inspired by *The Origin of Species*. Parliamentary government, whose very existence had been imperiled thirty years before, still flourished, although a new group of sober statesmen realized that another leap in the dark must be the end. In this solid world writing that dealt with dandies, *salons*, knee breeches, and quadrilles must have seemed fragile, tinseled stuff. The neat stucco of Georgian squares was being darkened by the sober brick Gothic of Victorian London. Decorum reigned over streets protected by the bobbies, and the superannuated Charlies of an earlier, rowdier London were forgotten except by oldsters who had been raffish youths.

A decade or two later, Locker-Lampson, wearied, perhaps, of the unrelieved dazzle of Meredithian heroines and the self-searchings of George Eliot's folk, murmured regretfully, "What has become of that witty old ghost of the silver-fork school, Mrs. Gore?" For she was gone, finally, almost the last literary link with the high world to which the Reform Bill had seemed the end of civilization. Thackeray had become its laureate; *Vanity Fair*, an account of that world by a contemporary who had traveled far in spirit, if not in time, had supplanted the stories written with no such eye for perspective.

Found today only in copyright repositories like the British Museum, vanished almost utterly from the shelves of the dealers, and even from the penny barrows on Faringdon Road, the fashionable novels have not failed to leave some impress on the English novel. In Jos Sedley, Rebecca Sharpe, Rawdon Crawley, and George Osborne we can still see likenesses, transmuted by genius into imperishable figures. Created only six years earlier than *Vanity Fair*, *Cecil* is laid in the same period, yet mustiness pervades it, while the toys of *Vanity Fair* shine as undimmed and fresh as though the author had put them away only yesterday.

Why this should be—why not only *Cecil*, but also *The Diary of a Désennuyée*, *Granby*, *The Young Duke*, and even *Pelham* and *Vivian Grey* are best read in the yellowed paper of the original editions, is a lesson in the values which make for permanence. Some novels, of course, as current as a newspaper when written, reveal traces of the old freshness after the dust and cobwebs of a century have been removed. Others, as historical as *Vanity Fair*, lack the notes either of contemporaneity or of historical convincingness. One cannot re-create the past by the simple subtraction of years from the almanac. In attempting to interpret 1815 in the terms of 1840, the fashionable novelists too often forgot the winnowing effects of time. Their characters, amusing enough for a single puppet show, began to bleed sawdust after repeated performances. Thackeray, regarding the same world, distinguished the permanent from the transitory. Today, only he remains, but countless leaves, some of them delicate and lovely, drifted into the mold out of which grew the sturdy trunk of *Vanity Fair*.

BIBLIOGRAPHY

Adams, Herbert B., The Life and Writings of Jared Sparks, Boston, 1893.

Ashton, John, The History of Gambling in England, London, 1898.

Aurevilly, Barbey d', Du dandysme et de Georges Brummell, translated by D. B. Wyndham Lewis, The Anatomy of Dandyism, London, 1928.

Beattie, William, Life and Letters of Thomas Campbell, London, 1849.

Beavan, A. H., James and Horace Smith, London, 1899.

Bentley, Richard, Some Leaves from the Past Swept together by R. B., Privately printed, 1896.

Blessington, The Countess of, The Belle of a Season, 1840.

——— The Confessions of an Elderly Gentleman, 1836.

——— The Confessions of an Elderly Lady, 1838.

——— Conversations of Lord Byron with the Countess of Blessington, 1834.

——— Country Quarters, 1850.

——— Desultory Thoughts and Reflections, 1839.

——— Flowers of Loveliness, Twelve Groups of Female Figures Emblematic of Flowers, 1836.

——— The Governess, 1839.

——— The Idler in France, 1841.

——— The Idler in Italy, 1839.

——— Journal of a Tour through the Netherlands to Paris in 1821, 1822.

——— The Lottery of Life, 1842.

——— The Magic Lantern, or, Sketches of Scenes in the Metropolis, 1822.

——— Marmaduke Herbert, or, The Fatal Error: a novel founded on fact, 1847.

——— The Memoirs of a femme de chambre, 1846.

——— Meredith, 1843.

——— The Repealers, 1833.

——— Sketches and Fragments, 1822.

——— Strathern, or, Life at Home and Abroad, 1845.

Blessington, The Two Friends, 1835.

———— The Victims of Society, 1837.

Blessington Papers, The, Collected by Alfred Morrison, 2d series, Privately printed, 1895.

Blunden, E., Leigh Hunt, London, 1930.

Brightfield, Myron F., Theodore Hook and His Novels, Cambridge, 1928.

Brillat-Savarin, J. A., La Physiologie du goût, Paris, 1825.

Bulwer-Lytton, Edward George Earle Lytton, Alice, or, The Mysteries, 1838.

———— Devereux, 1829.

———— The Disowned, 1828.

———— England and the English, 1833.

———— Ernest Maltravers, 1837.

———— Falkland, 1827.

———— Godolphin, 1833.

———— Greville (unfinished), 1822.

———— Ismael and Other Poems, 1820.

———— Paul Clifford, 1830.

———— Pelham, 1828.

———— The Pilgrims of the Rhine, 1834.

———— The Siamese Twins, 1831.

———— Weeds and Wildflowers, 1825.

Bulwer-Lytton, Edward Robert, first Earl of Lytton, The Life, Letters, and Literary Remains of Edward Bulwer, Lord Lytton, by His son, London, 1883.

Burney, Fanny, Cecilia, London, 1782.

———— Evelina, London, 1771.

Bury, Lady Charlotte Susan Maria, Alla Giornata, 1826.

———— The Baronets, 1864.

———— Conduct Is Fate, 1822.

———— The Devoted, 1836.

———— Diary, Illustrative of the Times of George IV, 1838.

———— The Disinherited, 1834.

———— The Divorced, 1837.

———— The Exclusives, 1830.

———— Family Records, 1841.

———— Flirtation, 1828.

———— The History of a Flirt, 1840.

———— Journal of the Heart, 1830.

———— Journal of the Heart, 2d series, 1835.

Bury, The Lady of Fashion, 1856.
—— The Lady's Own Cookery Book, 1844.
—— Love, 1837.
—— The Maneuvering Mother, 1842.
—— A Marriage in High Life, 1828.
—— Poems on Several Occasions, by a Lady, 1797.
—— The Roses, n.d.
—— Self Indulgence, 1812.
—— The Separation, 1830.
—— Suspirium Sanctorum, or Holy Breathing, 1826.
—— The Three Great Sanctuaries of Tuscany, Valombrosia, Camoldoli, Taverna, a poem, with historical and legendary notices, 1833.
Byron, Lord, George Gordon, Beppo, 1818.
—— Don Juan, 1819, 1821, 23.
—— Journal.
Carlyle, Thomas, Sartor Resartus, 1833-34.
Collins, A. S., The Profession of Letters, London, 1928.
Dilke, Charles Wentworth, Papers of a Critic, London, 1875.
Disraeli, Benjamin, Coningsby, 1844.
—— Contarini Fleming, a Psychological Romance, 1832.
—— Endymion, 1880.
—— The Infernal Marriage, 1834.
—— Ixion, 1833.
—— Popanilla, 1828.
—— The Star Chamber, April 19–June 7, 1826.
—— Vivian Grey, 1826-27.
—— The Young Duke, 1831.
Doyle, J. A., Memoir and Correspondence of Susan Ferrier, London, 1898.
Edgeworth, Maria, Belinda, 1801.
—— Tales from Fashionable Life, 1809–12.
Egan, Pierce, Life in London . . . London, 1821–28.
Ellis, S. M., William Harrison Ainsworth and His Friends, London, 1911.
Ferrier, Susan, Destiny, London, 1830.
—— Inheritance, London, 1824.
—— Marriage, 1818.
Goethe, J. W. von, Wilhelm Meister's Apprenticeship, translated by Thomas Carlyle, 1824.

Gore, Catherine Grace Frances, The Abbey of Laach, in S. H. A. Tales of All Nations, London, 1827. The editor's Preface is signed H. S. S.
—— Adventures in Borneo, 1849.
—— Agathonia, a Romance, 1844.
—— The Ambassador's Wife, 1842.
—— And Ye Shall Walk in Silk Attire, guitar song, 1867.
—— The Banker's Wife, 1843.
—— The Birthright, and Other Tales, 1844.
—— The Bond, a Dramatic Poem, 1824.
—— The Cabinet Minister, 1839.
—— Castles in the Air, 1847.
—— Cecil, or The Adventures of a Coxcomb, 1841.
—— Cecil, the Peer, 1841.
—— The Courtier of the Days of Charles II, with other Tales, 1839.
—— Dacre of the South, a drama in 5 acts, verse, 1840.
—— The Dean's Daughter, 1853.
—— The Débutante, 1846.
—— The Diamond and the Pearl, 1848.
—— The Diary of a Désennuyée, 1836.
—— The Dowager, 1840.
—— The Fair of Mayfair, 1832.
—— Fascination, and Other Tales, 1842.
—— A Good Night's Rest, a farce in 1 act, 1825. In Duncombe's edition of the British Theater, Vol. XXXIX.
—— Greville, 1841.
—— The Hamiltons, 1831.
—— Heckington, 1858.
—— The Heir of Selwood, 1838.
—— The Historical Traveller, 1831.
—— Hungarian Tales, 1829.
—— The Inundation, a Christmas Story, illus. by George Cruikshank, 1848.
—— King O'Neill, prose comedy in 2 acts, 1837. In Dick's Acting National Drama, Vol. VII.
—— The Lettre de Cachet, 1827.
—— A Life's Lessons, 1856.
—— The Lost Son, 1854.
—— The Lover and the Husband, 1841. From the French of "Gerfant" by Chas. de Bernard.

Gore, Mammon, 1855.
—— The Maid of Croissey, Drama, 1835. In Dick's A. N. D., Vol. VI.
—— The Man of Fortune, and Other Tales, 1842.
—— Mary Raymond, and Other Tales, 1838.
—— Memoirs of a Peeress, 1837.
—— Men of Capital, 1846.
—— Modern Chivalry, 1843.
—— Modern French Life, 1842. A collection of tales from the French, ed. by Mrs. Gore.
—— The Money Lender, 1843.
—— Mothers and Daughters, 1831.
—— Mrs. Armytage, 1836.
—— New Year's Day, a Winter's Tale, 2d ed., 1846.
—— The Opera, 1832.
—— Peers and Parvenus, 1846.
—— Pin Money, 1831.
—— The Popular Member, The Wheel of Fortune . . . London, 1844.
—— Polish Tales, 1833.
—— Preferment, or My Uncle the Earl, 1840.
—— Progress and Prejudice, 1854.
—— The Queen of Denmark, an historical novel trans. from the Danish of T. C. Heiberg, 1846. Ed. by Mrs. Gore.
—— The Queen's Champion, Melodrama, in Dick's A. N. D., 1834.
—— Quid pro quo, or The Days of Dupes, the prize comedy, 1844.
—— Richelieu, 1826. Attributed to Mrs. Gore.
—— Romances of Real Life, 1829.
—— The Rose Fancier's Manual, 1838.
—— Self, 1845.
—— Sir Roger de Coverley's Picture Gallery, The Tale Book, 1859.
—— The Sketch Book of Fashion, 1833.
—— Sketches of English Characters, 1846.
—— The Snow Storm, a Christmas story illus. by Geo. Cruikshank, 1845.
—— The Song of the Highland Chiefs, 1827.
—— Stokehill Place, 1837.
—— The Story of a Royal Favorite, 1845.

Gore, Temptation and Atonement, and Other Tales, 1847.
—— Theresa Marchmont, 1824.
—— The Tuileries, 1831.
—— The Two Aristocracies, 1857.
—— Women as They Are, 1830.
Gronow, Rees, Last Recollections, London, 1866.
—— Reminiscences, London, 1863.
Hall, Samuel Carter, A Book of Memories, London, 1871.
—— Retrospect of a Long Life, New York, 1883.
Haydon, Benjamin, The Autobiography and Memoirs of Benjamin Robert Haydon, edited by Tom Taylor, New York, 1926.
Hayward, A., The Art of Dining, London, 1852.
Hazlitt, W. C., Four Generations of a Literary Family, New York, 1897.
Hemphill, Barbara, Lionel Deerhurst, or, The Days of the Regency, edited by Lady Blessington, 1846.
Hook, Theodore, Sayings and Doings, 1824, 1825, 1826.
Howe, Susanne, Wilhelm Meister and His English Kinsmen, New York, 1930.
Jeaffreson, John C., Novels and Novelists from Elizabeth to Victoria, London, 1858.
Jerdan, William, Autobiography, London, 1852–53.
Jerrold, Walter, Thomas Hood, His Life and Times, London, 1907.
Jesse, William, Life of Brummell, 1844.
Kemble, Frances, Records of a Later Life, London, 1882.
Knight, Charles, Passages of a Working Life, London, 1864.
—— Shadows of the Old Booksellers, London, 1865.
L'Estrange, A. G. K., The Life of Mary Russell Mitford, New York, 1875.
Lister, T. H., Arlington, London, 1832.
—— Granby, London, 1826.
—— Herbert Lacy, London, 1828.
Luttrell, H., Advice to Julia, London, 1820.
Madden, R. R., The Literary Life and Correspondence of the Countess of Blessington, London, 1855.
Maginn, William, Whitehall, or, The Days of George IV, London, 1827.
Mallock, W. H., Memoirs of Life and Literature, London, 1920.
Martineau, Harriet, Autobiography, Boston, 1877.
Mathews, C. J., Life, London, 1879.

Mead, E. W., The Grand Tour in the Eighteenth Century, Boston, 1914.

Melville, Lewis, William Makepeace Thackeray, London, 1910.

Molloy, J. Fitzgerald, The Most Gorgeous Lady Blessington. London, 1897.

Monypenny, W. F., and Buckle, G. E., Life of Disraeli, New Rev. Edition, London, 1929.

Moore, Thomas, Memoirs, Journal and Correspondence, 1855–56.

Morgan, Lady, Passages from My Autobiography, New York, 1859.

Napier, Macvey, Selections from the Correspondence . . . edited by his son, London, 1879.

Normanby, Lord, Constantine Henry Phipps, Matilda, a Tale of the Day, London, 1825.

Oliphant, Mrs., William Blackwood and His Sons, London and Edinburgh, 1897.

Patmore, P. G., My Friends and Acquaintance, London, 1854.

Redding, Cyrus, Fifty Years Recollections, London, 1858.

Reid, T. Wemyss, The Life, Letters, and Friendships of Richard Monckton Milnes, London, 1890.

Rogers, Samuel, Recollections of the Table Talk of Samuel Rogers, New York, 1856.

Sadleir, Michael, Bulwer, a Panorama: Edward and Rosina, Boston, 1931.

——— The Strange Life of Lady Blessington, Boston, 1933.

Saintsbury, George, A Consideration of Thackeray, London, 1931.

Shepherd, R. H., Life of Carlyle, London, 1871.

Southey, Robert, Sir Thomas More, or, Colloquies on the Progress and Prospects of Society, London, 1829.

Thackeray, W. M., Codlingsby, Punch, April 24, May 15, 29, 1847.

——— Lords and Liveries, Punch, June 12, 26, 1847.

——— The Newcomes, London, 1853–55.

——— Pendennis, London, 1849–50.

——— Vanity Fair, London, 1847–48.

Toynbee, William, Glimpses of the Twenties, London, 1909.

Trench, R. C., Letters and Memories, London, 1888.

Veblen, Thorstein, The Theory of the Leisure Class, New York, 1899.

Walker, Thomas, The Original, 6th edition, London, 1885.

Ward, Robert Plumer, De Clifford, or, The Constant Man, 1841.
—— De Vere, or, The Man of Independence, 1827.
—— Pictures of the World at Home and Abroad, 1839.
—— Tremaine, or, The Man of Refinement, 1825.
Westmacott, Charles Malloy (Bernard Blackmantle, pseud.), The English Spy, London, 1825.

INDEX